HISTORICAL THEORY

Practising historians claim that their accounts of the past are something other than fiction, myth or propaganda. Yet there are significant challenges to this view, most notably from postmodernism. In *Historical Theory*, a prominent historian develops a highly original argument that evaluates the diversity of approaches to history and points to a constructive way forward.

Against naïve empiricism, Mary Fulbrook argues that all historians face key theoretical questions, and that an emphasis on the 'facts' alone is not enough. Against postmodernism, she argues that historical narratives are not simply inventions imposed on the past, and that some answers to historical questions are more plausible or adequate than others. The argument of *Historical Theory* is illustrated by numerous substantive examples and its focus is always on the most central theoretical issues and on real strategies for bridging the gap between the traces of the past and the interpretations of the present.

Historical Theory is essential and enlightening reading for all historians and their students.

Mary Fulbrook is Professor of German History at University College London. Her numerous books include *A Concise History of Germany* (1991), *Anatomy of a Dictatorship: Inside the GDR, 1949–89* (1995), *German National Identity after the Holocaust* (1999) and *History of Germany 1918–2000: The Divided Nation* (2002).

HISTORICAL THEORY

Mary Fulbrook

London and New York

First published 2002
by Routledge
11 New Fetter Lane, London EC4P 4EE

Simultaneously published in the USA and Canada
by Routledge
29 West 35th Street, New York, NY 10001

Routledge is an imprint of the Taylor & Francis Group

© 2002 Mary Fulbrook

Typeset in Galliard by The Running Head Limited, Cambridge
Printed and bound in Great Britain by
TJ International Ltd, Padstow, Cornwall

British Library Cataloguing in Publication Data
A catalogue record for this book is available from the British Library

Library of Congress Cataloging in Publication Data
A catalog record for this book has been requested

ISBN 0–415–17986–6 (hbk)
ISBN 0–415–17987–4 (pbk)

IN MEMORY OF HOWARD (1949–2001)

CONTENTS

PREFACE

This book addresses essential issues about the nature of historical knowledge. It is not about 'approaches to history' in the sense of distinct theoretical traditions, nor is it a 'history of historiography', nor a guide to varying 'historical skills and methods'. There are many good books on all these sorts of topics. Rather, it is about the ways in which all historical writing is inevitably theoretical; and about the ways in which we can hope to make progress in developing enhanced accounts of selected aspects of the past in the light of the interests and perspectives of the present, while yet being able to devise criteria for saying that some accounts are 'better', more empirically adequate, than others.

My primary concern is thus to explore just how far, and under what conditions – or with what qualifications – we can hold a view of history as saying something true (however limited, temporary, inadequate) about a real past (however essentially 'unknowable' in any totalising sense), even in the wake of the postmodernist challenge and in the light (if that is the right word in this context) of the political 'noise' which surrounds all historical writing. These are questions which have bothered me for a long time, as a practising historian who is committed to a notion of history as trying to say something true about the past, and yet is highly aware of the ways in which different historical traditions and conflicting interpretations of the past are closely linked to political and moral positions.

One of my more specific purposes has been to construct a theoretically tenable route out of the rather entrenched positions of an arguably increasingly sterile debate between empiricists and postmodernists. I do not find the variety of postmodernist positions acceptable or convincing, for a number of reasons outlined below; but I do not feel that they have as yet been adequately answered by historians coming from a basically empiricist position. A related purpose, against any simple empiricist view, is to establish that all history writing inevitably entails taking a stand on key theoretical issues, whether or not the historian is aware of these – and many practising historians are not. There is no escape from having a theoretical position, whether explicit or implicit. But I argue that it does not follow from this that all historical approaches are in principle equally acceptable – or equally fictional, as the relativist case would suggest. It may be possible to agree on criteria for preferring one historical approach or interpretation to another; and these criteria need not be, as the postmodernists would have it, purely based on moral, political, or aesthetic considerations.

Cumulatively, this book seeks to establish the character of historical investigation as something distinct from fiction-writing, political ideology, and indeed also the old bogey man of (an idealised view of) the natural sciences. I make no claim to have resolved all the problems inherent in these long-running debates, but rather hope to have clarified – or at least to have offered some productive ways of thinking about – what any given position on these issues must entail.

I have sought in this book to draw examples from a wider chronological and geographical range than that of my own current field of research in modern German history. My examples are nevertheless still drawn from those areas of largely European and occasionally American historiography with which I am most familiar, and do not range widely over terrain where I feel too uncertain of my ground to warrant sensible discussion. But the implications of the discussion relate to key issues in all historical investigation, and are, I believe, applicable to a far wider body of examples than those selected for illustrative purposes in this book.

Critics often impute attributes to the authors of particular books by which they think they can categorise and critique the arguments. The debate between the Cambridge historians E. H. Carr and Geoffrey Elton in the 1960s, for example, is often set up as one between radical and conservative historical approaches; American 'identity historians' make great play of various types of 'underdog history' or history written from particular perspectives, such as working class, black, feminist, gay, subaltern and so on. I do not actually think that the personal attributes of the author are or should be relevant to the evaluation of a particular theoretical approach, as I shall seek to argue below (particularly in Chapter 9), and I would hope that my arguments in this book will stand or fall on their own merits – no doubt an illustration of my underlying faith in intellectual rationality. Nevertheless, I have been encouraged by my publishers to make some comments about myself if for no other reason than to pre-empt some of the most basic possible biographical fallacies.

I write this book, inevitably, from my own standpoint both as an individual and as a scholar. The latter is probably more relevant in critique. In discussing paradigms, I operate from within my own paradigm: namely one which has constructed paradigms as a useful framework for inquiry. I do not, then, think it is possible to 'stand outside' any or all theoretical approaches. In a wider sense, I no doubt start with innumerable assumptions rooted in a western European and North American background and education. As far as any possible personal 'identity politics' are concerned, I am essentially a cosmopolitan white mongrel, born in Wales to a Canadian father and a German mother, herself a Christian *Mischling* who left Nazi Germany because of its racist politics. I have greater faith in collective communities rooted in ethical and political choices than in those based on the accidents of biological or geographical heritage. I have a somewhat transatlantic educational background, having studied first at Cambridge and then at Harvard. Thus I am committed to certain notions of truth and rationality which are probably in large part products of a western post-Enlightenment education. My own field of research, modern German history, is littered with particularly politicised controversies which point up in often highly dramatic ways the interactions between politics, morality, and historical interpretations. As something of an outsider as far as personal involvement in these controversies is concerned, I have always been bothered by the high degree of heat and indeed personal vituperation occasioned by debates among German historians over issues of contemporary history. I have also been intrigued by the degree of ferocity sometimes aroused in debates among Anglo-American historians over far more distant periods of history – the notorious 'rise of the gentry', or the origins of (and even the very designation of) the English Revolution or Civil War, for example. I hold relatively strong political and moral views on a range of issues, but have always wanted to work out ways of ensuring that such views do not influence choices with respect to the relative adequacy of competing historical interpretations. So in a sense this book is about exploring the extent to which all the kinds of biographical detail I have just given have – or should have – absolutely no bearing on the ways in which the relative merits of different historical arguments are evaluated.

Acknowledgements

I am immensely grateful to John Breuilly, David D'Avray, Peter A. Hall, Victoria Peters, David Roberts, and an anonymous reader for Routledge, for their extremely perceptive and helpful comments on parts or all of successive drafts of the manuscript. As always, they bear no responsibility for the inadequacies of the eventual result; as they will be well aware, this book could have been written in many different ways. In the interests of exploring what I conceive to be the primary issues, I have chosen not to pursue some of their suggestions which might have led me too far astray into other fields of inquiry; there is much else that could be said on all the topics discussed below, and some of it will have to be said in other contexts. In the end, the way I have chosen to write this particular book is the way in which I could best clarify the arguments for myself – and hence, hopefully, for the reader.

I have thought about the issues discussed in this book over a long period of time, and it would be inappropriate to thank all those who have contributed in some way to the development of my current views on these matters (although I would probably want to include Geoffrey Hawthorn, Theda Skocpol and Daniel Bell in this wider long-term list of those who have particularly stimulated and guided my interest in matters to do with historical theory). I would, however, explicitly like to thank those who commented very fully and helpfully on the original proposal for this book: Patrick Joyce, Allan Megill, Alun Munslow, David Welch, and an anonymous referee. I have also learnt from the comments and reactions of colleagues in Washington, DC, where I presented some of the arguments in the 1999 Annual Lecture of the German Historical Institute Washington, and was particularly challenged by Konrad Jarausch's written commentary on my lecture. I have also benefited greatly from conversations with my students and colleagues at UCL, particularly an MA class on theory taught jointly with Stephanie Bird, and a history class at Birkbeck College where I gave a series of seminars on these issues.

My husband and children have, as always, supported me unreservedly throughout the writing of this book. They have been more or less willing companions on visits to most of the historical sites I mention, and have often seen things with very different eyes. I have particularly enjoyed conversations on many of these issues with Conrad, whose growing philosophical, historical and literary interests accompanied some of the stages of my own thinking and writing (he will recognise the traces). He is also responsible for suggesting the cover picture.

I dedicate the book to the memory of my brother Howard, whose goodness and generosity meant so much to us.

Part I

INTERPRETATIONS: APPROACHES TO HISTORY

1

INTRODUCTION

Reading certain theoretical works of the past few decades, one might be forgiven for thinking that until the later twentieth century, everybody had agreed that historical accounts were simply accepted as True Stories containing Important Facts about Things Which Really Happened. History was, at least since the more scientistic turn of the twentieth century, a discipline quite distinct from literature. Literature was about things that had not happened, and history was about things that had. Literature was about imagination and invention; history was about telling the truth. Historians wrote about facts, to be clearly distinguished from fiction and myth. And, on this allegedly traditional view, historians were trained to do it properly, objectively; using appropriate sources and methodology (known by critics as 'source fetishism'), with appropriate time spent sweating in the archives ('archive positivism'), their results could be trusted. Then along came some theoretically sophisticated postmodernists, much influenced by French post-structuralism, who mounted a mortal attack on this happy picture of historians earnestly in pursuit of truth. With the 'linguistic turn', history dissolved into relativist discourse; the 'truth' could not only never be known, but was indeed itself merely an article of faith. Historical works were essentially fictions written in realist mode, with conventions such as quotations from sources and scholarly footnotes serving to bolster the reality effect. Meanwhile, however, the vast majority of practising historians ignored the unintelligible theorists, and simply got on with the job of reconstructing the past; and their readers continued to read their books as if they had something interesting and accurate to say about the past.

Of course such widespread agreement on the nature of history never existed. Differences over the character of history as a discipline for acquiring knowledge of the past are hardly a recent development. Debates over approaches to knowledge, understanding and explanation in the historical and social sciences have been going on for generations, indeed centuries.[1] Recent skirmishes over postmodernism have merely added some new twists to old scepticisms. In the context of current debates, I seek in this book to argue a case for historical knowledge as distinctively different from fiction or propaganda, but to argue this without falling into a naïve empiricism resting on a simplistic appeal to 'the facts'. I seek

3

to explore the extent to which historical knowledge can in some sense be 'true', testable, capable of progress within certain parameters; the extent to which, and the bases on which, there will remain fundamental and irresolvable differences of approach and assumptions among different historical communities; and the extent to which the human imagination and capacity for inter-subjective communication have roles to play in bringing knowledge of aspects of the past to different audiences in an ever-changing present.

My underlying premise is that theory is fundamental to historical investigation and representation. Part of my aim in this book is to raise certain theoretical issues to the attention of those who remain relatively blind to the importance of theory in history. All history writing is, whether historians acknowledge this or not, an intrinsically theoretical as well as empirical enterprise. There are historians who consciously claim to be theoretical – who claim that their work is informed by explicit bodies of theoretical debate such as Marxism, structuralism, discourse theory, or feminism. And there are historians who, in contrast, claim to be simply 'doing history', exploring the archives, trying to find out as best they can 'what really happened' or 'how it really was'. Implicitly they, too, are working within bodies of assumptions of which they may be more or less aware: assumptions about what is already 'common knowledge', assumptions about how best to pose and frame the questions guiding their inquiry, assumptions about what to look for and where to look for it, assumptions about how to define who are the key historical actors (social classes, 'great men'?), and assumptions about what would constitute satisfactory answers to their questions. These often hidden, implicit assumptions are as much bodies of theory as are the concepts and strategies of those operating within an explicitly theoretical '-ism'.

This book is thus about the ways in which all historical writing is inevitably theoretical. It is not about 'history and theory', as though the latter were in effect an optional add-on; such an approach is based in a fundamental misunderstanding about the nature of historical inquiry, as though 'history' could simply choose whether or not to 'borrow' theories and concepts from cognate disciplines in the social sciences, such as anthropology, sociology, psychology, geography, or economics. As I hope to show, even the most wilfully 'a-theoretical' historians actually operate – and have to operate – within a framework of theoretical assumptions and strategies. Nor is the book about particular 'theories of history', 'theoretical approaches to history', or substantive historical controversies. There have been many such books, serving to introduce readers to particular bodies of debate and controversy; I take these as given and have no desire to seek to replicate the often excellent surveys and introductions to particular approaches to history or bodies of substantive historical work.[2] Finally, the book is not in the nature of an introductory methodological survey, however sophisticated, where again there are a number of useful primers.[3] This book is, rather, about the intrinsically theoretical nature of historical investigation and representation. More particularly, it seeks to explore and come to a view on two specific issues which have concerned and puzzled me over a long period of time, and it is written in the context of a more general challenge to the nature of history.

The two major issues which puzzle or bother me may be put quite simply, although it is far harder to work through to a satisfactory solution of the questions they raise. I have in part written this book because I wanted to work out an answer to the conundrums they pose. The first issue is precisely that of the multiplicity of theoretical approaches to historical investigation referred to above. If we believe that historical investigation is the pursuit of true accounts of selected aspects of the past, and yet we have competing accounts of the same phenomenon – for example, Marxist and non-Marxist accounts of the origins of the French Revolution, or 'functionalist' and 'intentionalist' accounts of the genesis of the Holocaust – is there some way of deciding between them on grounds that are not purely rooted in political, moral, aesthetic or personal preferences and prejudices? How, in other words, do we deal with the plethora of competing theoretical approaches or 'paradigms' of historical inquiry? The second issue is closely related to this. If we (want to?) believe that historical investigation is the pursuit of truth about the past, and yet competing paradigms seem to be closely related to particular positions on the political spectrum – left-wing, radical, conservative and so on – what, if anything, is left of notions of 'value-freedom' or 'objectivity'? Should such notions be simply jettisoned as intrinsically unattainable, even undesirable, and replaced with a wilfully situated, partisan notion of historical inquiry? But what then – if anything – distinguishes history from myth, ideology, propaganda? What is left of a notion of history as the pursuit of truth about the past?

The more general context of current debate is that of the new twists provided by postmodernist challenges to long-running controversies about relativism, radical scepticism, and the possibility of saying anything at all about the past which is not in some sense fictional, constructed, contestable, unstable, incapable of any form of rational verification (if only in the sense of being in principle open to falsification). In the past few decades, a number of scholars have brought insights from linguistics and literary theory to bear on history, seeking to argue that history is in some senses merely another form of fiction. These challenges have taken several different forms: some postmodernists argue that we can never really know anything about the 'past as such'; others concede that individual factual statements about the past may be true, but hold that the infinity of possible ways in which we can 'emplot' individual facts into coherent narratives, or 'impose' stories on the past, indicates that historical interpretations are essentially constructions in the present, not – as traditional historians would claim – reconstructions of the past.

The debates about postmodernism have recently provoked a number of quite heated responses, many of which seem to me not to deal adequately with the issues raised by the more serious postmodernist theorists. A thread running through this book, therefore, will be that of responses to postmodernism. But I do this alongside trying to grapple with what seem to me the more fundamental questions raised by the issues of paradigms and politics mentioned above. I seek to provide a view of historical investigation as a matter of collective and theoretically informed inquiries into selected aspects of the past, in which it is possible to make 'progress', at least within given parameters of inquiry, and to be clear about the roots of or bases for residual differences in fundamental – metatheoretical – assumptions.

It seems to me that part of the problem lies in the way in which recent debates have become unnecessarily polarised, both in terms of substance and in terms of tempers. While empiricists tend to focus on the evidence of past reality, driven by a degree of optimism about their capacity to evaluate and make good use of that evidence, postmodernists tend to focus rather on issues relating to the lability and unrootedness of current representations of that past (whether or not they have much faith in the 'evidence'). The two barely meet. In particular, postmodernists tend to emphasise heavily the gap between an essentially unknowable past and an imposed (and, it is often implied, almost arbitrarily constructed) representation in the present, while empiricists often tend almost to ignore the character of this gap altogether. Meanwhile, walls of values separate a variety of general approaches from one another, less on theoretical or empirical grounds than on political and personal ones. There has been a relatively widespread temptation to be content with simple assertion, enumeration or juxtaposition of opposing views. This book seeks to analyse the nature of the gap between the 'facts' and empirical traces of the past, so heavily emphasised by empiricists, and the constructions, interpretations or even 'fictions' of the present on which postmodernists tend to lay most emphasis. The gap, I believe, can be bridged only by developing a degree of theoretical awareness.

The facts of the matter?

Why do these issues matter? Why bother our heads with often abstruse theory? Should not historians simply 'get on with the job', rather than engaging in introspective examination of their own enterprise; should they not leave theorising to intellectual historians and philosophers who, by not engaging in the hard slog of substantive research, have the luxury of time to spare for such ruminations? Many practising historians arguably share Geoffrey Elton's 'suspicion that a philosophic concern with such problems as the reality of historical knowledge or the nature of historical thought only hinders the practice of history'.[4] By and large, probably a majority of historians persuade themselves that postmodernist positions, in particular, are rather extreme and need not be taken seriously, although views vary as to whether there is a real threat or not. Lawrence Stone's beleaguered perception of a 'crisis of self-confidence' among practising historians, and his fear that history might become 'an endangered species', are disputed by postmodernist Patrick Joyce, who suggests that, at least in Britain, 'rank indifference rather than outright hostility' is 'the dominant response'.[5] Would it not be better, then, just to turn to practical manuals of 'how to do it', guides to 'source criticism' and the like?

There are several reasons why answers to perennial questions about the nature of history matter, and should matter even for those historians who think they can ignore such questions. Most historians make at least an implicit claim for some degree of truth value for what they are saying. They are generally viewed by the public as 'experts' whose accounts should be distinct from, and superior to, those of myth-mongers, propagandists, pleaders for special interests. Those historians with paid positions in the education system and in what may be termed the 'public history' industry bear a degree of public responsibility and accountability for the ways in which they spend their time. Lay readers on the whole turn to the works of historians with the assumption that they have some expectation of (to use the much-cited quotation from Ranke) finding out 'how it really was': not how someone imagined it might have been, with a combination of inspiration, invention, rhetoric on the one hand, and selection, exploitation and collation of the flotsam and jetsam of surviving 'evidence' on the other; nor how someone would prefer one to think it had been, in order to argue a political or moral case for one side or another in a particular controversy, or to construct an acceptable identity in which a previously underprivileged or marginalised group can take pride.

Yet the very plurality of approaches in history suggests that there is in fact no single disciplinary approach: that 'history' actually only refers to the subject matter – that which has gone, the past – and not to a distinctive set of theories and methodologies. Even what is worthy of constituting an object of inquiry in the past is itself often a matter of controversy: for example, the narrow definitions of their subject matter by historians of high politics have increasingly come under fire from those who view other aspects of human experience as being equally valid or at least potentially illuminating objects of study. But also, and more importantly: if mutually competing accounts are produced, from different theoretical (or political, or personal) perspectives, of the *same* phenomenon in the past, and there appears to be no rational – or at least mutually agreed – means of adjudicating between these approaches, then what is the status of any notion of historical truth? Are not the competing accounts simply acts of faith? If there is no agreement on the character of the phenomena to be studied, then what has become of a 'discipline' which cannot even agree on its object of inquiry, let alone any mode of interpretation or explanation?

A familiar, if somewhat extreme, example will serve to illustrate some of the basic issues. In Nazi Germany, around six million people were murdered on grounds of 'race', politics, religious belief, or alleged physical 'inferiority' (the Nazi notion of 'life unworthy of living', *lebensunwertes Leben*). There are an almost infinite variety of ways of trying to recount and represent this horror – none of them, arguably, adequate to its reconstruction and explanation. Any notion of history writing as mimesis – an accurate reproduction of the past in its entirety, or in its 'essence' – instantly breaks down in face of this tragedy. This extreme example also presents an extreme challenge to notions of history as rational explanation in terms of a complex combination of causes under particular circumstances, or as interpretive understanding of the motives of actors. Even the very construction of a single *explanandum* – the Holocaust – rests on the assumption that millions of different individual acts of brutality and murder, scattered across different parts of a continent over an extended period of years, can be brought together under a single conceptual heading positing some unity and cohesion to these disparate events. As such, constructions and interpretations of the Holocaust would appear to give important fodder to the postmodernist case.[6]

Those historians coming from an essentially empiricist position would place primary emphasis on empirical accuracy. It is of course important to ensure that 'the facts' are correct – as illustrated in the notorious libel case brought (and lost) by David Irving against Deborah Lipstadt and the publisher of her book on revisionist interpretations of the Holocaust, Penguin Books. The facts are clearly essential building blocks in the development of historical accounts. But investigating history is about more than simply digging up 'true facts' about the past, and jettisoning false assertions or exposing fraudulent misrepresentation. Even a very brief glance at historical controversies over Nazi Germany will reveal that there are a wide range of positions which may be held by historians who do pay appropriate respect to the evidence. There is, for example, the so-called 'intentionalist/functionalist' controversy over the way in which Nazi racism developed into mass genocide, with major differences in theoretical assumptions between those placing primary emphasis on Hitler's intentions, on the one hand, and those explaining increasing radicalisation in terms of the way the regime functioned, on the other.[7] A quite different approach is developed by those such as Daniel Goldhagen, who effectively resurrects older notions of 'national character' by positing some form of German collective mentality characterised by 'eliminationist anti-semitism' persisting over centuries.[8] Similarly, in explaining Hitler's rise to power, there are worlds of theoretical difference between those who emphasise long-term structural features such as Germany's alleged 'special path' to modernity, or *Sonderweg*; those who put a heavy explanatory burden on the medium-term consequences of Germany's defeat in the First World War and the provisions of the Treaty of Versailles, or the weak structure and development of the Weimar economy; those who lay primary emphasis on the alleged charisma of Hitler, coming as it were out of nowhere; or those who highlight the political narrative of short-term decisions and mistakes of individual politicians in the closing years of Weimar democracy. Thus, even among historians with a serious respect for the evidence, the self-same historical facts can be emplotted in many different kinds of narrative.

Thus, while an emphasis on empirical evidence, and on the skills of critical evaluation and interpretation of sources, is highly important, it is not in itself sufficient as an argument for history being more than ideology or myth, a belief system akin to any other. This is the somewhat unsatisfactory position which, at heart, Richard J. Evans' *In Defence of History* boils down to.[9] I agree with Evans that it is essential to get the facts right. But I do not think that he has dealt adequately with related arguments about varieties of possible ways of emplotting the same facts. Nor is it sufficient to say that there may be many perspectives on a phenomenon, all potentially of equal value, as some other commentators argue. Historical knowledge and interpretations are too important an aspect of our lives for us to rest content with a view that history is all 'just perspectival', or that, essentially, 'anything goes' and that evaluation is more a matter of where one's political sympathies lie than of the (essentially unattainable) 'truth' of any given account. Oddly, Ludmilla Jordanova's recent account, *History in Practice*, combines both these views. She places a great deal of emphasis on the essentially 'common sense' skills of the practitioner, and brushes off very lightly the problem of personal moral and political sympathies, simply acknowledging and accepting these as an element in adjudicating competing accounts. This is also the central problem with the attempt to rescue some notion of truth presented by Joyce Appleby, Lynn Hunt and Margaret Jacobs, in *Telling the Truth about History*.[10] Their essentially whiggish (though transposed to American history) account of the development of historical approaches culminates in the proposal that we should simply celebrate a democratic, multi-cultural, multi-perspectival, pluralism of historical approaches without seriously addressing the – still – relativist implications of this view, which (if taken to its logical conclusion, which they fail to do) would imply that only political sympathies can ultimately adjudicate between 'better' (= underdog, enabling, empowering, etc.) and 'worse' (= conservative, elitist, etc.) accounts.

If historians agree on the facts – dates, events, 'what happened' – but do not agree on the broader framework of interpretation or explanation, should we simply accept that all accounts are merely 'perspectives', in principle equally valid (or equally fictitious)? Or can we develop some means of looking, not merely at the accuracy of the individual building blocks, but also at the wider interpretive framework? It is the latter which primarily concerns me in this book. And historical theory, in this sense, is not a purely 'academic question'.

To return to our example: it is clearly desperately important, for a whole variety of reasons, for historians to continue the attempt to gain as accurate – and as objective and unbiased – an analysis and explanation of the Holocaust as possible. For explanations of this mass murder are at the same time attributions of culpability or guilt on the one hand, and declarations of exoneration on the other. And these attributions have played a major role in the societies which have come after Hitler. From war crimes trials to the facilitation or blighting of professional careers, from radical sociopolitical restructuring to kicking over the traces, from private and public commemorations to selective reinterpretation and repression of memory, interpretations of the past are inevitably also a part of the present.[11] It is all the more important, then, to be aware of the parameters and claims to truth of historical scholarship; of the ways in which the production of historical knowledge is an integral part of an ever-changing present; and of how historical consciousness affects the ways in which we engage with the present and help to shape the future.

The organisation of the argument

The book is broadly divided into three parts, although all of these overlap. The rest of Part I examines approaches to history, both in the sense of the discipline of historical investigation, and in the sense of historical perspectives on the past. Chapter 2 introduces recent theoretical debates about 'the nature of history' in the light of longer-term disagreements over the contested character of historical inquiry. At the end of that chapter will be found a guide to what I intend to argue in relation to those debates throughout the rest of the book; an argument which requires some knowledge of current debates and which therefore cannot so easily be placed here, where it might otherwise belong. Readers familiar with the theoretical background and the issues around postmodernism (and who are no doubt used to skipping about on CD-Roms) can easily hop directly to this summary of arguments at the end of Chapter 2 if they so wish. Chapter 3 turns to what I consider to be the most important and difficult challenge: that of the sheer variety of historical traditions, the diversity of approaches, or paradigms, in history. Rather than simply recounting the histories of different theoretical traditions, I seek to examine the ways in which different paradigms in the present affect the diversity of routes into the past, and explore the underlying bases of the current plethora of theoretical positions, some of which are more compatible with one another than others.

Part II then turns to analyse the diverse ways in which historians can seek to investigate the past, paying particular attention to strategies for seeking to bridge the gap between present concerns and assumptions, on the one hand, and the complexities of myriad aspects of the past, on the other. I look explicitly at the essentially theoretical problems – which are common to historians of all theoretical persuasions, including those who claim to have none – of framing questions, devising appropriate conceptual frameworks, assessing what is always theoretically netted 'evidence', and constructing answers which serve to satisfy curiosity. Chapter 4 argues that, contrary to the position of postmodernists, the much vaunted 'death of metanarrative' does not logically entail that any narrative is merely a fictive construct imposed almost arbitrarily at the whim and fancy of the historian in the present. Rather, historians work within given frameworks of questions and puzzles, seeking to find answers to such communally defined problems using sets of concepts and methodological tools which are more or less open to amendment and development. In the process of seeking answers to questions, they may develop new approaches, insights or theories. Chapter 5 looks at the issue of concepts as the nets through which we seek to capture the traces of the past. It argues that there are serious theoretical issues which all historians need to address with respect to the selection and development of appropriate conceptual frameworks for netting the evidence. Chapter 6 then examines the ways in which historians do not arbitrarily 'emplot' titbits of evidence or individual factual statements into a continuous narrative, but rather search for conceptually netted evidence or clues in order to try, rationally and logically, to answer their theoretically informed questions about the past. Both individual factual statements and wider historical pictures or theories are thus, *contra* the views of postmodernists, potentially 'disconfirmable' (to use the neologism favoured by one of their prime exponents, Hayden White). Chapter 7 draws attention, however, to the rather diverse ways in which curiosity may be satisfied, depending often on far wider assumptions which are not rooted in the empirical evidence. In particular, historians and their audiences differ greatly with respect to underlying assumptions about such questions as the relative roles of structure and agency, of wider constraining and constructing forces versus individual motives, decisions and actions, or the underlying drives and emotions of a hidden psyche. Depending on wider philosophical assumptions about what it is to be human, and other beliefs which may well be beyond the scope of empirical or rational argument, different historians will appeal to, or rest content with, very different types of analysis. While there may be no obvious rational means of choosing between different approaches at this level, at least it will be possible to be clear about what such choices might entail by way of wider beliefs or leaps of faith.

Part III then turns to aspects of bringing selected, interpreted knowledge of the past to the present, examining issues of representation, reception and political implications of our knowledge of the past in the present.

I argue that, while all historical knowledge is inevitably situated, we need to work towards a more complex understanding of the ways in which historical accounts are coloured by contemporary political and other connotations than has so far been available in analyses focussing primarily on the attributes and assumed prejudices of individual historians. Historical investigation, representation and reception are collective endeavours. I conclude by exploring the status of partial (in all senses) historical knowledge as a central part of our lives as human, social beings. I argue throughout for the possibility of inter-subjective communication across cultures separated by time (history) as well as – but in different ways from – inter-subjective communication between different individuals, social groups and places in the contemporary world. As a creative, sociopolitical and cultural endeavour, history is no less subject to vicissitudes and failures of communication (difficulties of translation, inaccuracies, indeterminacies, ambiguities and loss of meaning, unintended distortion or downright dishonesty) than any other form of mutual understanding; but this does not mean that, in the babel of tongues, ideals cannot be articulated, standards enunciated, progress made. In short: *pace* postmodernism, but without rushing to join the anti-theoretical barricades of some empiricists, I think it is possible to seek responsible, accountable ways of investigating and representing the past – all the more so if we know the implications and limits of the theoretical language in which we are talking. It is the purpose of this book to explore some of the parameters of those collective conversations.

2

THE CONTESTED NATURE OF HISTORICAL KNOWLEDGE

Historians have never agreed about the nature of their craft; and yet this has never prevented people from continuing to engage in historical investigation and debate. For centuries, western conceptions of history have combined, in different measures, views of history as a branch of literature or poetry, an ingredient of politics in the sense of praising heroes and denouncing villains, a contribution to collective memory in the keeping of chronicles and annals, and an essentially religious stamping ground for moral lessons for the present and future. Debates over questions such as 'how did this state of affairs come to pass' or 'who is to blame' or 'let us now praise famous men/fallen heroes' are inevitably ones which arouse high emotions and violent disagreements. Such disagreements inevitably spill over into questions not merely of substance but also of method. Historical understanding, in short, has for centuries been an integral and contested element of human life in an ever-changing present.

Even when the notion of history as scientific investigation of the past became widespread, historians continued to disagree dramatically over the character and implications of their investigations. While some sought for the 'laws' of human development, others sought merely to reconstruct unique aspects of the past 'for its own sake'. Some thought, with Marx, that rather than merely investigating the world, the point was to change it; others followed Ranke in eschewing any political role at all in the attempt at modest reconstruction of the past 'as it actually was'. Most recently, some theorists of history have posed fundamental queries as to whether the past can be known at all – or whether we are not essentially back with history as literature, politics and myth.

The diversity of historical traditions

With the eighteenth-century Enlightenment recognisably 'modern', 'scientific' versions of recounting and exploring the past began to appear, as in Montesquieu's *Spirit of the Laws*, which sought to identify and explain in secular terms regularities and variations in types of government. Yet even in the writings of the great German Enlightenment philosopher Hegel an older, fundamentally religious framework was present: the heritage of the Judeo-Christian tradition,

12

with its notions of the original fall and the progressive struggle towards redemption in the 'final day of judgement' can be clearly discerned in Hegel's key notion of historical stages in terms of 'World Spirit realising itself'. Many of the great historical works of the later eighteenth and nineteenth centuries continued to be marked by a combination of moral engagement and literary endeavour; many historical analyses were also prompted by serious political engagement with the key issues of their time (Tocqueville, Burke and others on the French Revolution; Tocqueville on America). These features of history – its engagement with the past from the perspective of the present – continued to be central even with its establishment as an academic discipline in the nineteenth century.

With the new faith in positivist conceptions of science, history was established as a university subject, worthy of study in its own right alongside other academic disciplines. A key figure in this 'scientisation' of history, and founding father of what is often confusingly termed 'historism' or 'historicism' (a term subsequently deployed in a very different sense by the philosopher Karl Popper, as we shall see in a moment) was the German historian Leopold von Ranke. While his very substantial body of historical works have faded into a dusty distance, he is extraordinarily well-known for one brief phrase: his oft-quoted dictum that historians should show 'how it really [or actually] was'. Given the odd grammatical construction of Ranke's oft-quoted phrase, *wie es eigentlich gewesen*, which always feels as if it is missing a final verb (*ist*), it is perhaps worth for once quoting the full sentence, which could roughly, if somewhat inelegantly, be translated as follows: 'History has been ascribed the office of judging the past in order to teach the contemporary world for the use of future years; the present attempt is not subservient to such high offices; it only seeks to show how it actually was.'[1] The thrust of the comment is thus to emphasise history as a modest endeavour concerned solely with retrieving the evidence and reconstructing the past irrespective of any moral judgements or potential uses for contemporary purposes.

Yet such a notion was not universally shared, even within Ranke's own German cultural environment. At precisely the time Ranke was promoting a notion of investigating the past 'as it actually was', his more radical contemporary, Karl Marx, began – as he saw it – to uncloak bourgeois notions of history (and particularly heroic narratives of high politics) as disguised ideology. Struggling free from the Hegelian heritage of German Idealism, Marx sought to show that history was at heart the record, not of some mystical 'World Spirit realising itself', but rather of the collective struggles of real people. In effect, Marx simply replaced one metanarrative with another. In place of World Spirit came the progressive history of humankind to produce and reproduce, in the process entering into distinctive sets of social relations (or class relations), constantly developing the technical means of production, and proceeding through revolutionary struggles to ever higher stages in the history of human emancipation. Without entering into any detail here over the massive corpus of Marx's work and the continuing debates over its interpretation, it is worth highlighting three general features of the Marxist heritage.

First, despite his reaction against the substance of Hegel's idealist view of history, Marx inherited the somewhat metaphysical 'grand narrative' in terms of historical progress towards an ultimate goal, the 'end' of human history: in his case, this was to be an indistinctly defined, because as yet unrealised, communist society of plenty. There have been many subsequent reactions against this, often simply replacing one grand narrative with another, such as the rise of liberalism, democracy, 'Progress' – or, in the case of postmodernism, with a narrative of chaos and indeterminacy. Second, Marx wrote in the positivist context of nineteenth-century faith in science, and belief in the possibility of discovering underlying social and economic 'laws'. Again, while reacting against any general notion of historical or social 'laws', there have been subsequent variations on the theme, questioning whether it is possible to develop valid historical generalisations or provide causal explanations which do not give much – or indeed any – weight to the actors' perceptions and ideals. Third, Marx was (at least in his early writings) acutely aware of the importance of human agency, and the power of people to affect and change circumstances: his notion of revolutionary 'praxis', in contrast to mere philosophical understanding of the world, effectively challenged any notion of merely observing the past 'for its own sake'. This too has proved to be an extraordinarily fertile source for future notions of historical interpretation as interventions in the present – and has been massively opposed by those coming from the Rankean tradition of history as a documents-based study of the past 'in its own terms' or 'for its own sake' (however laden these latter phrases might also be).

Despite the often extraordinarily prescient insights, detailed theories and ambitious scope of his work, Marx failed to integrate these three features (some of which have been submerged into general 'common sense', others of which are rooted in wider quasi-metaphysical presuppositions which very few would share today). It is important to note, however, that Marx's attempt to construct a truly 'scientific' alternative, allegedly revealing the hidden 'laws' of social development – which yet required a little helping hand from a politically enlightened vanguard – shifted attention away from the motives and actions of individuals to underlying economic and social structures and collective class actors. This faith in the possibility of 'scientific analysis' of what was 'really' the case, beyond the expressed ideas and values of individual historical participants, combined with an activist notion of political intervention to effect future change, inaugurated radically different traditions of historical writing in the twentieth century from those emanating from other nineteenth-century academic currents.

Thus, even as history began to be established as an academic discipline, it was one with remarkable internal diversity of objects of inquiry, and notions of methods and goals. In the form of Marxism-Leninism, Marx's approach was institutionalised in the historical academies of twentieth-century communist states, and also became, in the rainbow colours of western neo-Marxisms, highly influential among left-wing circles in many capitalist states, although with dramatic variations and much internal factionalism. While Marxist historians were among the most prolific and engaged writers in some national contexts, they were well-nigh outcasts in others. At a philosophical level, Karl Popper's famous critique of the 'poverty of historicism' (note the misnomer) accused Marxism – and Freudian psychoanalysis – of being an essentially unfalsifiable belief system on a par with religion. Nevertheless, a combination of Marx and Freud fed into, for example, the highly influential writings of the Frankfurt School of Critical Theory. The critiques of the Enlightenment heritage, and more activist notions of praxis, initially developed by Adorno and Horkheimer, fed into later twentieth-century historical and social analyses in the United States and Germany, most notably in the works of Herbert Marcuse and Jürgen Habermas. Quite different forms of Marxism which almost wrote human agency out of human history entirely were to be found among the structuralists associated with Louis Althusser in France, who, in turn, clashed violently with humanistic Marxist historians such as the British historian E. P. Thompson. Thus the ambiguous legacy of Marx was one to which many heirs laid claim.

In western states, a wide variety of alternative non-Marxist theoretical traditions proliferated. The sustained attempts of Max Weber to develop a methodologically self-aware approach to problems of world history resulted in a highly sophisticated set of concepts and theses. Weber sought to combine the systematic pursuit of valid historical generalisations with an emphasis on the need for an 'interpretive understanding' of the internal meanings of human behaviour, both in the sense of individual motives for action and in the wider sense of collective belief systems which could not be reduced, as in Marx's work, to some 'underlying' material base. Weber also sought to separate academic analysis from political prescriptions, with his notions of 'value neutrality' and objectivity.

In the course of the twentieth century, the growth of higher education in the western world sustained – even, with its emphasis on originality, actively fostered – a wide variety of competing theoretical approaches, squabbling heirs, in different ways, to the Rankean or Enlightenment heritage, with often cataclysmic differences in underlying assumptions. This is not the place to provide any kind of history of historical scholarship; but it is important simply to note the sheer diversity – and continuing diversification – of historical traditions and approaches. Historians focussing on high politics and international diplomacy were challenged by others seeking to pay attention to labour history, social history, women's history; these in turn were challenged by those seeking to refocus attention on issues of mentality or culture. Nationally defined histories were viewed in new ways by those coming from post-colonial perspectives. Differences over subject area were cross-cut by theoretical and methodological debates. Those writing 'traditional' historical narratives couched in terms of individual motives, actions, contingencies, combinations of circumstances, unintended consequences and unique chains of events, were challenged by those proposing a more analytical approach to history in terms of 'factors' and generalisations, often based in explicitly formulated hypotheses and systematically assessed by means of stringently comparative or quantitative analyses. There remained major differences over the extent to which historical research and writing could or should be value-free.

Thus, over the course of the past two centuries, a wide diversity of approaches to history have developed in the educational establishments of the industrialised world. To bowdlerise only slightly, the historical landscape of the later twentieth century might appear to a Martian observer roughly as follows. While pragmatic stalwarts sought to hold the terrain of objectivity or value neutrality, and some continued the pursuit of 'governing laws' on a widely prevalent model of the natural sciences, theoretical ambushes were mounted on all sides. So-called 'hermeneutic' theorists pointed to the importance of 'interpretive understanding' of rule-guided behaviour, in contrast to notions of causal explanation, arguing that there were key differences between interpretations of human actions and explanations of natural phenomena. Those influenced by anthropology entered the thickets of meaning in quest of 'thick descriptions', picking up on a much-quoted notion of Clifford Geertz. Non-Marxist structuralists of one variety or another engaged in underground exploration of 'deep structures', whether of the economy or the 'human mind'; others looked rather at structures in terms of visible social relations, facets of political organisation and institutional arrangements. Meanwhile, some dogged historians simply plodded on, empiricist hats on heads to protect against the dazzling glare of theory, spades in hand in order to dig up the empirical facts of the past and explain what had happened by providing a simple chronological narrative of what they had found. Then, finally, in the closing decades of the twentieth century, along came the postmodernists: to tell everyone that it is in principle impossible to access the 'signified' behind the 'signifier', itself a mere product of 'discourse'; that reality can never be tapped in representation.[2]

Such a brief sketch of course entails massive oversimplification of the past two centuries of theoretical controversy. But it does perhaps serve to point to a long-standing and rather startling state of indecision (or, to put it more strongly, fundamental disagreement in principle) about the nature of historical investigation. Underlying these different approaches are quite diverse assumptions about the nature of historical actors, the character of historical inquiry, and the relations between investigation of the past and standpoint in the present. Many of these debates revolve too on comparisons between modes of investigation and the production of 'knowledge' in history and natural science. Differences in historical approach have also frequently been fundamentally linked to different positions in the political spectrum. Narratives of high politics have often been linked to conservatism, for example, while social history, labour history or feminist history have often been associated with self-professedly left-wing or radical historians. Yet for many decades a notion of objectivity nevertheless held sway among probably the majority of western professional historians.

Recently, there has been – and note the paradox of the way I am about to describe this – a marked re- or de-politicisation of history for extraneous, world-historical reasons. Commentators vary as to the direction in which they think this trend is going: while right-wingers see the 'death of Marxism' as heralding a de-politicisation or 'death of ideology', left-wingers see the 'triumph of conservatism' as rather a politicisation in the other direction. Whichever way one cuts into these debates, there is a startling formal symmetry, roughly running along the lines of 'my history is objective and true; yours is ideological and false'.

The critique of western 'bourgeois' history as ideology had of course long been a refrain of Marxist historiographical approaches, particularly those sustained by the communist regimes of the former Soviet bloc. In practice, historians under communist regimes had varying degrees of leeway, and not all Marxist history written under the constrained and censored circumstances of different eastern European communist regimes adhered to the bald tenets of the ruling parties.[3] This was of course even less the case among the wide variety of western forms of neo-Marxism, many of which developed almost entirely unconstrained by political considerations (and some of their more abstruse proponents apparently barely aware of any real world outside the ivory tower exchanges, virtually unintelligible outside the charmed circles of the converted). Ironically, the end of the Cold War has in some areas simply shifted, rather than removed, the political barriers in history. The collapse of the communist regimes of eastern Europe in 1989–90 of course carried with it a rejection of Marxism as the legitimating ideology of dictatorships now discredited, not only by the western 'victors of history' in charge of the 'restructuring' of institutions of teaching and research in the former Soviet bloc, but also in the eyes of those who had formerly lived in, even many of those who had sustained, these regimes. But, in the process, an interesting shift began to be notable at least in certain corners of western historiography not previously associated with political intent: there was a more overt politicisation of much western historical writing, a more explicitly condemnatory or laudatory tone than had been fashionable for some time in quarters previously noted for their claim to 'objectivity'. The end of détente signalled a return to quite strident – victorious – overtones in many conservative quarters in the West. On the right, there has recently been a vociferous rejection of the long-held postulate of 'value-free' scholarship. The resurrection of 'totalitarianism' as a concept, once utterly discredited as an instrument of Cold War propaganda, is indicative of this trend towards the explicit and wilful repoliticisation of history on the right.[4] So too, of course, is the proclamation of the 'end of history'; the triumph of western liberalism as the (quasi-Hegelian?) goal towards which all of History had been striving.

The diversity of historical perspectives, and the close links between particular theoretical approaches and political standpoints, have presented a major challenge to any notion of history as the pursuit of truth. This is not limited to the long-running debates between 'left' and 'right', but has diversified with the plethora of 'new approaches' to history in the later twentieth century. Some have gladly acknowledged and even celebrated the inevitably situated character of historical knowledge, including for example the challenges to 'traditional' historical narratives mounted by those coming from feminist or post-colonial perspectives.

Others have clung to a notion of historical truth as unrelated to contemporary political standpoints. Some have implicitly assumed that competing interpretations can in some way be combined in principle in a wider synthesis, as 'new perspectives' serve to widen old horizons; others have taken the dazzling, ever-changing mosaic as indicative of the kaleidoscopic character of contemporary pictures of the past, which can itself never 'really' be known. On the latter view, history is about the imposition of interpretations, the construction of meanings: endowing and investing selected remnants of the past with meanings in the present, not reconstructing it 'as it actually was'. The issues raised by this diversity of assumptions and approaches will be addressed throughout the rest of this book.

The postmodernist challenge

The currently fashionable theoretical terrain for debating these rather longstanding questions about the character of history is that of postmodernism, which has shifted attention to the relations between history and literature. A growing sense of unease with both the positivist and the Marxist traditions led many historians in the 1970s to pay greater attention to issues of language, culture, and 'discourse'. But this was no mere shift of subject matter or substantive area of interest, as had been the case with many previously heralded 'new approaches', such as labour history, economic history, women's history, social history, the history of everyday life. Rather, it posed a fundamental challenge to the very possibility of doing history at all – at least in the versions which had predominated, across a wide range of areas of historical inquiry, for the preceding two centuries. It was premised on quite different notions both of 'knowledge' and of ontology, or modes of being in the world. As David Harvey puts it, 'fragmentation, indeterminacy, and intense distrust of all universal and "totalising" discourses (to use the favoured phrase) are the hallmark of postmodernist thought . . . [and] a rejection of "metanarratives" (large-scale theoretical interpretations purportedly of universal application).'[5] This shift inaugurated – or was accompanied by – a widespread scepticism about being able to know and/or say anything about the real past which was not in some sense fictional.[6]

There is a very widespread view that history is about real people and real events, which really happened, and from the surviving traces of which a relatively accurate account can be constructed. This is without doubt the most prevalent view among lay people, who read history books, go to museums, look at exhibitions, watch documentaries, in the faith that they can rely on the professionals to present to them some approach to an accurate picture of the past 'as it really was'. It is also a view which embodies a belief in the possibility of progress, of cumulative advances in knowledge, as professional research tells us more about things which we only imperfectly knew about or understood before. It places faith in the professional expertise, hard work and skills of historians to pursue the empirical quest and present the results with integrity. And it is precisely this faith which has been challenged head-on by postmodernists. So, whatever one makes of some of their more abstruse formulations and ontological claims, it is important to attain some clarity about what precisely they are saying and whether or not it makes sense. If it does, the enterprise of historical investigation cannot deliver what most people, particularly lay consumers, think it can; if postmodernist claims do not make sense, then we need an explicit articulation of where precisely postmodernists have gone wrong.

On some views, postmodernism is less a theoretical position than an inescapable contemporary condition. To take the example of one vocal exponent (following Lyotard's notion of the 'postmodern condition'), in Keith Jenkins' view, whether we like it or not, we have no choice: 'Today we live within the general condition of *postmodernity*. We do not have a choice about this. For postmodernity is not an "ideology" or a position we can choose to subscribe to or not; postmodernity is precisely our condition: it is our fate.'[7] On Jenkins' view, our only choice appears to lie in whether we celebrate and enjoy our condition, or grumble, mutter, and ineffectually seek to resist the inevitable. But not all would share this analysis of our age and our intellectual condition. Others (including myself) might prefer to conceive of postmodernism as a claim – or, rather, a loose set of only partially related and seriously contested claims – rather than a *fait accompli*. I should emphasise – and the reader should take it as given throughout – that a lot more goes under the amorphous label of postmodernism than is relevant in this context: in an architectural and design context, for example, postmodernism has been defined as 'anti-Bauhaus'.

My concern here, in any event, is not to define postmodernism as such (a definitional game which would be both of little import and doomed to disintegrate in qualifications), but rather to focus on certain questions posed by self-proclaimed postmodernists which are of direct relevance to the practice of history. In particular, there seem to me to be two separate issues raised under the banner of postmodernist approaches to history, which do not necessarily always go together. One has to do with the possibility – or otherwise – of unmediated access to a real past; the other has to do with what is done with the surviving traces (whether deemed to be 'texts', or considered as essentially unproblematic 'events' or 'facts') of that past in the present. The focus of postmodernist critiques of 'traditional' history varies according to whether they are more concerned with the former or the latter, or, in the more radical versions, both.

There are some rather extreme proponents of the 'all the world's a text' variety – or, to use Derrida's now popular formula in French, '*il n'y a pas de hors-texte*' – who suggest that all we have in history is a series of constructed texts commenting on constructed texts commenting on constructed texts, in a seemingly endless circle of constructed meanings which cannot be directly assessed against an unmediated 'real' past. The past is on this view simply not available as an objective criterion for adjudicating among discourses.

F. R. Ankersmit, for example, has presented this view. He disputes that one can go back to a still extant written text from the past – he uses the example of

Thomas Hobbes – to adjudicate among competing interpretations of that written text, which is actually still available to us in the present (in a way in which actions, emotions, personalities, relationships, indubitably are not): he states with direct reference to the example of Hobbes that 'we no longer have any texts, any past, but just interpretations of them'.[8] The situation is even worse with respect to comparisons of different interpretations of the same historical topic; in Ankersmit's view, there is simply no way of appealing to some independent court of evidence, the past:

> There is no past that is given to us and to which we could compare these two or more texts [competing interpretations of the same topic] in order to find out which of them does correspond to the past and which does not . . . [T]he past as the complex referent of the historical text as a whole has no role to play in historical debate . . .[!] Texts are all we have and we can only compare texts with texts . . . [W]e can never test our conclusions by comparing the elected text with 'the past' itself . . . [N]or is such reference [to 'the past'] required from the point of view of historical debate.[9]

On this view, history acts not as a window on, but rather as an artistic substitute for, the past which it seeks to replace. The criterion for judging any historical account is thus not whether it is faithful to some real past, but whether one likes it or not – on political or aesthetic grounds, rather than the criteria of accuracy or explanatory power favoured by more empiricist historians. Keith Jenkins – at least in his very widely read incarnation of the 1990s – acts as a useful secondary exponent of postmodernist views developed by Ankersmit and others. Jenkins tells us that postmodernism entails:

> an understanding of the past which asserts that such an understanding is always positioned, is always fabricated, is always self-referencing and is never true beyond peradventure; that history has no intrinsic meaning, that *there is no way of privileging one variant over another by neutral criteria* and which sees histories located at the centre, or on the margins, not necessarily by virtue of their historiographical rigour and/or sophistication – for brilliant histories can be variously marginalised – but by their relationship to those that have the power to put them there.[10]

Historians, on Jenkins' view, have always only been able to engage in some form of intertextuality; what he finds suspicious are the imputed motives for resistance to acknowledging that this is what historians do and always have done.[11] (Jenkins does not consider the possibility that his own views, which he appears to hold with more passionate conviction than clarity of argument, might legitimately be challenged.) The only arbiters here of 'truth' appear to be personal and political sympathies.

These are views plucked from the more extreme end of the spectrum, denying any kind of access to knowledge of the past 'as it really was' (to return to Ranke's useful phrase). There are also less extreme versions of this emphasis on textualism. Patrick Joyce, to take a relatively rare example of one who not only preaches but also seeks to practise postmodernist history, does not dispute the reality of a past. However, that past is only present to us in a discursive, textual form:

> At one level we may of course posit a dualism between the 'real' . . . and representations of it. The 'real' can be said to exist independently of our representations of it, and to affect those representations [note the concession, unlike Ankersmit and Jenkins!]. But this effect is always discursive, and it must be insisted that history is never present to us in anything but a discursive form, here taking 'discursive', of course, to denote all forms of communication, including those beyond the verbal alone . . .
>
> The major advance of 'postmodernism' needs to be registered by historians: namely that the events, structures and processes of the past are indistinguishable from the forms of documentary representation, the conceptual and political appropriations, and the historical discourses that construct them . . . There is no overarching coherence evident . . . Gone . . . are the grand narratives that historicised the notion of social totality.[12]

The emphasis here is on the discursive, in the sense of pre-interpreted, character of all social reality. There can be no access to any putative 'past as such'.

There is another version of postmodernism, particularly associated with Hayden White, which focusses less on the character of the surviving traces of the past (as in the Joyce example just quoted) than on what the historian does with these traces in the present. Many people whom one might call postmodernists do *not* deny that the past was real, or that real evidence has survived from it.[13] In that sense, they do not disagree with the empiricists, who often weaken their case by punching an extremist straw man. (It might also be noted in passing that, while Hayden White's classic text on *Metahistory* of 1973 is often seen to have heralded the advent of postmodernism in history,[14] the question of what constitutes a historical 'fact', and how it is plucked from the past and actively woven into a constructed story in the present, is far from new: even Carr and Elton batted this particular topic about.[15]) In its postmodernist incarnation, this view claims that while individual statements may be true (or false), the way the historian shapes them into a coherent interpretation or representation is a product of the present, imposed in an almost infinite variety of possible ways on the traces of the past. What Hayden White and his followers have done is thus to focus less on the sources themselves than on the uses the historian makes of them when making a selection from them and imposing a constructed account in re-presenting them: it is the extraordinary lability and range of interpretations possible in the mode of

representation, rather than problems concerned with evidence from the maelstrom of an undisputed past *reality*, which is the prime focus of their concern.

Hayden White has highlighted what appears to him to be the devastating revelation that stories are not given in the wealth of material that has survived from
the past. The past did not unfold as narrative; this has to be superimposed on it,
to give it coherence and meaning, in retrospect. Thus the form which historians
impose in reconstructing and representing the past is itself essentially also a content. Hayden White puts it thus: the 'traditional view' is that

> what distinguishes 'historical' from 'fictional' stories is first and fore-
> most their content, rather than their form. The content of historical
> stories is real events, events that really happened, rather than imaginary
> events, events invented by the narrator. This implies that the form in
> which historical events present themselves to a prospective narrator is
> found rather than constructed . . . The story told is a mimesis of the
> story lived in some region of historical reality, and insofar as it is an
> accurate imitation, it is considered to be a truthful account thereof.[16]

Hayden White argues that:

> this value attached to narrativity in the representation of real events
> arises out of a desire to have real events display the coherence, integrity,
> fullness, and closure of an image of life that is and only can be
> imaginary.[17]

There are variations in the ways in which this imposition of narrative on selected
events from the past is conceived, and some of Hayden White's own analyses
seem unduly symmetrical and arbitrary (unlike the more traditional historians'
penchant for the number three – causes, course and consequences; beginning,
middle, end – White has a proclivity for dividing things into four). The problem
here is less the inaccessibility of a real past than the general implication that there
are a wide, if not quite infinite, variety of ways in which the 'same' past can be
differently recounted, as different 'emplotments' are imposed on historical material, leading to a potentially dizzying relativism in which it is hard to discern any
rational criteria for prioritising any one interpretation or representation over
another. (Hayden White has in fact subsequently conceded that certain emplotments of the Holocaust – for example, as comedy – are simply not acceptable;
and while Roberto Benigni's often very humorous film, *Life is Beautiful*, may at
first blush appear to contradict this, on further reflection it does not constitute
'comedy' in the classical definition.)[18] This is little different, in effect, from
Ankersmit's notion of 'narrative substances' or historical concepts (such as 'the
Cold War') which are imposed on, rather than given in, the past.[19]

On this view – and not without reason – history has begun to collapse towards
literature, as theorists have adopted some of the tenets and concepts of literary

criticism to analyse the writing of history, and been struck more by similarities than by differences. As we shall see further in later chapters, scholars such as Hans Kellner have developed more fully the notion that history cannot be about 'getting the story straight', because there is simply no story 'out there' to be told.[20] Others, such as Robert Berkhofer, have deeply unsettled any view of history as we traditionally have known it, whether as writers or readers, without yet being able to present any stable or clearly defined alternative.[21]

There is clearly a problem for notions of historical knowledge if these views are accepted. As three American commentators, Appleby, Hunt and Jacobs, have put it, the question for the postmodernist is:

> how does the historian as author construct his or her text, how is the illusion of authenticity produced, what creates a sense of truthfulness to the facts and a warranty of closeness to past reality (or the 'truth-effect' as it is sometimes called)? The implication is that the historian does not in fact capture the past in fruitful fashion but rather, like the novelist, gives the appearance of doing so.[22]

They also note that the term itself is uneasy: 'post-' is not a declaration of what it *is*, but rather what it is *against*, what it *comes after* but does not securely replace. To quote Appleby, Hunt and Jacobs again:

> At the heart of modernity is the notion of the freely acting, freely knowing individual whose experiments can penetrate the secrets of nature and whose work with other individuals can make a new and better world.
>
> Postmodernists' primary goal has been to challenge convictions about the objectivity of knowledge and the stability of language . . . Postmodernism renders problematic the belief in progress, the modern periodisation of history, and the individual as knower and doer.[23]

This is rather curiously linked to a degree of what might be called perspectival pluralism. Since an almost infinite number of stories can be told about (or constructed from, or imposed upon) the 'same' past, from an almost infinite variety of perspectives, and since there is no means of access to the 'real' past beyond texts or discourses about it, there is no metatheoretical means of adjudicating between stories. So what at first sight appears to be a principled (and arguably 'politically correct') support of pluralism, of 'multi-culturalism', of telling stories from the point of view of 'the Other' (women, the underdog, the marginalised) rather than only the victors of history, reveals itself in the end to be extraordinarily a-political: one can hardly take up cudgels on behalf of a cause or an interpretation which is as good or as bad, as true or as mythical, as any other. It is also, ultimately, intellectually self-contradictory: when criteria for adjudicating between better and worse accounts, adequate and less adequate interpretations, dissolve, then why should one prioritise a postmodernist version over any other? Why should those who dispute the very notion of truth be deemed themselves to be uttering the truth on the nature of knowledge? Again, political and moral affinities appear to be the only arbiter.

These are complex issues, and there have been many attempts to engage with the multiple challenges to notions of history posed by postmodernism. Scholars across Europe, North America and Australia (and probably elsewhere in literatures of which I am unaware) have provided responses either expanding on or reacting to a multiplicity of points.[24] Some have been openly combative, as in Gertrude Himmelfarb's spirited defence of 'the proposition that there are such things as truth and reality and that there is a connection between them'.[25] Some have sought to deal in detail with particular philosophical points taken separately, as in specialised debates over issues of epistemology, narrative and evidence.[26] Some have tried to incorporate at least an account of postmodernism into their characterisation of approaches to history, as in a number of new or recently reissued revised editions of textbooks on the nature of history.[27] Without trying to summarise what is now a large literature, it is worth making a few general points about some of the key protagonists and the general thrust of recent debates. In particular, it is worth attempting, perhaps, to characterise the often merely implicit empiricism of many of those who feel most under attack by postmodernists.

The empiricist target

The empiricist view of most practising historians is not always naïve, and is certainly a little more differentiated than the widespread lay faith in the truth of professional historical representations.[28] Very often, as we shall see for example with respect to sources and narrative, postmodernists are tilting at windmills; occasionally, however, their targets strike back with explicit defences of empiricist or pragmatic approaches. As useful straw men for postmodernists, Arthur Marwick and Geoffrey Elton represent rather combative spokespersons for a 'just-get-on-with-the-job' view of history.[29] While the ebullient tone (and on occasion near libellous comments) of some of Elton's and Marwick's writings may not be widely appreciated, many practising historians probably broadly agree with the general thrust of this pragmatic, empiricist approach. Even those who do believe in the importance of explicit theoretical debate, and whose sympathies arguably lie closer to E. H. Carr than to Elton, still share certain fundamental premises about the possibility of an empirically based history.[30]

Roughly, the view in this very wide camp (which encompasses an extremely broad range of methodological approaches and fields of research) runs as follows. The past can, it is freely admitted, never be 'really known': what we know of it is a reconstruction based on its traces, on evidence which has survived to the present. And that evidence is not imaginary, not merely a figment of a discourse: it is real. We have a sense of a past that really happened, and we have a simple desire to know more about it; so we look for appropriate traces to piece together a fuller picture, a more rounded story. Of course nothing is simply given: specific questions have to be explicitly formulated by the historian and posed to the sources; archives have to be exhaustively and honestly scoured, sources interpreted with a critical eye, compared with other sources, evaluated in the light of the contexts of production, intended effect and audience, and so on. But, to repeat: the sources are real traces, they constitute real evidence of a real past. New evidence will shed new light, and better, 'revisionist' accounts can be developed. History is thus cumulative: we get to know more and more about the past. The professional task for this group is in one sense simple: we get into the archives and libraries, and get on with the job. In another sense, however, this group recognises that historical research requires considerable skills, which can be taught and learnt, as well as acquired with experience; history is thus a professional discipline which requires appropriate training in skills and methods. And it is also a discipline which requires imagination, creativity, engagement. Geoffrey Elton often serves as a straw man to be castigated without re-reading; nevertheless, even Elton makes quite sensible remarks on the active character of historical writing, the ways in which the historian shapes the material, and the need for empathy and engagement rather than impersonality. In this area, Elton does not provide a good example for critiques of history as an intrinsically flawed attempt at mimetic representation.[31]

Cumulatively this sort of approach generally amounts to the view which Hayden White has dubbed the 'craft notion of historical studies . . . [held by those] who view narrative as a perfectly respectable way of "doing" history . . . or "practising" it'. Hayden White comments that 'this group does not so much represent a theoretical position as incarnate a traditional attitude of eclecticism in historical studies – an eclecticism that is a manifestation of a certain suspicion of theory itself as an impediment to the proper practice of historical inquiry, conceived as empirical inquiry'.[32] It does seem to be the case that many – but far from all – adherents of this general approach dislike 'theory' in the grand sense. Many, though far from all, tend to be explicitly anti-Marxist, and also somewhat hostile to the writings of other explicitly theoretical approaches, particularly the work of those who do not appear to have dirtied their hands in the archives. Quite apart from their political standpoint, Marxists are accused of trying to constrain all of reality into a predetermined procrustean bed, irrespective of mountains of evidence to the contrary. Not only Marxists come in for criticism: Marwick manages to conflate Marxism, structuralism, post-structuralism, and postmodernism, with a few swipes at other manifestations of 'metaphysical' approaches along the way; Windschuttle includes a range of social theorists as well as literary critics in his sights; Elton is particularly irritated by what he castigates as 'sociological' approaches. 'Theory' is generally seen as an extraneous impediment to real work, and certainly 'not what Real Historians do'. Additionally, for many of this sort of a- or anti-theoretical empiricist, the values of the historian can and should only enter into the picture in so far as individuals have particular personal viewpoints, which they would be well advised to declare, and thus supposedly neutralise, at the outset.

Not all non-postmodernist historians can be bracketed under the rather over-simplified ideal type postulated by postmodernist critiques. Hayden White himself, in the essay just cited, in fact distinguishes five different groups with respect to views on narrative: in addition to the 'craft' protagonists, he lists the 'Anglo-American analytical philosophers', the 'social-scientifically oriented historians', the 'semiologically oriented literary theorists', and 'certain hermeneutically oriented philosophers'; by no stretch of the imagination could any of the latter four be accused of theoretical naïvety.[33] The straw man version of naïve empiricism critiqued by postmodernists fails entirely, for example, to cope with a Lawrence Stone or a Richard J. Evans, both of whom combine belief in the possibility of investigating a real past, and evaluating real evidence, with an explicit, theoretically informed conceptual apparatus.[34]

There are many historical approaches which do *not* proceed by the narrative mode of 'telling the story'. Part of the problem with postmodernist attacks on their particular construction of 'naïve empiricism' is that they have tended to focus on just one particular version of 'doing history', that of the allegedly theoretically innocent narrative form, at the expense of a wider engagement with alternative, often theoretically far more sophisticated, approaches. However, in terms of current debates there does tend to be an undue polarisation and what might be called (to readapt a famous term of Hexter deriving from earlier debates on the English gentry) a 'lumping' of positions which are not intrinsically, logically, connected to one another. Hence narrative history has often slipped forward to a position of standing in for all of a-theoretical empiricist history. In fact, however, as we shall see, by no means all non-postmodernist history adopts the narrative mode of representation; and, more importantly, not even the most dogged empiricist of any persuasion can evade theoretical issues.

There are also unresolved problems to do with the political character or otherwise of history. Most historians lying on what one might roughly call the 'empiricist' side of the divide broadly hold to some notion of 'value-freedom', if only in the unexamined sense that they believe in history as an honest attempt to find out 'what really happened', whether one likes the answer or not. Postmodernists of various shades have – to different degrees – fundamentally challenged such a notion of truth, asserting that it is simply a situated truth for those who hold positions of dominance and influence, and that, at the level of 'discourse', there is an intrinsic link between power and what is characterised as a 'knowledge'. Thus, Foucault's linking of knowledge and power is central for postmodernists who focus on the political situatedness of a (collective) 'discourse' rather than on the work of individual scholars; by contrast, most 'traditional' historians hold to some notion of value neutrality or 'objectivity' in a more individualist sense.[35] When Marwick talks of 'society's need to understand particular aspects of the human past', a need which is to be met by its 'professionals', he easily lays himself open to the charge of failing even to see, let alone seriously address, the questions of what is 'society', who defines the 'need', who identifies which 'particular aspects' are worthy of exploration – to which the answer of a Keith Jenkins is, of course, those in a position of economic and political power to determine whose stories get told and whose get marginalised or suppressed.[36] Yet even those who, like Appleby, Hunt and Jacobs, or more recently Jordanova, wish to rescue some more sophisticated notion of 'telling the truth', have not developed adequate principles for adjudicating among a multiplicity of competing accounts of the same phenomenon. Unlike Ankersmit, they do believe in an appeal to the past; but their own accounts provide so many alternative pasts, from multiple perspectives, that they appear to leave no space for any neutral court of arbitration where these accounts conflict.

Not all historians or those interested in their products have paid much, if any, explicit attention to the philosophical challenges of the postmodernists, preferring to dismiss them as 'fashionable nonsense'.[37] It would probably be fair to say that by far the most widespread response has been that of sheer lack of interest in postmodernist scepticism. Probably most practising historians – whatever their specific, substantive area of study – adopt a rather pragmatic approach to digging up and re-presenting the past. They either take for granted, or bracket out, the questions raised by the sheer diversity of approaches and philosophical doubts about the nature of history. They assume that attention is most profitably focussed on analysis of substantive problems with respect to particular periods or topics in the past. There is widespread faith among practising historians in the possibility of progress: in providing ever more adequate answers to historical questions through the discovery of new evidence and/or the application of new techniques. But it seems to me that there is a wider need to be more explicit about theoretical issues in history: that repeated appeals to 'reality' and 'the facts' are not sufficient to deal either with the radical doubts of the philosophical sceptics, or with the challenges posed by the diversity of historical approaches outlined above.

Partial history: the issues and the argument

My purpose here has not been to summarise the development of these debates in detail, but merely to introduce some of the key themes and issues prevalent in the current theoretical malaise of many western historians.[38] We shall deal in detail with some of these as they arise in the chapters which follow. I do not want the structure of the argument that follows to be determined by the ways in which the debates over postmodernism (or indeed any particular 'isms') have developed. I want rather to focus on key issues which I think all historians must face. In addressing these central issues, I believe a way can be found both to circumnavigate some of the real naïveties of those empiricists who deny the postmodernist case any credibility, and at the same time to salvage a view of history which does accord it a degree of truth value, a status apart from fantasy and myth.[39]

Let me then briefly disentangle some of the key points or questions which it seems to me are at issue in these debates, and which underlie the chapters which follow.

1. History as a window on, or substitute for, the past

Is history deemed to be a transparent or reflective means (metaphors vary – window, mirror and magnifying glass have all been popular) through which one can glimpse at least some elements of the 'real' past, however imperfectly; or is history rather an opaque product purely of the present, to 'substitute for' or 'replace' a past which can only be 'constructed', not 'reconstructed'? Put fundamentally: Is past reality – which by definition has gone forever – in principle in some way 'accessible' through surviving traces, or not?

2. Historical pictures: trues stories or fictive constructs?

Is there an imposition or invention of a narrative in the present, or do historians genuinely reconstruct stories which are clearly rooted, if not actually 'already existent', in the traces of the past, and which can be rationally revised in the light of new traces? What are the implications of the difference between individual 'statements' – which may be true or false – and the pictures of wholes which are constructed by historians (White's 'emplotments', Ankersmit's 'narrative substances')? In short: how do tales told in the present relate to the complex realities of the past?

3. The role of political and moral values

What roles do political and moral sympathies and standpoints play in the production, evaluation and reception of historical accounts? If they are not recognised as legitimate arbiters among competing accounts of the same historical phenomenon, what theoretical arguments can be deployed to sustain some notion of objectivity or value-freedom – or should this concept be jettisoned?

Let me briefly preview my own argument in the light of these questions. Most current postmodernist and empiricist positions would now have in common the premise that historical research is no longer (if it ever was) about the pursuit of one single true master narrative. Despite major differences among both postmodernists and many of those seeking to resist their challenge (for example, Himmelfarb, or rather differently, Appleby, Jacobs and Hunt in the United States; Windschuttle in Australia; Ludmilla Jordanova, Richard J. Evans, and Arthur Marwick in Great Britain), they also have in common a difficulty with addressing the problem of multiple competing narratives, to which they then provide different answers. For most postmodernists, all historical narratives are equally plausible, or equally untrue, or characterised by what Hayden White rather inelegantly but usefully terms 'nondisconfirmability'; the criteria for choice among competing historical accounts then rest not so much on some measure of verisimilitude or measurement against an (inaccessible) past, but rather on contemporary aesthetic, moral or political grounds. Those historians who have sought to critique postmodernism have generally dealt quite well with certain difficulties and inconsistencies in the postmodernist position (as in Richard Evans' lampooning), and have then simply reiterated an essentially empiricist, if theoretically sophisticated, belief in the accessibility of traces of the past, or empirical evidence, which will allow for a source-based reconstruction of the past. They have on the whole failed adequately to address the more difficult question of adjudication among competing accounts, often retreating to essentially rather fuzzy notions of 'historical multi-culturalism' or 'let a thousand flowers bloom'. They have tended to conceive the issues as related to the perspectives and values of individual historians, rather than as one of competing collective historical traditions (or what I shall define in the next chapter as paradigms or paradigm candidates). The current state of the debate is overly polarised, often premised on false dichotomies, and unduly focussed on the background and values of the individual historian rather than on the language communities of groups of historians working in particular traditions.

This book seeks to shift attention rather to the more collective level of competing paradigms of historical inquiry. I intend to argue (first in partial agreement and then in partial disagreement with the various positions outlined above) that:

1   Along with postmodernists, we can now agree that there is no single true master narrative or overarching metanarrative.

2   We can also agree that there can in principle be an infinite number of 'partial narratives', constructed as answers to particular questions phrased in specific ways about selected aspects of the past.

3   However, against the postmodernist view, I shall argue that not all candidates for 'partial narratives' are equally acceptable, illuminating or true; it is therefore not merely a matter of the personal, aesthetic, moral or political preferences of an individual historian, nor of the dominant politics and/or 'discourses' of the day, as to which accounts are prioritised and which marginalised.

4   In partial agreement with the empiricist view, I shall agree that we can in principle develop and apply mutually agreed criteria for 'disconfirming' particular partial accounts (or parts thereof), using appropriately interpreted empirical evidence of a variety of sorts.

5   However, against naïve empiricism I shall argue that we cannot do without a degree of theoretical sophistication and debate. 'Empirical evidence' can only be captured through certain conceptual nets which must themselves be the object of analysis and critique.

6   We can in principle – at least, within the very broad compass of 'western'

notions of scholarship – develop and apply mutually agreed criteria for evaluating different accounts against each other, in terms of, for example:
– range, comprehensiveness and interpretation of sources, netted within an appropriate conceptual framework which must itself be open in principle to critique and revision;
– capacity to account for (= satisfy curiosity about) a particular *explanandum* in the light of our existing contextual knowledge and particular interests;
– presentation and accessibility of historical accounts for a range of purposes to different audiences in the present.

7   Where there are discrepancies and incompatibilities between competing partial accounts, we can be explicit about criteria for exploring further the extent to which differences can be mutually resolved, or for identifying the metatheoretical, metahistorical (and possibly metaphysical) assumptions in which bedrock disagreements will persist.

In other words, I shall seek to show, against certain postmodernist positions, that historical accounts are not simply narratives which are more or less arbitrarily imposed on (rather than found in or constructed from) selected traces of the past (whether this is deemed to be knowable or not), and are then presented in a form and style designed to achieve some sort of 'reality effect'. Against some empiricist positions, I shall argue that there are theoretical and conceptual choices which filter what historians working within different traditions of inquiry will look for by way of 'empirical evidence', which is not such a simple matter as many discussions of 'source criticism' might suggest. I shall also suggest some of the other ways in which historical consciousness and knowledge is informed not only by the traces of the past but also by the concerns of the present.

In this way it is possible to attain greater clarity about the bases for disagreements between different historical accounts; to clarify ways in which different theoretical and conceptual frameworks and associated substantive accounts can be operationalised, tested, amended, or discarded; and/or to identify the respects in which they are rooted in essentially untestable propositions on which they may be accepted or rejected for metatheoretical, rather than substantive historical reasons. Thus, rather than wafting into vague notions of multiple, simultaneous, competing perspectives among which one can only choose on grounds of personal preferences of one sort or another, or (worse) arguing the impossibility of any real sort of historical knowledge at all, it may be possible to develop a theoretically grounded notion of 'progress' in historical understanding.

3

HISTORICAL PARADIGMS AND THEORETICAL TRADITIONS

In 1962, Thomas Kuhn caused quite a stir with the publication of his *The Structure of Scientific Revolutions*.[1] This overturned the previously held and very widespread view that the natural sciences were simple, cumulative enterprises, success stories of straightforward advance in which each generation of scientists built on the achievements of the previous one. Instead, Kuhn argued, key scientific breakthroughs took place when one world view – one way of seeing, describing and explaining the world – was radically rejected and replaced by a completely different world view, or, in a more specific sense, a 'paradigm'. Thus, the flat earth was replaced by a round earth; the sun circling the earth was replaced by the earth circling the sun; Newton was replaced by Einstein.

Each world view, or paradigm, entailed a particular set of assumptions about the nature of the world, a corresponding set of analytical concepts for describing the world, and a number of hypotheses purporting to explain how the world worked. With the institutionalisation of western science, one specific paradigm would become dominant: the one taught and researched within the establishment. 'Mature science' – in the sense of the western natural sciences – was supposedly distinguishable from would-be sciences, or intellectual candidates for scientific status (such as the social sciences) by the predominance of one specific paradigm at any given time.

Within any given paradigm, there would be features which remained unexplained: 'puzzles'. 'Normal' scientific activity within the paradigm was thus one of 'puzzle-solving': filling in the gaps, completing the circle, nibbling away at the edges. All of this was 'cumulative' within the specific paradigm, and constituted in some sense 'advances in scientific knowledge'. But major advances took place not through 'the discovery of new facts' facilitated by this puzzle-solving activity, but rather when a revolutionary change in world view took place: when the dominant paradigm was challenged, and ultimately overthrown, by an alternative, completely different and mutually contradictory, way of seeing things – a *Gestalt* switch. The classic example of this was the replacement of Newtonian physics with Einstein's theory of relativity.

Kuhn's controversial thesis was by no means universally accepted, even as an account of the recent history of western science, let alone in its implications for the thus designated intellectually 'immature' social sciences.[2] Leaving aside here the question of Kuhn's applicability to the natural sciences (where incompatibilities between the determinist implications of Einsteinian concepts of time-space and the apparently infinite possibilities for free will in quantum mechanics suggest at least major paradigm competition, if not an impending revolution), there are nevertheless intriguing and suggestive implications for our analysis of the nature of history.

A notable phenomenon in the human sciences, and in particular in history, is the existence of a plethora of different theoretical approaches, which may or may not constitute mutually incompatible 'paradigms'. (Strictly speaking, these should be called 'paradigm candidates', in that no one of them alone commands the field, in the Kuhnian sense; however, for simplicity I shall continue to call them paradigms in what may perhaps be allowable as a 'post-Kuhnian' sense.) If one examines, for example, the history of historical writing in the United States and western Europe over the past half century or so, it becomes quite clear that, at any one time, a wide range of approaches to the analysis of history are present, even if only one or two such approaches are institutionally predominant at any one time.[3] Over time, these approaches rise and fall in overlapping waves, with competition both within and between traditions, and intellectual cross-fertilisations spanning quite different intellectual traditions and substantive disciplines. Thus exponents of a traditional form of diplomatic and political history might argue quite strongly against what they perceive as subversive or intellectually charlatan Marxists; but a cursory analysis of unfolding debates within western neo-Marxism, structuralist Marxism, and more culturalist forms of Marxism, will readily reveal even more frayed tempers and more explosive controversies.[4] Similarly, intellectual fashions are no respecter of boundaries between disciplines: consider, for example, the varieties of structuralism and post-structuralism in disciplines as diverse as linguistics, literary theory, anthropology and history.

All of this may be very interesting in its own right, and many courses on historical theory simply aim to expose students to a range of such approaches, most often through key illustrative works of major practitioners of these approaches. In an educative sense, it is of course very important to know what we are talking about – to have read Christopher Hill or E. J. Hobsbawm or E. P. Thompson when talking about a particular version of later twentieth-century British Marxist social history. But, however educated we are about who has said what, and what critiques have been levelled against this view, and who has subsequently said what about these critiques (a very easy and widespread way of teaching the subject of theory, and of structuring books about theory), and however essential this basic knowledge is to conducting a rational conversation about such matters, it does not fully serve to address the wider, more fundamental issues at stake. If we want to hold the view that the task of professional history (in contrast to myth, ideology, memory) is to find out the 'truth' about the past, then the existence of a range of potentially mutually incompatible approaches poses something of a problem. If different paradigm candidates (to use the term loosely for a moment) give us different versions of the same past, which version is 'best' and on what grounds? Does this mean that other paradigms should be jettisoned as mere 'ideology' (as some approaches would in fact argue)?

In short: if we (even only implicitly) agree that there are a range of theoretical perspectives in history, and that the task of courses on historical theory is simply to expose students to this range, but we have no means – other than appeal to political or personal preferences – of adjudicating between these competing perspectives, then we (again, perhaps only implicitly) land up adopting one of two possible (and in my view undesirable) positions. The first of these positions runs essentially along the lines that: 'my approach to history is the right one, the pursuit of the truth about the past; yours/theirs is basically myth, ideology, politics, masquerading as history'. The second version is less dogmatic about there being one truth, one perspective from which to start, and adopts instead some version of 'all perspectives are equally valid'; this form of supposed tolerance and pluralism in fact amounts to a relativist view in which, if all are equally valid, then none is actually valid (it is all a matter of opinion).

This chapter seeks to address much more directly than is usual the nature of historical approaches or paradigms in history. It is not intended as any sort of comprehensive survey of competing theoretical approaches (of which there are many). Rather, the chapter seeks to analyse the bases and types of paradigm that are (or have been) available and/or fashionable. More particularly, I want to develop the argument that perspectives in history are not – or not only – about the personal or political viewpoints of the individual historian, but are filtered through a more complex theoretical net. We need, in other words, to break out of the debates about 'self-reflexivity' (to use the term fashionable in postmodern quarters), or the longer-running discussions circling around E. H. Carr's injunction that 'before you study the history, study the historian'.[5] It is a theme running throughout this book – and to which I shall return more explicitly in Chapter 9 – that the 'politics of history' is about more than the personal proclivities of individual historians. Secondly, I want to argue that paradigms are not only about the situated collective perspectives of groups of historians in the present, but also about the inevitable theoretical structuring of ways of constructing and investigating the past. Analysis of 'approaches in history' thus cannot rest content with highlighting the alleged biases, viewpoints and blind spots of individual observers. Nor can those who see themselves as primarily empirical historians with little or no interest in 'theory' escape the issues quite as easily as they might like.

While showing that there is no such thing as 'a-theoretical history', I want also to show, however, that some approaches are more open, more mutually compatible with one another, and more susceptible to 'improvement' in the light of (conceptually netted) evidence, than others. This broader argument cannot be developed in this chapter alone; what follows here is the general framework which underpins the arguments of the rest of the book.

It may be helpful first to distinguish between three different levels or aspects of paradigm choice, as follows:

A. Theoretical

Paradigms (or paradigm candidates) in the strict sense of the word might be defined as articulate theoretical frameworks based on an explicit set of assumptions about 'how the world works'. These include: the 'naming of the parts', the vocabulary of concepts through which to capture reality; assumptions about the relationships among these constituent parts; and assumptions about priority, causality, relative importance, weighting, and so on. Crucial work will already have gone on, producing apparently promising and illuminating results; but puzzles remain to be solved, allowing for movement, progress, revisions within the paradigm.

It is worth listing some of the constituent elements separately, so that later we can more easily look at the issue of compatibility or not across paradigms:

- a framework of given questions and *puzzles*
- presuppositions about what to *look at*: the constitution of the 'subject' of inquiry; a set of analytical concepts for 'describing' the character of past worlds
- presuppositions about what to *look for* (clues, also known as 'sources'): and an associated set of methodological tools and concepts through which to capture and analyse the 'evidence'
- a notion of what will serve *to answer* the question
- a notion of the *principal purpose(s)* of historical reconstructions, and hence of appropriate *forms of representation* for different types of audience.

This chapter will introduce the different types of paradigm in a very general way, and subsequent chapters will then examine in somewhat more detail each of these aspects of paradigms with reference to examples of specific historical questions and topics.

B. Contextual

As far as historical inquiry is concerned, however, there are also some more external and anthropological criteria involved in differences of theoretical approach. Specific paradigms are often associated with particular scholarly or political communities, with particular connotations which may influence 'membership' in a particular theoretical tradition or scholarly language community. Here we should include not only the political associations or connotations of particular theoretical language communities, but also the identities and/or biases of individual observers and investigators as members of particular groups in the present, which may lead them to prefer one approach to another.

C. Metatheoretical

Underlying both the specific theoretical and the contextual elements there are elements of what might be called a 'philosophical anthropology'. By this I mean, for example: very broad, general assumptions about 'the nature of man' (or, in less sexist language, being human); assumptions about the relations between the individual and society; assumptions about the 'motors of change', the 'character of history' (in the sense of how things changed in the past); assumptions about the nature of the intellectual enterprise. These might be seen as integral to A, above, since they are fundamental to what the subject matter is about; but I am distinguishing them here, because they are in some ways broader, more deeply held, and integral to the constitution of the observer's viewpoint. It is thus more in the nature of 'metatheory'.

On the basis of different assumptions at each of these levels, one can distinguish several different types of paradigm in history. It seems to me that, within the field of historical study, at least four major variants may be discerned, which I shall discuss with examples in this chapter: 'implicit paradigms'; 'perspectival paradigms'; 'paradigms proper'; and 'pidgin paradigms'.

Implicit paradigms

A-theoretical historians, if provoked sufficiently, may be brought to enunciate the view that Theory Is Not History and historians should get on with The Real Job of Doing History. Now for the bad news.

Even those who have no interest in theory are actually operating with implicit paradigms. In fact, the rest of this book is devoted to unpicking the various elements involved even in implicit paradigms. We have just introduced some of these elements, which, if unpacked a little more, include: the constitution and categorisation of 'facts'; the selection of which 'facts' to include and exclude; notions about the relationship among elements; the significance and weighting given to each element; the constitution of what might be called a *Geschichtsbild*, the historical picture of the whole, and the emplotment, the tale told about the combination of selected elements (sometimes called the metanarrative); and the general evaluation and emotive colouring given to the final product, the representation of history (including the use of language through which to write and represent selected aspects and interpretations of the past).

Since implicit paradigms underlie all historical writing, we shall be looking at all these elements throughout the rest of this book. Here, I shall just give a couple of examples to illustrate what is meant by the use of implicit paradigms even when historians think they are not operating with theory in any very explicit sense.

For example, how should one approach characterisation and explanation of the English Civil War – or English Revolution, as Marxist historians (used to) like to call it? At one level, it is about the imputed motives, acts and decisions of particular individuals. There are key *dramatis personae* – King Charles I, Archbishop Laud, Oliver Cromwell, to name only the most obvious. The tale can be told as a narrative of individual clashes, decisions, battles, 'accidents of history'. At another level, it can be told as a tale of a split within the ruling classes over relatively parochial matters such as taxation or religion. And at a far broader level, it can be set within the wider comparative context of early modern rulers across Europe seeking to develop new forms of personal rule without reference to the late medieval intermediary bodies or estates. The general background paradigm, or framework of inquiry, will determine which set of historical actors (individuals, classes, groups) are those set to play upon the stage; and what kind of explanation will satisfy a particular sort of curiosity. The relatively stronger economic and political position of the English gentry in contrast to the Prussian *Junkers* will play a role in explaining the failure of Charles I in contrast to the later successes of Prussian absolutism if one is operating within a paradigm having reference to general structural patterns and political trends in early modern Europe; the personalities of key individuals will bear a heavier explanatory weight if one is operating within the complex single narrative paradigm.[6]

Similarly with the example of the collapse of democracy in early twentieth-century Germany. While some historians focus on the detailed machinations of key individuals in the closing days of the Weimar Republic, others shift attention and lay explanatory weight on selected structural and conjunctural factors (the effects of the First World War, the weaknesses of Weimar political and economic structure, in conjunction with the strains consequent on the Wall Street Crash). Yet others would spread the explanatory net far wider. Some might focus specifically on long-term features of German history, castigating the alleged cultural consequences of German inwardness from Luther through Kant, or the supposed structural dislocations of the peculiar German route to modernity (variations on the *Sonderweg* thesis). Others might lay the blame at the door of 'modernity' per se, rather than German history in particular, and point to the effects of the French Revolution which unleashed demotic forces not adequately contained by traditional authorities, on which 'totalitarian' leaders such as Hitler, Mussolini and Stalin could capitalise. From a quite different perspective, the blame might be laid, neither on matters specifically German, nor on 'modernity' in general, but rather on modern capitalism, emplotting Weimar and Nazi Germany within a tale of 'late monopoly capitalism'. It is only with a select few of these examples that we arrive in terrain which is wilfully and self-consciously 'theoretical' (proponents of the *Sonderweg* thesis and Marxist historians would in different ways lay claim to the use of 'theory'); most exponents of the other metanarratives just listed would profess that they were simply presenting history 'as it was'.

These are but very brief indications of some conflicting implicit paradigms, varying on what is brought into the historical lens and where explanatory weight is laid. I leave open for the time being certain fundamental questions, of which the most important are perhaps the ones concerning how far such implicit paradigms are open to amendment (or potential jettisoning) on the basis of the evidence, and whether or not at least some of them are mutually compatible. We shall return to these major questions later on.

For the time being it is important simply to note the fact that any historical explanation entails choices about selection and explanation, whether or not it is considered by its proponents to be theoretical. And what satisfies one historian's curiosity (analysis of key meetings, the specific motives or actions of particular individuals) may seem just a matter of irritating or even trivial detail from the perspective of another historian. Underlying these differences are fundamentally different views on, for example, issues such as the constitution of the historical period or problem, or the respective roles of structure and agency, discussed further in some of the following chapters. And, far more broadly, we may note the ways in which certain perspectives tend to be linked with certain political standpoints in the present – conservatives often tending towards short-term narratives of the actions of key individuals, sometimes embedded in wider notions about 'modernity', while liberals or left-wingers seem more comfortable with structural frameworks of one sort or another. This political 'noise' around the edges is also a subject to which we shall return very explicitly in Chapter 9.

Perspectival paradigms (or subjects of inquiry)

Let us now turn to more explicit 'theoretical approaches'. A number of 'new approaches', new '-isms', often turn out to be what I call 'perspectival paradigms', which can be characterised as, not so much 'new approaches to old questions' (as they often claim) but rather 'old approaches to new questions'. These are paradigms which, on closer inspection, may be distinguished from one another by virtue of the fact that they seek to illuminate different 'segments of reality' or, more simply, different subjects of inquiry.

When one looks at the history of history, one often finds that, for a while, historians define their approach in terms of one particular set of questions to which they want answers. Thus, the history of 'high politics' (the chronological framework of the succession of kings, chancellors, or whatever) was for a long time a major focus of historical attention in much of western European and Anglo-American history. Associated with 'great men theories of history' was, slightly oddly, also a collective actor of history, 'the nation' – which was simply assumed to exist, as a composite subject of history, the unfolding story of which could be narrated in almost anthropomorphic fashion. 'Nations' as well as great individuals could, in what has often been dubbed the 'traditional approach to history', be primary actors in historical narratives.

Then, for a variety of reasons, other topics began to intrude – or come into the focus of the historian's lens. In other words, what was deemed to be the proper subject of history was challenged and partially displaced. Histories of great men and great nations were knocked from their pride of place as the obvious or primary subject of historical accounts. There was not a little political intent behind this iconoclasm, but the serial challenges from previously marginalised groups and areas were various and often saw themselves as mutually competing, for all their real degrees of overlap. 'New perspectives' emerged alongside the 'traditional approach'. Let us just briefly mention a few examples.

Subfields such as social history of course had a long and distinguished tradition alongside the history of high politics and diplomacy. Often they were seen as precisely that; mutually complementary subfields. To quote one of the best-known 'classic' exponents of social history, G. M. Trevelyan: 'Social history might be defined negatively as the history of a people with the politics left out . . . [But] without social history, economic history is barren and political history is unintelligible.'[7] In the later half of the twentieth century, however, not only did social historical approaches begin to proliferate, but successive new variants made bold claims for shedding radically new light on the world of the past. Labour history, the history of the organised working classes, began to be counterposed in often quite heated terms to political and diplomatic history. This was, however, relatively soon found to have its omissions and blind spots; new forms of 'history from below', of 'everyday life', of subcultural underworlds beyond the reach of organised labour, began to come into view. A previously overlooked and forgotten fifty per cent of the population was also suddenly noticed, as 'women's history' was identified as a further area of investigation which had previously been silently absent from historical accounts. Hence new sub-disciplinary subject areas began to carve out distinctive debates and lines of inquiry, sometimes with a noticeable degree of hostility towards those approaches which they critiqued and appeared to be seeking to replace rather than complement.[8]

Some perspectives involved more than just the addition of new groups or areas to look at. The distinctiveness of the French *Annales* school of history was precisely that it stood out, in its emphasis on the *longue durée* and slow sea changes in underlying structures, against the 'traditional' focus on the motives and deeds of relatively small numbers of prominent individuals. This focus on the actions of the privileged few, or of great men, was challenged also by the totalising approach to 'societal history' (*Gesellschaftsgeschichte*) favoured among German historians of the so-called 'Bielefeld School' (the location where prominent exponents such as Hans-Ulrich Wehler were based), seeking to encompass whole social and economic structures as providing at least the constraining conditions, if not the full explanation, for developments and events in the sphere of high politics. Here, it was not the actions of a few named individuals, or even of whole classes, but entire structures that seemed to dominate the account.

One might perhaps place 'societal history' in the next section on paradigms proper – and, of course, these categories have fluid boundaries, as we see with other approaches which reappear under different headings. But, interestingly societal history was in turn challenged not because – or not solely because – of its structural approach, but rather because it was deemed to have 'left something out'. Hard on the heels of an often quantitative societal history came a rediscovery of culture, in the allegedly 'new' cultural history.[9] In other words, the major challenge arose because of the perceived need to illuminate an inadequately explored perspective or 'segment of reality'.

Very often perspectival paradigms had at first to engage in considerable practical struggle to gain any institutional foothold. Once a particular academic industry was well underway, with a gaggle of research students and established disciples of major historians exploring, for example, a particular view of Tudor government (Geoffrey Elton and acolytes) or the Namierite intricacies of personality politics in eighteenth-century England, then those who chose instead to look at the rise and fall of particular classes or patterns of marriage and family formations might find it quite difficult to find a secure academic foothold. Nevertheless, however frustrating the battle may have been for some practitioners to convince the academy of the importance of their chosen field of study, topics such as witchcraft and magic, or the struggles of the emergent working classes, or women's history, succeeded in establishing their own niches – often quite prominent – in the academic landscape.[10] Moreover, many of these perspectival paradigms luxuriated in their claims to represent theoretical breakthroughs, sometimes signalled by attaching 'new' to their label (as with the 'new cultural history').

It is not my purpose here to provide a chronologically ordered bibliographical essay on these waves of historical focus, which has been done often enough by others. I want briefly to raise explicitly the more general point. These perspectival paradigms differ from one another largely in terms of at least some of the elements listed under *A*, above: namely, what to look at, what vocabulary to use, what questions to ask. They also often differ quite a lot with respect to *B* (variants of underdog history often being professed by those who see themselves as professionally marginal and/or left-wing, and so on). But on the whole perspectival paradigms are not premised on fundamentally incompatible metatheoretical assumptions (*C* above). Many perspectival paradigms could be seen as mutually complementary, enhancing an ever more multi-faceted and complete knowledge of the past, as in Trevelyan's view of social history, although explanatory weight is often laid in quite different places. A decision about whether the explanatory emphasis lies with individual motives or with enduring structures is a classic example of where the boundaries between perspectival paradigms and paradigms proper are particularly fluid.

The issue arises as to whether most perspectival paradigms genuinely represent new theoretical approaches; or whether they are not, in fact – to use a photographic metaphor – simply taking photos of the same clump of trees, with the same camera, but from different perspectives. Closer inspection reveals that there is not one answer to this question. Sometimes it is just a case of the same trees being photographed from different angles; sometimes there are genuinely different theoretical approaches to the same topic (or, to continue our metaphor, the same trees are taken from the same angle, but with a different kind of camera and lens); sometimes even the trees are constructed differently. As the cliché has it, while some are concerned to reconstruct the shape of the whole wood, others 'cannot see the wood for the trees' – and may be looking at different trees, at that.

Let us get away from the trees metaphor, and take another example, in order to distinguish perspectival paradigms from what I shall come on to next, paradigms proper. We have noted the emergence of something we called, for the time being, simply 'women's history' – defined initially as the history of a previously ignored group, namely women. This is rather different from what now goes under the term 'feminist history'. If we look even for a moment at 'feminist history', we find a multitude of different possible approaches: Marxist feminists, psychoanalytic feminists working in a post-structuralist, Lacanian tradition, liberal feminists, and so on, might all be focussing on what, to a mundane outsider, might appear to be the 'same' subject: women. But they construct this 'subject' very differently in terms of their theoretical concepts of gender (as opposed to biological sex). Gender history could be as much about men as about women – for example, it could focus on the construction of masculinity, rather than 'women's work' (or any other traditional subject of 'women's history'). And 'feminist history' could refer to the standpoint and ideals of the historian rather than to the substantive object of investigation. So here we are straying from the area of 'perspectival paradigms' into something rather different, namely 'paradigms proper'.[11]

Similarly with another recent fashionable area: post-colonialism.[12] This, it seems to me, might be categorised not so much as a genuinely new theoretical approach, but rather as a perspectival paradigm, in the sense that a whole new area of study has been discovered or established (although there are debates, among those working in this field, over what constitutes the area and whether it refers to the period after the end of colonisation, or to the colonial period proper as well). The issues have to do with the interactions between the voices of the colonialists and those of indigenous people, particularly subordinate or 'subaltern' classes. Analysis may focus on the ways in which – or even whether at all – it is possible for the subaltern to 'speak' in their own voices, to allow their experience to be heard uncontaminated by the traces of the colonial rulers' linguistic and cultural vehicles of expression. But theoretical approaches to this object or field of study vary dramatically. Very often even within the work of one author there are conceptual borrowings from a number of theoretical perspectives. We shall consider this again in a moment when we come to the question of 'pidgin paradigms' or 'magpie theories'.

However, what basically distinguishes perspectival paradigms is their choice of what to look at, accompanied sometimes by inflated claims for the importance of their area for a reconsideration of previous approaches which had neglected the chosen topic.

Next, however, we need to consider the strongest version of paradigms: paradigms proper.

Paradigms proper

What is distinctive about what I here call 'paradigms proper' is that they differ from one another on all three levels: internal, contextual and metatheoretical. Working upwards from the most general level to the more specific: at level C, paradigms proper are based, ultimately, on a set of very strongly held metatheoretical premises akin to a belief system; one either holds these truths to be self-evident (to borrow the immortal words of the American constitutionalists) or one does not. At level B, paradigms proper often have particular connotations in terms of the political sympathies and cultural identities of the particular language communities specialising in and developing each tradition. And, at level A, from the underlying assumptions follow a whole set of explicit theoretical propositions and concepts, and related applications and investigations.

The underlying assumptions may be based in deep sets of political, moral and philosophical beliefs about society, the future, human nature, human development. These 'metatheoretical assumptions' may be more or less irrefutable: simply tenets of faith, which one may like or dislike, share or reject; they may thus be beyond the realms of rational discussion and refutation. The traditions of faith may become very closely allied with the name(s) of leading theorists or founders of the tradition (Marx, Freud, Lévi-Strauss), and with particular institutions or parties and political viewpoints. Let me give some examples.

Marxism

Marxism can come in many variants, which we shall meet again in many guises. The original ideas of Karl Marx were extraordinarily rich, inspiring, and full of self-contradictions. A veritable industry has grown up exploring the antinomies between the 'early' and the 'late' Marx, between the 'voluntaristic' and the 'determinist' or 'structuralist' Marx. It would be not only foolish, but also simply wrong, to try to lay down fundamental tenets of Marxism, which has proved to be a very broad church indeed. However, some attempt at definition of range, if not specificity, must be made.

Fundamental to Marxism is the commitment to a more egalitarian future, and to the analysis of society with respect to assisting change towards that better future. ('Philosophers have only interpreted the world . . .; the point, however, is to change it.') Fundamental to Marxism, too, is a notion of historical materialism: that (even if only 'in the last instance') the 'mode of production' is in some sense either determining, or at the very least conditioning or constraining.

Even within these two sentences, a whole host of debates have been adumbrated. Take simply the second of these sentences. Note, for example, that 'historical materialism' does not imply 'economic determinism': the Marxist term 'mode of production' includes both 'means of production' (level of technology and so on) and 'relations of production' (defined both in terms of the ownership or non-ownership of the given means of production, and in terms of class consciousness, that is consciousness of common interests in opposition to other classes). Already the sphere of ideology is present; for, although 'it is not consciousness that determines being, but on the contrary social being determines consciousness', at the same time 'the ruling ideas of the age are the ideas of the ruling class'. So – even in this thumbnail sketch – we stand before a host of potentially self-contradictory issues, which provide the roots for the very different strands of twentieth-century Marxism. Marxism-Leninism – with its emphasis on the 'vanguard Party' which provides the fount of all wisdom on behalf of the supposedly duped masses who are suffering from 'false consciousness' – can as easily come from these antinomies as can the more voluntaristic Marxism of Gramsci or the Frankfurt School theorists.[13]

Analysis of recent 'Marxist' historical writing suggests that there is a very wide range of what is theoretically possible under the rubric of 'Marxism'. If one looks, for example, at the works of E. P. Thompson or Christopher Hill, one finds a fascination with the role of ideas in history that is almost worthy of Max Weber.[14] Put perhaps only a shade too simply, the complexities and self-contradictions of Marxist theory are ultimately predicated on a common substantive concern with class as a key historical factor and actor; but beyond this, issues to do with class formation and class consciousness allow an enormous latitude with respect to the role of ideas in history. Indeed, one sometimes has the impression that huge theoretical effort is devoted to rescuing some version of 'materialism' in face of acknowledgement of the key role of ideas, by finessing the explicit theoretical framework regarding the 'superstructure'.

Others, of course, have gone to a quite different extreme in pursuing the often self-contradictory opus left by the master. The structuralist Marxism of Louis Althusser, Étienne Balibar, and Nicos Poulantzas picked up on Marx's fascination with structures and the alleged 'laws' of history which operated whether or not human beings were aware of them.[15] In the frequently opaque structuralist Marxist writings of the 1960s and 1970s – at the time when the British Marxist social historians were also at their peak – these continental theorists developed a bleak view of the world in which there appeared to be no human actors, no real ideas (with the exception, of course, of the ideas of the theorists themselves). And, as the exchanges between Althusser and Thompson demonstrated, they could make their more empirical and idealist colleagues in Britain very angry indeed.[16]

What does this display of diversity mean for the 'bottom line', the 'lowest common denominator' of 'Marxist' historical accounts? Clearly the political commitment – in the most general terms – to radical critique of capitalism and the quest for an alternative and more equal or just society has to be an element. This then plays some role in the choice of subject matter (often expressed in sympathy for the underdog, who is to be rescued from the 'infinite condescension of posterity'; occasionally the upper classes, but from the perspective of class struggle) and the style and purpose of writing, topics to which we shall return in later chapters. It may also entail a set of assumptions about the importance of class and class struggle as the substantive focus of historical accounts. Depending on the inclination of the historian, it may or may not also entail a degree of theorising, or revising theory almost against the evidence, in order to sustain the commitment irrespective of the apparent evidence. Thus, as new features emerge which pose problems for the classical heritage of Marxist theory (nationalism, feminism, culture) the theory is revised and adapted so as to salvage it from possible wreckage or simple abandonment. For *aficionados*, the debates can be obsessively compelling; for those outside the charmed circle of the committed, the jargon-ridden and generally heated arguments may be largely unintelligible and rebarbative, akin to medieval controversies over how many angels can dance on the head of a needle, a closed circle of debate for the converted.

Whatever one makes of it, either intellectually or politically, the multi-stranded theoretical tradition collectively known as Marxism has provided a major paradigm for twentieth-century historians, whether as template or foil. It has occupied different places in the western academy at different times – from radical outcaste to intellectual chic, from student attics in Frankfurt and Berlin to the Parisian Left Bank, from object of McCarthyist persecution to Ivy League preserve of political correctness, from the British academic fringes to the Master of Balliol College, Oxford (in the person of Christopher Hill) – but it has been hard to ignore as an intellectual force. The framework has exerted a fascination which one might have thought would long hence have been spent; only the perversions of the original ideal in the distortions of self-professedly Marxist-Leninist regimes of the twentieth century, and the ultimate collapse of the Soviet empire in 1990–1, may have dealt the paradigm a more definitive death blow than the million and one empirical challenges to the metatheoretical assumptions.

Psychoanalytic approaches

Even so, Marxism has had a more general impact on the way we analyse the world: the need at least for some sensitivity to issues such as 'class', or perhaps society and economy in a broader and looser sense, is now widely taken for granted among historians, whatever their political persuasion. The same is to some extent true of Freud's ideas. The full Freudian doctrine and practice of psychoanalysis is perhaps shared, again, only by the minority band of true believers; and among the heirs of Freud and Jung there are many different schools. But certain ways of thinking about the human personality – notions of repression, of the unconscious, of neurosis, of the significance of the apparently non-rational in behaviour – have simply become part of a set of western assumptions about the nature of being human.

Freudian theory, in the strict sense, has not had much of an impact on mainstream historical interpretations, although there are some quite explicit examples: including psychoanalytic interpretations of Martin Luther, of witchcraft beliefs and accusations in early modern Europe, and of the collective social psychology of East Germans.[17] More specifically, through certain often rather tortuous circumnavigations, via – again – continental theory and particularly philosophy and literary theory, psychoanalytic insights have returned, in a fashion, in the works of Foucault, Derrida, and Lacan. These theorists, along with the version of psychoanalytic interpretation associated with Melanie Klein, have particularly influenced certain versions of gender history. Their radical rejection of conventional western notions of the subject, of the conscious self, are hardly imaginable without the prior and pathbreaking analyses of Freud. On the other hand, they have also drawn from – and in their designation as 'post-structuralist', have broken with – another major paradigm of twentieth-century thought: structuralism.

Structuralism

Structuralism is a prime example of a 'strong' paradigm in the strict sense, which has been of major intellectual significance across a number of disciplines through the middle part of the twentieth century. Originating in large part from the grammatical work of Ferdinand de Saussure before the First World War, which was taken up in the structuralist linguistics of Roman Jakobsen, structuralism spread through an astonishing variety of disciplines, from linguistics through literary criticism to anthropology, history and sociology, and proved no respecter of political boundaries either.

What are the fundamental tenets of structuralism? Perhaps there are three of unavoidable significance for structuralism in the strong sense (there are other versions of structural analysis and structural explanation, which we will come on to later).[18] First, structuralists are interested in looking at the structure as a whole, and at the relationships among elements in the structure; they are, thus, interested in the totality, not in any of the individual parts. Secondly, structuralist analysis tends to be synchronic, rather than diachronic; that is, it looks at the ways in which, when one element in the structure changes, other elements have to change accordingly. It is more interested in the transformational rules which govern the relationships among elements, rather than in the causes or historical antecedents of the current structure and its constituent elements (although some structuralists do search for 'theories of transition' from one set of structural relationships to another). Thirdly, and perhaps most importantly, the purpose of this paradigmatic version of structuralism is to analyse 'visible' structures not for their own sake, but in order to search for the 'deep structures' that generate 'appearances'. The fundamental goal is to penetrate beyond the level of observed realities to the underlying and ultimately determining deep structures that are beyond the consciousness of the human actors who play out the effects, like puppets on strings. Indeed, the consciousness of human actors (as expressed, for example, in myths or religious beliefs) is often deemed to be *prima facie* 'wrong', an ideological mask serving to disguise rather than reveal the deeper realities beneath. There are also some subsidiary principles or characteristics of some (but not all) versions of structuralism. One is the analysis of what are deemed (often rather arbitrarily) to be binary oppositions, on the grounds that these are the basis of all codes. Another is the belief that the aim of structural analysis is to reveal fundamental 'universals of the human mind'.

Structuralism in its heyday spread from the structural linguistics of de Saussure and Jakobsen, through fields as diverse as psychology (Piaget) and literary theory.[19] Its major exponent in anthropology was Claude Lévi-Strauss, who claimed as the key intellectual influences on his own development the three strands of Marxism, psychoanalysis and geology. (Commentators have also noted his interest in music.)[20] On Lévi-Strauss' view, 'primitive societies' lay, like geological fossils, scattered around the world, revealing contemporaneously different stages of human development; all that was required was not extensive field work in any one place (Lévi-Strauss was notable among anthropologists for his very short-lived exposure to arduous inquiry among non-literate peoples) but rather the application of formidable brain power in cracking these codes. In his extraordinarily clever, and arguably completely unfounded, analyses of topics such as culinary codes (counterposing such alleged 'binary oppositions' as the raw and the cooked, the fresh and the rotting), kinship systems, myths and rituals, Lévi-Strauss thought that the analysis of 'primitive societies' could lead him to unlock the secret 'universals of the human mind'. There was, for Lévi-Strauss, a difference between 'conscious models' and the 'real models' which they disguised; and each was in turn ordered in relation to others, such that any society had, when all codes were juxtaposed, an 'order of orders'. Myths and rituals might serve to disguise and 'explain' the economy, the stratification system, the kinship system; each order was in itself a means of communication and circulation, whether of goods and services, women, ideas, gifts and food (goodies to think with).

This sort of structuralist approach stood in total and explicit contrast to what is often termed 'structural-functionalism': the analyses of 'surface structures' carried out by, for example, Bronislaw Malinowski and Radcliffe-Brown. Lévi-Strauss derided Radcliffe-Brown's empiricist approach to what one might call 'actually existing' kinship relations. That sort of anthropological approach was predicated on the fact that since, in a non-literate society, there were no written records on which to base a history of institutions, one had to resort to explanation in terms of the functions performed by a particular institution or practice for the maintenance of social cohesion. This was not at all what was intended by the search for 'deep structures' or the 'grammar' of the human mind.

However, this does not mean that the apparently more mundane and empiricist approach of structural-functionalism was not, itself, predicated on distinctive metatheoretical assumptions. For example, as Steven Lukes has pointed out, the notion of *anomie* popularised by one of functionalism's founding fathers, Émile Durkheim, was deeply rooted in a philosophical anthropology which held that human beings required some sort of social norms to 'contain' and keep them within bounds. This version of the relations between individual and society was more or less diametrically opposite to that underlying Marx's notion of *alienation*, which presumed that a healthy state of being 'truly human' required, not subjection to externally imposed social norms, but rather release from such external constraints.

Structuralism entered the world of historical analysis in several ways. In its strong version, just described, it influenced particularly certain Marxist historians such as Nicos Poulantzas. In a much weaker version, it had a broader influence over a whole range of historical analyses, including the influential works of American scholars such Barrington Moore and his one-time student, Theda Skocpol. It has also, in an ironic and back-handed sort of way, been important recently via a roundabout route: the development of post-structuralism in literary theory and philosophy had major influence on certain historians who jumped on the post-Marxist, post-structuralist bandwagon of discourse theory and the 'linguistic turn' of the 1980s.

Acts of faith? The incommensurability of paradigms proper

My purpose here, however, is not to present a history of currents in intellectual thought, but rather, by this relatively brief survey of a few contrasting approaches, to highlight the importance of different metatheoretical presuppositions underlying certain paradigms. The paradigms which we have considered so far under the heading of 'paradigms proper' do represent more or less mutually incompatible ways of viewing the world – and their incompatibilities rest on fundamentally different anthropological assumptions. To seek for 'deep structures' which give rise to the surface appearances, in pursuit of the 'universal structures of the human mind', is to pursue what from another set of assumptions is a pot of gold at the end of the rainbow, or the holy grail. Either one assumes that there is such a thing as fundamental, universal structures of the human mind; or one does not. If one does, then one looks at overt, visible kinship structures, or at myths and rituals, as akin to codes which conceal the real, hidden logic of the deep structures, the secrets of which can only be cracked by the code-breaker (in the person of Lévi-Strauss). If one does not, then one may perhaps adopt a functionalist point of view and look at kinship relations, or myths and rituals, for the functions they perform in sustaining and reproducing a given form of society. Or, from a version of Marxism, one may look at the very same phenomena from the point of view of the unequal socio-economic and power relations they serve to disguise, mask, and reproduce – this time, not in the interests of a reified 'society as a whole', but rather in the interests of a particular dominant class. Thus, the very same social 'facts' – who is allowed to marry whom, what lines of descent there are, what sorts of creation stories are told, and so on – may be subjected to radically divergent, mutually incompatible forms of analysis and explanation.

How does one decide among these different forms? Does one engage in an act of faith; or of faithful discipleship to a particular teacher adhering to a particular school of thought; or choose on the basis of what is currently fashionable; or of what accords with one's prior inner convictions (whether on the basis of upbringing, parental influence, schooling, or whatever)? Thus, one may choose with post-structuralists to engage in the act of faith required to agree with the decentering of the subject (for post-structuralists would be self-contradictory if they asserted their own authority as absolute); or one may savagely critique this as a western-centric pseudo-intellectual self-indulgence in light of the real oppression and material misery of the majority of the world's population, for which a Marxist analysis may be more appropriate. It is hard to say what sways most people who choose one or another 'strong paradigm' or 'paradigm proper'. Very often it may be a combination of a number of totally extra-theoretical matters – institutional pressures and constraints, peer group pressure, the cultural and political connotations of following a certain line of theory, or the pressures to reject it – rather than any rational argument that sways the individual towards one school or another.

The problem arises for all of these that, if one does not share the underlying premises or act of faith, or one does not like the associated politics, one cannot enter into the mental world of the paradigm – and, as a result, one is likely to be at least somewhat sceptical (if not downright suspicious and dismissive) of any alleged 'findings', interpretations, or results of inquiries undertaken within this paradigm. It certainly means that analysis in competing paradigms cannot be deemed to be in some sense a cumulative enterprise engaged in fruitful dialogue.

Pidgin paradigms and magpie theories

Finally, let us look at approaches which often claim to 'use theory', but often do not in fact constitute coherent theoretical approaches in and of themselves.

In many areas of western academia at least, it is fashionable to be 'theoretical', and particularly to offer a 'new approach'. (This was of course quite different in communist states, where the only theoretical possibility was to work within the given constraints of the official version of Marxism-Leninism.) Often concepts are borrowed, like glittering titbits, from one theoretician or another, and transposed to new contexts in what can be a highly eclectic fashion. Hence the term 'magpie theory'; or, to point out just how much the concepts may change as they are transposed to construct a new and hybrid tongue, 'pidgin paradigm'.

Particularly insightful or promising concepts may be transported with extraordinary fluidity across wide intellectual boundaries; thus we all, to some extent, employ terminology first deployed extensively by Marx and Freud, without necessarily acceding to the whole theoretical framework from which these concepts are plucked. We speak quite happily, for example, of 'repression', 'neuroses', 'Freudian slips', the 'subconscious' and so on, often without either being aware of, or agreeing with, the whole set of theoretical assumptions within which these concepts were located. They have simply entered the everyday parlance of post-Freudian western discourse.

Some are more explicitly plucked out for redeployment in different mental contexts. Thus one often finds articles making use of one or another apparently promising concept, taken in isolation: Bourdieu's notion of 'habitus', Foucault's concept of 'power', and so on. This theoretical eclecticism does not seem bothered by the abandonment of the rigorous set of inter-related assumptions which constituted the original theoretical framework, and may indeed simply assume that the concepts may be deployed in some form of additive fashion to provide a more comprehensive analysis.[21] There may be an issue to do with primary focus here. Historians are generally more interested in illuminating some aspect of the real world in the past than in refining a set of theoretical concepts about that past. Thus, they may deploy a concept because it seems a helpful way of talking about a particular feature that they are interested in (such as applying Weber's notion of 'charismatic authority', for example, in talking about Hitler); they are not as interested in seeing whether the 'reality' they are analysing suggests amendments to the concept – or whether, indeed, the variety of conceptual frameworks on which they are drawing might or might not be mutually incompatible.[22]

This use of concepts borrowed from other theoretical frameworks can, it has to be said, sometimes be simply a substitute for original thought, verging on the pretentious, even obfuscatory. But deployed well, such usage can be exceedingly illuminating. The deployment by Ian Kershaw of Weber's notion of charismatic authority to describe Hitler's power provides an excellent example of the way in which a theoretical category derived from a particular conceptual armoury can genuinely open up fruitful avenues of inquiry and interpretation.[23] Weber's concept of charisma neatly combines a focus both on the extraordinary individual and on the conditions under which that individual can command a following; it is thus a social, or social psychological, and not a purely psychological concept. Applied to Hitler by Kershaw, in the context of his notion of 'working towards the Führer', it serves beautifully to move forwards the previously somewhat sterile debates between the so-called intentionalists, who focussed primarily on Hitler's intentions, and the 'structuralists' or 'functionalists' who laid emphasis on the structure and functioning of the regime.

More generally, the existence of magpie theories or pidgin paradigms is of some significance because it indicates that, provided there are shared meta-theoretical premises (level C), and a willingness to talk across elements in levels A and B, it is possible in principle to translate across different paradigms or frameworks of inquiry. In other words, at least some paradigms are not enclosed systems of thought, and at least some practitioners can develop a facility for dialogue across paradigms. Even if – as we shall see in the following chapter – we can never develop any 'theory-neutral data language' allowing us to converse with one another, and examine the evidence of the past, in the framework of some 'super-paradigm', we are still capable of at least certain cross-paradigm conversations that make mutual sense.

Paradigms and paths to the past

There are many overlaps between the categories I have elaborated above, which, as I have attempted to emphasise, are not watertight; but the distinctions made in this chapter have not been developed for purely typological, classificatory purposes. Rather, they may help to determine just how far different paradigms are or are not intellectually mutually contradictory. Let me return, then, to the general discussion at the start of this chapter.

There are several rather crucial questions relating to the plenitude of competing approaches in history. On what different, metatheoretical, assumptions are particular approaches based? What determines whether scholars choose to operate with one set of assumptions rather than another? Are some approaches in principle complementary while others are mutually incompatible; and, if so, are there rational criteria – or criteria which can be mutually agreed – for adjudicating between those which seem to give conflicting answers to the same questions? To what extent do political values and often unexamined cultural predispositions, moral postulates or other underlying premises affect choice of theoretical approach? To what extent are such approaches the result of socialisation into particular scholarly 'language communities'? How do paradigm shifts occur?

Essentially, we can summarise these diverse questions as all fundamentally relating to three basic, underlying questions which we shall address throughout the remainder of the book:

1   To what extent are paradigms rooted in essentially metatheoretical assumptions, which one either accepts or rejects, but which are beyond the bounds of rational debate?
2   To what extent are paradigms open to change rooted in some form of belief in the possibility of extra-paradigmatic access to the 'real past'?
3   Is there some way of adjudicating among them and searching for a single 'super-paradigm' (in the Kuhnian sense of a mature science); or is there something about the nature of historical inquiry which means that there will inevitably, and always, be a number of separate, competing, coexisting, mutually incompatible paradigms among which one cannot choose on mutually agreeable grounds? If the latter is the case, what does this mean for the nature of history, or the status of historical knowledge as 'truth' about the past?

These are the big questions we shall be concerned to address throughout. As we have seen already, however, answers to these questions must be somewhat differentiated.

There is a spectrum of degrees of political colouring of paradigm choices, or openness to alteration on the basis of rational argument, although the extent to which one can say 'empirical evidence' affects paradigm change has to be qualified in the light of our discussion of concepts in the next chapter. There may be certain general criteria of validity, and criteria for critique, which are above or beyond particular implicit, perspectival, or pidgin paradigms. The latter may in turn be sufficiently loosely held to be open to revision and change. Thus some traditions of inquiry may be much more open to revision, dialogue, and amendment than others.

Across those approaches where there are shared general criteria, one can develop what might be called a basic code of historical practice, such as:

1 commitment to basic honesty and integrity rather than deceit;
2 absence of wilful distortions or omissions;
3 commitment to accepting the possibility of revision of particular interpretations in the light of further evidence (though subject to certain theoretical qualifications, to be discussed further below);
4 and perhaps also (though this is less often explicitly articulated by practising historians) commitment to enjoyment of the creativity of the historian as writer while still adhering to some notion of faithfulness to the past.

However, it has also to be said that some paradigms – particularly paradigms proper – remain resolutely incompatible. This may be because of distinctions on the basis of prior assumptions, or metatheoretical presuppositions – about the nature of relations between the individual and society, or between 'consciousness', culture, ideas, and material conditions; and about whether one should look 'beyond' or 'below' the level of 'surface appearances', and so on – which are not necessarily open to rational debate or falsification (level C, in my initial analysis). And all paradigms tend to develop as discrete 'schools', 'language communities' of scholars with specific institutional bases and communication networks; these schools may develop a political dynamic of competition which cross-cuts other bases of distinction between paradigms.[24] Let us now take our analysis into more detail, and start to look at different aspects of routes from the present to the past.

Part II

INVESTIGATIONS: ROUTES FROM THE PRESENT TO THE PAST

4

BEYOND METANARRATIVE

Plots, puzzles and plausibility

To write history requires a leap of the imagination. To write history requires a degree of creativity. To write history requires active, critical powers of selection, analysis, representation. From disparate pieces of material, historians form coherent shapes which they present in ways which will be accessible, interesting, even entertaining, for contemporary audiences. But it does not follow from all this – as some highly influential theorists would have it – that history is little different from fiction, and that we must concede a degree of relativism in which any historical account is in principle as good as any other, and the only criteria of choice are aesthetic considerations or political or moral or other personal preferences.

The basic problem in recent discussions has been an illogical leap: from registering the 'death of metanarrative' (whether in the form of old-style teleological histories of whatever ideological and political colour, or in newer 'totalising' syntheses) to a premature celebration of history as virtually indistinguishable from fiction. This leap relies on a false dichotomy and a widespread failure to consider alternative possibilities. I shall argue that the death of metanarrative does not necessarily entail a view of history as fiction; rather, historical investigation is more akin to puzzle-solving within a particular conceptual and methodological framework. Within given parameters, historical explanations and interpretations – whether or not they are written in narrative form, or presented in more analytic style – are subject to empirical refutation.[1] This chapter will seek to establish the nature of history as a primarily puzzle-solving rather than fictional endeavour; subsequent chapters will look more closely at the character of the parameters within which such puzzle-solving takes place.

Telling tales? History as the imposition of narrative

One of the most influential voices in the debates over the character of historical representation in the later twentieth century was that of Hayden White. His seminal work on nineteenth-century historians, published in 1973, highlighted the ways in which their literary choices or style not only influenced the emotive character of the stories they told, but indeed imposed, through their very form, a particular kind of content.[2]

White himself did not dispute the possibility of empirically accurate knowledge about the past; on his view, individual factual statements (such as those which, when listed sequentially, constitute a 'chronicle' or 'annals') can be true or not true. Rather, White disputed the possibility of acquiring any meaningful interpretation of the interrelatedness and significance of this factual knowledge in any form outside the literary conventions of the present. There are, it seems to me, two rather different strands to his argument.

The first relates to significance and interpretation, or the meaning of the past for the present. All historical narratives, according to White, operate by selecting and re-producing specific historical facts, encoded in one of four possible literary forms: tragedy, comedy, romance and satire, which in turn endow meaning and significance on the previously disparate facts. As he put it: 'a historical narrative is not only a *reproduction* of the events reported in it, but also a *complex of symbols* which gives us directions for finding an *icon* of the structure of those events in our literary tradition'.[3] (What might be made of such a statement in a culture relying more on popular television series than literary classics he does not consider.) In an essay characterised more by circular assertion than by reasoned argument, White continues:

> Our knowledge of the past may increase incrementally, but our understanding of it does not . . . Like literature, history progresses by the production of classics, the nature of which is such that they cannot be disconfirmed or negated, in the way that the principal conceptual schemata of the sciences are. And it is their nondisconfirmability that testifies to the essentially *literary* nature of historical classics.[4]

This unfounded and unexamined circular assertion of supposed 'nondisconfirmability' (a nice double negative never proven by White) is used to buttress both premises and conclusion.

Secondly, White suggests that historical accounts produce relationships among these disparate events which were not actually given in the past:

> Histories, then [*though nothing previously has demonstrated this – M.F.*], are not only about events but about the possible sets of relationships that those events can be demonstrated to figure. These sets of relationships are not, however, immanent in the events themselves; they exist *only* in the mind of the historian reflecting on them.[5]

This is, if anything, an even stronger claim; for here White's argument is tantamount to denying the possibility of finding (rather than inventing) any form of real causal linkage between different historical events whatsoever. He is in effect suggesting that more or less any set of relationships can be imposed at the whim and fancy of the historian, as mere chronicle ('one-damn-thing-after-another') is transformed into narrative (that is, endowed with iconic significance within one or another literary convention, and shaped into a story with interrelationships among constituent elements). Neither the alleged 'nondisconfirmability' of historical classics, nor what we might call the supposed 'non-immanence' of relationships among different individual elements in an account are anywhere actually demonstrated convincingly by White. As we shall see, however, the practice of professional historians – even across different paradigms and coming from quite different premises – is precisely to seek honest mechanisms for 'disconfirming' not only individual factual statements but also more general explanatory frameworks concerned with relationships among elements in a wider historical picture.

For reasons which seem almost unfathomable in retrospect, White's initially quite limited assertions with respect to selected nineteenth-century historical classics were generalised to the practice of history *per se*, and became very influential in subsequent decades. What might at first have been an attempt to bring a little more self-confidence, imaginative pride and literary flair back into the increasingly dry, quasi-scientific practice of history backfired badly. White professed that he was attempting, not to undercut, but rather to *rescue* history: 'history as a discipline is in bad shape today because it has lost sight of its origins in the literary imagination. In the interest of *appearing* scientific and objective, it has repressed and denied to itself its greatest source of strength and renewal.'[6] But he ended up in a position where the power of history to say anything true at all was seriously damaged by his claim that history was 'essentially literary', that its theses were not subject to empirical refutation and that in any event literature, too, was about something 'real', or had deeper truths to transmit.

The confluence of White's views with several initially quite disparate intellectual and cultural traditions, including French post-structuralism, fed into more extreme positions where the possibility even of accurate knowledge about individual events (those fundamental building blocks of history, which when un-narrated and unrelated, in juxtaposition serve to produce White's chronicles or annals) began to be fundamentally queried, and in some cases completely denied.[7] In one version of post-structuralism, influenced by Derrida, the arbitrary relationships between 'signifier' and 'signified' meant, at the most extreme, that not even individual statements about the past could be accepted as meaningful in any stable sense, open as they were to a multiplicity of alternative 'readings'. Thus the very nature of 'texts' meant that virtually nothing could be said about the past that was not open to an infinite number of alternative interpretations: there was no 'past as such' against which any interpretation could be measured and judged 'better' or 'worse' than any other. As far as historical representations are concerned, Roland Barthes' analysis of the 'discourse of History' (which rather oddly often seems for Barthes to act as a virtually autonomous subject) highlights the production of what he calls the 'effect of the real':

> the paradox which governs the entire question of the distinctiveness
> of historical discourse . . . [is that the] fact can only have a linguistic

existence, as a term in a discourse, and yet it is exactly as if this existence were merely the 'copy', purely and simply, of another existence situated in the extra-structural domain of the 'real'.[8]

Those theorists of history influenced by Barthes thus highlight the importance of scholarly conventions of representation – the use of the 'telling quotation', the abundance of footnotes with references to 'primary sources' as well as comprehensive guides to 'secondary literature' – as a means of producing the 'reality effect'. In different ways, the ways in which contemporary empiricist historians present their 'findings' are designed to produce in their readers a sense of confidence in the account, that this is the best approximation available to 'how it really was'. Thus the equivalent of (old-fashioned, nineteenth-century) realism in literature is found or maintained in modernist historical scholarship at precisely the time when literature has developed into postmodernist experiments with form and meaning.

Hans Kellner in a rather different way defines the contrast between those who see history as the representation of true past stories, based on careful collation of sources, and those who see it primarily as a linguistic construction imposed by an active story-teller in the present:

> Two polar points of view confront the issues of history, sources, and language. On the one hand there is the attitude that historical substance always rests upon the materials that make up its sources, and that any significant change in our vision of the past will result from an advance in research that unearths new facts . . . Quite a different picture emerges if we are to maintain that rhetoric, or more generally mental and linguistic conventions, are primary, and that consequently *they* are the actual sources of historical work. This reading suggests that history is not 'about' the past as such, but rather about our ways of creating meanings from the scattered, and profoundly meaningless debris we find around us.[9]

Kellner's own view is that he does

> not believe that there are 'stories' out there in the archives or monuments of the past, waiting to be resurrected and told. Neither human activity nor the existing records of such activity take the form of narrative, which is the product of complex cultural forms and deep-seated linguistic conventions deriving from choices that have traditionally been called rhetorical; there is no 'straight' way to invent a history, regardless of the honesty and professionalism of the historian.[10]

Thus those influenced by this strand of postmodernist thinking will tend to emphasise the sheer chaos, complexity and contingency of the vast and multifarious 'pasts', and the ways in which the representations of different 'stories' produced by historians are primarily active products of the present rather than 'discoveries' about real relationships among elements in the past.

Many of these theorists thus focus not so much on destroying any notion of the 'actuality' of a complex past (which is held to be in itself meaningless) but rather on highlighting the ways in which historical accounts are constructions imposing meaning in the present. But the implications of these kinds of analysis were taken further by derivative commentators jumping on the postmodernist bandwagon in the later twentieth century. In 1999, Keith Jenkins presented a position at the extreme end of the spectrum. In his view, the arguments of Hayden White and others amount to the complete demolition of the status of historical accounts as anything like approximations to, or even interpretations congruent with, a real past. Ultimately, for Jenkins, 'anyone can have a history to suit themselves, anyone and anything – and thus "everything" – is permitted'.[11] Jenkins not only does not try to write history himself; he even queries whether, from a postmodernist perspective, it would be worth the effort. In his own inimitable style, Jenkins argues:

> if . . . historical 'knowledge' has been fatally undercut by postmodern scepticisms and relativisms and pragmatisms anyway, then not only is the question indeed raised as to what would a 'viable' postmodern history look like, but the question of why bother with one at all looks not only attractive but positively compelling; I mean, why bother historicising a past any more? Thus it will be my argument here that we might as well forget history and live in the ample imaginaries provided by postmodern type theorists[12]

Not everyone would agree with Jenkins' total dismissal at this time of any form of historical knowledge or consciousness. Nor would everyone necessarily share Jenkins' (self-indulgent? irresponsible? passing?) preference for living 'in the ample imaginaries' of his favourite postmodernists to the struggle, however imperfectly executed, to acquire some real knowledge and understanding of what has gone before; that is, to engage in a reasoned inquiry into the character of certain aspects of the past, to seek to explain how selected elements or strands changed in the ways in which they did and not in other directions, and to attempt, with as much intelligence, imagination and discipline as can be mustered, to bring some sense of all this back to the present in order to satisfy the curiosities of today.

Let us assume for the moment that we need not adopt the extreme position that we cannot make any meaningful statements about an extra-textual reality, and that we can agree with Hayden White that it is possible to make individual meaningful statements which are at least to some degree communicable with others. (Actually the writings of even extreme post-structuralists are predicated on the view that there will be a market for their books and articles, implicitly confirming this premise.) The issue then becomes one of the nature of the historical account produced. It seems to me that there has been a slide from proclaiming the (undoubted) death of 'metanarrative', understood in a totalising, teleological sense, to the premature and illogical conclusion that therefore, among the infinity of possible partial narratives, any (or no) narrative goes. (This is, it seems, what Keith Jenkins means by his idiosyncratic distinction between 'History in the upper case' and 'History in the lower case'.) Examined a little more carefully, this anti-historical conclusion does not necessarily follow. Let us start by examining the old, rejected metanarratives a little more closely, before embarking on analysis of what, apart from Hayden White's imposed fictions, might replace them.

The death of metanarrative

Much has been made recently of the alleged 'death of metanarrative', or 'grand narrative': that is, of histories which claim to encompass and tell *the* story of *the* great unfolding pattern of the past, in the light of some greater metanarrative, some broader philosophical framework. On more detailed inspection, it becomes clear that the overall 'framing', the general philosophy of history or wider *Geschichtsbild*, can in principle be distinguished from more specific theories about particular periods and particular patterns of change. The former may quite readily be rejected as essentially theological in character, premised on deeply held but non-verifiable beliefs about the ultimate meaning and goals – or lack of them, in the case of postmodernists – of history and of human existence; and/or as essentially literary devices, there not because they in some way reflect the way things actually are or were, but rather purely to help orientate and instruct the reader as to the morals of the story. But the more specific theories, embedded within the broader picture, are more compatible (to phrase it rather cautiously for the moment) with the kinds of historical investigation that many historians who reject grand philosophies of history undertake all the time.

In other words: the death of grand narrative does not automatically entail the death of all narratives which lay some claim to explaining, in a manner subject to empirical disconfirmation (on which more later), selected features of some aspect of the past. The rejection of the possibility of one master narrative does not logically entail that the multiplicity of competing subsidiary narratives are all equally valid (or, conversely, all equally invented). The rejection of metaphysical master narratives does not mean that there is no possibility of comparing competing 'partial narratives', developing rational grounds for claiming that one interpretation (of a particular set of issues or events) better accounts for the (theoretically netted) 'facts' and 'evidence' than another. Put more positively: syntheses constructed on the basis of (always partial) answers to questions rooted in the specific concerns and concepts of the present can be constructed, developed, compared, critiqued.

This rather general set of statements harbours a host of issues, which will perhaps become clearer by analysing some examples. Let us start with the classic metanarratives.

A wide variety of metanarratives are possible in principle: for example, cyclical theories of history, and histories in terms of 'decline and fall' have been popular at different times and in different cultural settings. In some respects, the post-modernist emphasis on 'ruptures', lack of any real connections between different elements in the past, and the intrinsic meaninglessness of human history, can be seen simply as yet another metanarrative, a set of philosophical assumptions about the ultimate meaning – or rather lack of it – of collective human existence over time.

The classic metanarratives in western Europe in the nineteenth and earlier twentieth centuries were couched in terms of some notion of progress, whether that of the Unfolding of World Spirit Realising Itself (the Hegelian version), or its materialist inversion in terms of Class Struggles and Human Emancipation towards Pure Communism (the Marxist version), or the Onward March towards Liberty and Democracy (the Whig version).[13] These three grand narratives have in common a certain overriding view of history as one of an upward march, from worse to better. In different ways, they are all essentially secularised versions of the Judeo-Christian master narrative: from the Fall, through the dark satanic struggles between Good and Evil, to the ultimate Redemption and Final Judgement. They presuppose grand patterns in history, which will eventually (whether or not it has yet been achieved) culminate in something much better than what has gone before. In some senses they all share the nineteenth-century faith in evolutionary progress towards some ultimate goal, or *telos*, of all of human history. Hence when we no longer share the faith in the ultimate goals, it is incredibly easy simply to dismiss these metanarratives as 'teleological'. They also share a certain essentialism: in other words, they posit a view of history as consisting of a single 'real' story, which it is the task of the historian to explicate.

There are also a variety of more recent and arguably less teleological metanarratives which may seem more immediately amenable to at least some modern sensibilities. Twentieth-century modernisation theory – with its focus on patterns of industrialisation, urbanisation, democratisation, improved communications, declining mortality and rising literacy rates – can be seen as a secular variant of the classic nineteenth-century metanarratives of progress. This assumes of course that increased technological mastery of the world is A Good Thing – or at least a development of such major world-historical significance that it cries out for explanation. Conversely, critiques of modernity – whether from radical or conservative standpoints – could point to the shadow sides of the post-Enlightenment legacy. These competing metanarratives are more obviously constructed from particular perspectives in the present, and more readily critiqued as such.

Hence, from multiple standpoints in the present – when we reject the notion that there is only one 'real' story, only one present or future standpoint from which to write – the easy rejection of the classic 'master narratives' as the only story to be told. I think it is important nevertheless to make a clear distinction between the (teleological) imposition of a single 'plot' to the whole of human history, and the construction of subsidiary, specific theses about selected aspects of historical change. It is thus worth exploring in a little more detail just what is at stake, and what further elements are involved that all varieties of history share, before we are tempted to follow postmodernists in throwing out the metaphorical baby of historical analysis with the bath-water of grand narratives rooted in some version of teleological emplotment.

Let us take, as an important – and widely denounced – example, the classic 'great story' or master narrative of Marxism. Clearly there is, at the most general level, a metaphysical overlay: the assumption of 'stages' of history, from lowest to highest (yet to come), taken in part from Hegel and echoing, as indicated, the Judeo-Christian historical world view. In the Marxist version, the stages are of course defined not in idealist terms ('World Spirit realising itself') but in the materialist terms of 'modes of production'; that is, the specific historical combinations of 'means of production' (relating to levels of technology) and 'social relations of production' (patterns of ownership of the means of production, relations between the constituent classes). There is also, very strongly, a notion that this particular narrative is the way things 'really' are; any attempt to write history differently is 'ideological', a mask disguising – from the point of view of particular class interests – what is 'really' the case. All of this exemplifies the metaphysical and essentialist qualities of the original Marxist master narrative.

However, beyond this, there are some more specific assumptions, or, to put it another way, there is a quite detailed theory of history predicated on some quite specific, and what one might call secular, economic, social and philosophical theories (however untenable many of these may appear today). In Marx's view, we do not simply leap, in some unspecified way, from one stage to the next – as in Hegel's metaphysical redescription of stages in terms of 'World Spirit realising itself'; rather, for Marx, the 'motor of history' is essentially a very grounded set of processes rooted in class struggle.

Thus, if we pause for a moment to examine Marx's theory of the dynamics of capitalism (at least at the stage in which he knew it, though his theory was intended to be more generally applicable), we find the following set of scenarios.[14] Marx's economic theories (labour theory of value, tendency of rate of profit to fall, and so on) lead him to the view that there will be certain consequences for the class structure. In particular, Marx posits the polarisation of the two key classes in modern capitalism, namely the capitalists (or bourgeoisie) on the one hand, and the proletariat on the other, with a concomitant marginalisation of other social classes. This polarisation is accompanied by the (relative if not absolute) emiseration of the ever greater numbers of the proletariat in contrast to the (relative or absolute) growth in wealth of the ever fewer but wealthier capitalists, who are increasingly able to squeeze out the *petite bourgeoisie*, who must, in turn, sink into the swelling ranks of the lower classes. These changes in the 'social relations of production', taken in conjunction with concomitant changes in the technological 'means of production' – particularly industrialisation, mechanisation, the growth of factories – will, in Marx's sociological theory, have crucial consequences for class consciousness. For – to take Marx's own analogy – isolated peasants will have no more awareness of their common interests as a class than do potatoes in a sack; but once workers are brought together in the inhumane conditions of modern factories, they will soon begin to have a shared awareness of common miseries, common injustice, in common opposition to an oppressing class of capitalists, and will begin to develop forms of political organisation to overthrow the conditions of their common oppression. Marx then moves from these economic and sociological theories to a combination of political and philosophical assumptions. He posits the rise of the revolutionary class, possibly spearheaded by a vanguard party, a notion taken to extremes in Marxism-Leninism; and his theory of alienation leads him, by virtue of his own particular philosophical anthropology, to the view that once the proletariat has overthrown the conditions of its own oppression, it will have overthrown the conditions for the oppression of all humanity. At this point he enters the ill-defined arena of his hazy vision of future communism based on plenty.

There is an enormous amount that can be – and has been – said about this massively ambitious, internally self-contradictory, often downright wrong-headed but enormously stimulating intellectual edifice. My point here, however, is not to be tempted into any detailed exploration of the Marxist tradition, but rather to point out that it is in principle possible to separate out quite different levels of analysis within Marx's theoretical edifice. The wider metaphysical and essentialist framing can be stripped away, revealing an infrastructure of far more specific, and historically limited or contextualised, economic, social, political and philosophical theories. Each element of these, in turn, can be examined 'in the light of the evidence', debated, rejected, developed or reinterpreted in a variety of directions. Thus, for example, the labour theory of value has been dropped by modern economists; developments such as the separation between managerial and capital-owning classes, or the growth of trade unions and the welfare state, or the uncomfortable fact that the supposed communist revolution took place in a relatively underdeveloped country, Russia, have posed serious challenges to Marx's social and political theories about the ways in which capitalism should or would develop; Marx's philosophical theories about what it is to be 'truly human', and his quasi-religious views on ideology and false consciousness, have been radically attacked; and so on. At the most basic, it is quite clear that a basic political commitment to the improvement of the conditions of the oppressed can be separated from both the general theoretical framework and indeed also from the revolutionary (rather than reformist) political programme. Hence, perhaps, the extraordinary fruitfulness of the Marxist heritage, loosely interpreted, in the works of some twentieth-century social historians who have been too good at their empirical research to stick with some of the wider metaphysical framework. We shall return to these issues in a moment. What is of particular interest in the current context, however, is that – contrary to Karl Popper's blanket condemnation of Marxism in general as a belief system akin to religion which is in principle 'unfalsifiable' – many of the constituent elements actually are in the nature of empirical propositions about relationships between observable elements defined in terms of a particular, theoretically informed conceptual vocabulary. And it is important to distinguish clearly between those which are, and those which are not, in some sense empirically testable. If we strip away the over-riding 'grand narrative', we are left with some specific propositions which are more 'testable' than others. At one end of the spectrum we might put arguments about the tendencies for class polarisation and emiseration, which can be shown not to have occurred in the way the theory postulated they would (or at least, not within one country as Marx thought; the argument is sometimes made that, across the globe, the divisions between rich and poor nations, 'first' and 'third' worlds, echo some of Marx's predictions – but here we start falling prey to the temptation to amend the theory in order to salvage the general moral of the story in face of the evidence). At the other end of the spectrum of 'testability', we might put Marx's views about alienation and false consciousness – which really are untestable in Popper's sense.

What is important to note, however, is that there is a corpus of specific propositions in the midst of all this which might be called 'theories of the middle ground', potentially falsifiable, about real relationships and trends in history. This is also a crucial part or constituent element of what is at issue in the arguments about the nature of history, and we shall return to it in a moment.

The point of this excursion into a classic metanarrative is to illustrate the fact that we can in principle disentangle larger metaphysical views about the purpose and goals of history from more specific, historically grounded, propositions about the interrelations among particular elements in any given historical constellation. We need now to examine what is at stake when we move from single 'big pictures' or 'master narratives', with all their nineteenth-century overtones, to the question of competing narratives constructed from a multiplicity of possible 'endpoints' of history.

The many ends of history

Teleological and essentialist philosophies of history have, notwithstanding the joys of new discovery proclaimed by some postmodernists, never gone entirely unchallenged. As H. A. L. Fisher presciently put it, in his *A History of Europe*, published in the gathering political stormclouds of the mid-1930s:

> Men wiser and more learned than I have discerned in history a plot, a rhythm, a predetermined pattern. These harmonies are concealed from me. I can see only one emergency following upon another as wave follows upon wave, only one great fact with respect to which, since it is unique, there can be no generalisation, only one safe rule for the

historian: that he should recognise in the development of human destinies the play of the contingent and the unforeseen . . . The ground gained by one generation may be lost by the next. The thoughts of man may flow into the channels which lead to disaster and barbarism.[15]

Geoffrey Elton, too, had predictable uncomplimentary things to say about what he summarised as 'purpose in history' (though postmodernists would probably not wish to be unduly associated with Elton's views).[16] Nevertheless, the issue of 'rupture', of intrinsic meaninglessness and lack of what one might call 'inherent patternedness' has been central to postmodernist arguments. Any attempt to impose some metanarrative on selected aspects of the past has then been classified as 'emplotment', the function of which is to impose sense in the present but which bears little relation to any intrinsic characteristics of the past 'as it actually happened'.

The widespread explicit rejection of master narratives on the grand world-historical scale in the twentieth century did not always bring with it a rejection of what might be called quasi-teleological approaches in practice. Indeed, a large part (though far from all) of historical investigation is predicated, explicitly or implicitly, on the selection of some sort of endpoint which requires explanation. The difference between these sorts of partial narratives and the classic metanarrative lies in the fact that partial narratives do not claim to be 'the Whole Truth'. Occasionally they seek to present an alternative large picture on a massive world-historical scale, comparable in some ways to the classic metanarratives although less theological or essentialist in assumption; more often, perhaps, they are couched in terms of adding some previously neglected strand to 'the wider picture', or contributing a new thread; and sometimes they dispute the very possibility of any synthesis or larger picture, seeking rather to view some aspect of the past from a 'new perspective' which distorts the angle of vision, challenging the very notion of a 'wider picture'.

A more circumscribed secular version of the classic master narratives is to be found, as already indicated, in some theories of 'modernisation' which posit selected characteristics of western modernity as constituting, if not the *telos* towards which all 'development' is striving, then at least a set of developments which has had and continues to have profound effects on (most of?) the rest of the globe. What distinguishes this (and many comparable kinds of narrative couched in what, for want of a better word, I shall call 'something-centric' terms) from the grand narratives just mentioned is that these secular versions tend to be less essentialist in tone. That is, they do not say this is 'how it all really is', but rather that, if we are interested in this particular endpoint, defined in terms of these particular criteria, then these are the factors that seem to lead to it; or at least, these are the questions we need to be exploring in order to answer the big questions about how we came to live in a world like this rather than something else. Rather than being 'master narratives', they are perhaps better described as 'selective major narratives' which may be more or less conscious of the extent to which the endpoint selected is but one among many possible endpoints from which to write.

Thus, to select as an example a highly theoretically self-aware historian, Jürgen Kocka takes (as an endpoint which is of importance to him) the notion of 'civil society' in which there can be open democratic debate in a 'public sphere', and examines the conditions which gave rise to this at different times and in different places.[17] To some extent couched within an overall framework of 'modernisation theory', such an approach does not preclude the possibility of there being other equally valid 'endpoints' for which one might wish to explore the relevant conditions and causes. A multiplicity, or intrinsic pluralism, of possible narratives is thus conceded, in a way which would be anathema to the classic master-narratives of Hegel and Marx.

More obviously quasi-teleological are those 'underdog' histories which consciously, explicitly, wish to 'give back a past', or give a voice, to previously marginalised groups who had been more or less written out of mainstream ('hegemonic') histories. This is very obviously the case, for example, with histories of black Americans which seek to give former slaves a voice, and to celebrate their agency, their 'resistances', rather than casting them merely as passive pawns, the barely visible backdrop to 'real' history. The same is true of much of the women's history that was written about this previously marginalised group in the later 1960s and 1970s, as for example in Gerda Lerner's at the time pioneering works.[18] Similarly with the reinsertion of agency in accounts of the 'making' of the English working class, with E. P. Thompson's determination, in his oft-quoted and highly apposite phrase, to 'rescue the poor stockinger, the Luddite cropper, the "obsolete" hand-loom weaver, the "utopian" artisan, and even the deluded follower of Joanna Southcott, from the enormous condescension of posterity' in his classic work, *The Making of the English Working Class*.[19] Similar underdog histories can be found in the works of other Marxist historians – notably Christopher Hill for the seventeenth century.

Some of these could be characterised as essentially perspectival paradigms. Such approaches are essentially predicated still on a notion of a wider picture, into which these histories must be reinserted to produce a more comprehensive and more adequate, potentially unified 'synthesis'. (So, for example: histories of the United States which focus primarily on the ideas and actions of predominantly 'white anglo-saxon Protestant' males, or WASPs, must be supplemented by historical accounts of southerners, blacks, women and so on.) Yet the very notion of 'contributing to the wider picture' is challenged by those working within different theoretical traditions or what in Chapter 3 I have termed 'paradigms proper'. Thus for example, E. P. Thompson determinedly wanted to break away from notions of 'the working class' as a static category, a product of structure, an entity which could in some way be brought into a relationship with another class; rather, he wanted to emphasise agency, active self-formation through interaction and change in real historical circumstances. This is a very different paradigm from that of historians emphasising deep structures, or even of other Marxist historians who seemed to view classes as collective actors with fixed material interests over long periods of time, irrespective of cultural traditions and variations in degrees of class consciousness. Yet another theoretical paradigm underlies Joan Wallach Scott's critique, from a radical feminist perspective, of E. P. Thompson's very construction of the historical subject as a politically active male working class.[20] Here we enter the terrain of alternative categories or conceptualisations of – to put it rather crudely for the moment – what the past is made of. Once we start crossing conceptual boundaries in this way, it may no longer be simply a question of different possible endpoints in the present: there are also major issues to do with how we conceive of and hence investigate the past. These conceptual and explanatory issues will be explored further in the following chapters.

Thus, we cannot rest content with those attempted resolutions of the collapse of metanarrative which resort instead to some version of a 'celebration of pluralism' or what one might call a 'multi-cultural' version of history which argues that all stories are equally (in)valid, depending on one's standpoint in the present. The real issue here, it seems to me, is not so much one of multiple possible endpoints of history, but rather one of multiple possible theoretical approaches. We have, then, to think not so much in terms of substantive 'new perspectives' or perspectival paradigms (such as social history, women's history, black history) as in terms of competing paradigms proper. We also need to remind ourselves that there is a lot more to historical investigation than quasi-teleological metahistory and/or invented narrative.

If it is now very generally agreed that we cannot any longer (if indeed we ever did) share one Great Story about the past, then what should replace overarching views of the Onward March of History is far less uncontentious.[21] Several views are to be found in the literature, including: (a) that the coexistence of many stories, recounted from multiple endpoints, could still be compatible with the pursuit of a (possibly immensely complex and detailed but still in principle unified) synthesis of true (if never complete) knowledge about the past, with craft agreement on the appropriate means for assessing the relative value and/or need for revision of particular stories; (b) that the coexistence of multiple stories includes some which are not mutually compatible, and that, since there is no rational way of deciding between them, we decide among them on the basis of our personal preferences and prejudices; or – a rather stronger version of the previous view – (c) that since there is no way of accessing the past independently of any of these stories anyway, there is little point in pursuing history as a discipline dedicated to the pursuit of the truth about the past (though we may enjoy it as a form of fiction). The first position is the implicit working model underlying the practices of most western professional historians; the second is nevertheless adopted by some historians (on both right and left); the third is a strong version of postmodernist arguments (as represented, for example, by Keith Jenkins). I simplify somewhat, but I think it is worth making these distinctions.[22]

However, when we pursue matters in a little more depth, we soon find that the situation is rather more complicated. In particular, it is not so much the multiplicity of possible endpoints, but rather the multiplicity of possible theoretical perspectives or paradigms, that constitute the major difficulty in reconstructing a notion of history after the death of grand narratives. Let us explore this a little further by rephrasing the question of history as puzzle-solving rather than emplotment, and looking somewhat more closely at a specific example.

What's the story? Emplotment and puzzle-solving

Crucial to the Hayden White case is that stories are imposed, not given or found in the past. In White's view, relationships among historical events exist 'only' in the mind of the historian.

This is, as it stands, an extraordinarily strong assertion. If we really believed this in its full sense (and I can hardly think that even Hayden White or his followers actually conduct their own lives on this basis), we would have to say that there are (or were) no real connections between different things which happened in the past: that there are no real causes, or combinations of causes, for which we can look, when seeking to explain particular outcomes. Any attempt to recount a sequence of events as though earlier ones stood in some intrinsic relation to later ones would be merely an imposition by the person recounting.

In this strong sense, we could not say, for example, that there was any 'real' connection, actually 'given' in the past and 'found' (rather than invented) by the historian, between the appointment of Hitler as German Chancellor in January 1933, and the Holocaust of 1941–5. On the strong version of Hayden White's argument, any connection drawn between the events of 1933 and those of 1941–5 in a historical narrative arises 'only' from 'the mind of the historian reflecting on them'.

Similarly on a much smaller, everyday scale: very few individuals would assume that there are *no* intrinsic connections between developments in their own lives which are not simply figments of their own retrospective imaginations (gaining certain qualifications, preparing for and doing well at an interview, and then being appointed to a coveted job, for example; or suffering bereavement or financial strain, finding it difficult to sleep or to take decisions appropriately, with knock-on effects on work or domestic relationships). One of the totally disorientating and acutely miserable aspects of diseases entailing the loss of memory, such as Alzheimer's, is the very way in which such connections between past and present are lost – indeed, in which the details of the recent past become simply a cloudy fog, a series of moods and their aftermath rather than a memory of what caused them. Thus to posit the case that there are no real connections 'out there' between events at earlier and later dates is to make a very strong claim, which, I would contend, runs directly counter to the way most fully functioning human beings exist and live in the world.

The ostensibly weaker claim is actually the more subtle and the more interesting one: that there are a whole variety of possible 'real' connections, only some of which will interest us sufficiently for us to explore and seek to reproduce them in any detail. The potential infinity of (real, not imposed) interrelations also leads to the possibility of several different kinds of historical exploration.

These might include not only explanations couched in terms of an endpoint (as discussed above), but also diachronic exploration of interconnections within some historically constructed phenomenon (such as the 'Renaissance' or the 'Age of Enlightenment') which is itself open to analysis and revision as a historical construct, and also sequential analysis of some entity which is deemed to be in some way persistent over time (most obviously in the case of individual biographies, but also collective entities such as 'national histories').[23] It is important to note, in each of these cases, that historians are not simply plucking elements out of thin air to construct their accounts – whether explanatory, diachronic or sequential – but rather are operating within pre-existing, collectively developed frameworks of assumptions, knowledge (or lack of it) and questions. So for example recent works have sought to query previous assumptions about a singular phenomenon which can be termed 'the Renaissance'; or have addressed the relations between elite and mass culture in different geographical locations in the Enlightenment; or have revisited witchcraft accusations and trials in the light of alternative frameworks of interpretation.[24]

In short, historians work within collective traditions of inquiry which set certain parameters and puzzles for which they seek solutions. They do not start, as it were, with a blank sheet of paper, looking at a selection of historical 'debris' and wondering how to 'emplot' this into a coherent story (however much this may be what a relatively under-prepared examination candidate feels like when scouring his or her mind for any useful 'facts' to throw at an answer about which they have little real idea). Rather, they pose questions about problematic aspects of the past within pre-existing collective frameworks of assumed knowledge, theories, and moot points or dark spots for further investigation. Historians frequently work, whether explicitly or implicitly, within the context of collective 'controversies'.[25]

The key questions here are concerned, then, not so much with the more or less arbitrary individual 'imposition of narrative', but rather with possible ways (however imperfect and incapable of definitive conclusion) of attributing degrees of relative casual weighting to different antecedents; ways, within certain paradigms, of trying to 'disconfirm' certain accounts on the basis of new evidence or the reconsideration of existing evidence in new ways; and with the limits of collectively agreed means of proceeding in these ways, because of wildly different assumptions across paradigms of inquiry.

A great deal of history is, thus, not so much about individual historians 'emplotting' the past out of the blue, as it were, but rather about puzzle-solving within the context of particular controversies or wider frameworks of investigation. And this, it has to be repeatedly emphasised, is within a collective context: that of a discipline (albeit one characterised by a diversity of theoretical paradigms) with relatively well-defined, clearly delineated, debates. It may be that 'knowledge' is only cumulative *within* the framework of any given paradigm (with associated concepts and questions); but it is certainly the case that, within any particular historical discourse or paradigm, particular accounts, interpretations or explanations *are* potentially 'disconfirmable' (to use Hayden White's term) in ways and under conditions that we shall explore in more detail in the following chapters. In other words, we are not just talking about 'story-telling', but about testing or challenging received interpretations – whatever the form in which they have been represented. Paradigms, as we have seen, begin from what they take for granted as a given body of knowledge, a framework of interpretation (or several competing sets of explanations); and they have some idea of what they need to look for, what puzzles need to be solved, what 'evidence' or 'facts' will be relevant to answering their questions.

Although some paradigms seem to attract zealous converts more than others, it is not necessarily the case that different theoretical approaches are always completely watertight theoretical 'languages', or that the 'speakers' of one will not be able to understand or even speak the language of another. Indeed, it is generally part of the training of historians to be exposed to competing 'approaches' to any given topic of inquiry. Moreover, it is also the case that significant numbers of historians, at least in democratic societies where controversy is not only permissible but even encouraged, will generally not only be in principle amenable to debate across paradigmatic boundaries, but will be actively encouraged to challenge previous approaches and existing presuppositions. In short: there is, at least in much of western academia, an in-built professional requirement to challenge, innovate, develop new modes of conceptualisation and approach. Theoretical paradigms are infinitely more susceptible to rapid change than are, say, the rules of German grammar (a fact which many non-native speakers of German may have cause to regret). Paradigms are somewhat like language communities; but the analogy should not be stretched too far. Moreover, theoretical debates in history may well move at least some sets of collective conversations about certain aspects of the past into fruitful directions of further research and the development of more adequate interpretations.

Some paradigms are more compatible with one another than others; some are more open to revision than others. Some may remain more or less incommensurable. Let us focus at some length on a specific example: that of the French Revolution of 1789, where we find some very nicely contrasting lines of analysis, with clear differences of explanation rooted in different theoretical approaches and 'paradigms proper'. It is less easy to see here how 'new evidence' could help to resolve certain differences at the level of metanarrative, even though research has massively refined the empirical basis over which competing interpretations fight.

Nevertheless, it is worth reminding ourselves that it is relatively easy to 'understand' (if not be a 'native speaker of') a variety of theoretical approaches. This is quite clearly the case with, for example, competing interpretations of the French Revolution. Following the pioneering works on this epoch-making set of events by the French Marxist historians Lefebvre and Soboul, it was perfectly possible for a historian such as Alfred Cobban not only to understand the frameworks they presented, but also to challenge and revise these frameworks by exposing the underlying assumptions and evaluating them in the light of the evidence.[26] This initial revisionist attack stimulated a great deal of further research and controversy, which any current contribution in the field must be able to take into account. And such taking into account is a great deal easier to accomplish – even when discussing approaches which the author does not share – than might be the case if there were no shared ground at all, no mutual basis for debate.

Thus for example standard texts on the French Revolution – such as Doyle's classic texts on the origins and on the course and consequences, or the briefer historiographical overviews by, for example, Blanning or Townson – explicitly guide students through 'Marxist' and 'revisionist' accounts, delineating the main lines of competing arguments and showing the ways in which the findings of recent studies have served to suggest amendments to (or even refutations of) received views.[27] Thus it is perfectly possible for an intelligent historian to translate across a number of approaches and bring relevant evidence to bear on the main tenets of each, in order to indicate the current historiographical 'state of play'.

It is not only student textbooks which seek to introduce a range of views or to situate themselves within a field of controversy. Particular monographs will be less concerned to provide the reader with a relatively balanced overview than to make a new case at some length within a given historiographical context. Let us consider a couple of examples at somewhat greater length.

First let us take a work by an exponent of the 'new cultural history', Lynn Hunt. Her book on *Politics, Culture and Class in the French Revolution* begins with an introduction surveying the state of debate at the time of writing.[28] She makes clear distinctions between what she sees as the three main interpretive frameworks. Marxist accounts prioritise the role of the bourgeoisie, either (classically) in the origins of the Revolution, or with respect to its outcomes in terms of unleashing the conditions for the development of capitalism; revisionist accounts query the Marxist class analysis and concept of a revolutionary bourgeoisie, and highlight instead the ambiguities and overlaps between nobility and bourgeoisie; and finally, the Tocquevillian approach focusses on weaknesses in pre-revolutionary state power and the ways in which the 'modernising' project of political centralisation and enhanced state power was an outcome of the Revolution.

These three frameworks of interpretation (or explanatory paradigms) are sketched as background to a presentation of Hunt's own approach, which is presented essentially as a shift in both perspectival paradigm (the segment of reality to be explored) and 'paradigm proper' (with respect to the way in which it is to be conceived, the underlying assumptions about relations between society and individual). Hunt argues that a focus on origins and outcomes misses key aspects of *process*; and that 'politics' must be defined more broadly than is accomplished in a simple narrative of events, or a cumulative description of the intentions of individual actors.

In Hunt's view, social actors or social groups, on the one hand, and political structures and process on the other, cannot be simply reduced to one or other end of the equation (depending on theoretical position); and what is required, instead, is attention to language, images, symbolic practices, gestures, rituals and daily political activities:

> Revolutionary political culture cannot be deduced from social struc-
> tures, social conflicts, or the social identity of revolutionaries. Political
> practices were not simply the expression of 'underlying' economic and
> social interests . . . In the process, [revolutionaries] created new social
> and political relations and new kinds of social and political divisions.
> Their experience of political and social struggle forced them to see the
> world in new ways.[29]

For Hunt, the 'chief accomplishment' of the French Revolution was neither laying the foundations for capitalist development, nor political 'modernisation', as in the Marxist and Tocquevillian views. Rather, it was 'the institution of a dra-matically new political culture':

> The language of national regeneration, the gestures of equality and fra-
> ternity, and the rituals of republicanism were not soon forgotten.
> Democracy, terror, Jacobinism, and the police state all became recurrent
> features of political life.[30]

This thesis Hunt goes on to demonstrate through detailed empirical analysis of imagery, rituals, revolutionary rhetoric and so on.

We have here a set of widely acknowledged and easily recognised (that is, readily labelled by well-known markers) competing metanarratives: the (socio-economic) growth of capitalism, or the (political) emergence of the modern state, or of modern political culture and ideology, are variously given prominence or indeed prioritised above all else in these divergent narratives (if, in the case of the 'revisionist' approach, often only in a largely negative manner). Any 'new' approach, such as the 'new cultural history' perspective of Lynn Hunt, must situ-ate itself in relation to pre-existing competing metanarratives. Indeed, it is part of the claim to importance of any new work that it makes a contribution to the revi-sion, development, or replacement, of pre-existing approaches; that it is in some way 'better than' previous interpretations by virtue of the discovery of new mat-erial (for example, classes were neither as distinct from one another, nor as driven by clearly opposing interests, as portrayed in previous accounts), or by a shift in focus, or a change in conceptualisation.

Even the attempted escape from metanarrative has to situate itself explicitly in relation to pre-existing paradigms. As Simon Schama puts it in his preface to his own account of the French Revolution, *Citizens*:

> The drastic social changes imputed to the Revolution seem less clear-cut or actually not apparent at all . . . Nor does the Revolution seem any longer to conform to a grand historical design, preordained by inexorable forces of social change. Instead it seems a thing of contingencies and unforeseen circumstances.[31]

Simon Schama's 'chronicle' of the contingent could of course be seen as just another metanarrative.

The different paradigms in the context of which Hunt and Schama variously set their own books are also distinguished by conflicting assumptions about such issues as: individuals or collective groups (such as social classes) as key actors in the drama; the relations between presumed long-term material or class interests, and political ideologies and actions; whether culture, broadly defined, should be conceived as a process interacting with, but not reducible to, social class bases or political structures; whether or not designation by consequences rather than causes is legitimate (as in the view that, if the conditions for the subsequent development of capitalism were an eventual outcome of the Revolution, then the fact that the nobility was unaware of what it was unintentionally unleashing is neither here nor there). To quote Schama again: 'Along with the revival of place as a conditioner have come people. For as the imperatives of "structure" have weakened, those of individual agency, and especially of revolutionary utterance, have become correspondingly more important.'[32]

Furthermore, related to such differences in broad background assumptions are differences in empirical focus and the question of what is deemed to constitute relevant 'evidence' and an appropriate methodology for testing hypotheses and demonstrating the case. There is a marked contrast in focus between, say, a revisionist historian analysing the economic and social fortunes of minor nobles and diverse members of the bourgeoisie in one French town, on the one hand, and Theda Skocpol's grand comparative historical survey of the structural and financial weaknesses of *ancien régimes* in challenging international systems, leading to breakdowns in elite control and the emergence of structural spaces in which discontent from below could erupt, on the other.[33]

What is anyone seeking to understand the French Revolution to make of this plethora of paradigms? This is a question which remains open. On the one hand, it is indisputable that, after decades of lively debate, much of which prompted further research on specific questions, there has been a considerable increase in the amount of empirical detail, or what we actually know, about the situations, actions and roles of groups and individuals in later eighteenth-century France. Such increase in knowledge has clearly rendered certain individual propositions untenable, or at least served to qualify them severely. Nor would it be fair to say that such enhancement of knowledge was not welcomed on all sides of the debates. The author of the classic Marxist account of 1962, Albert Soboul, for example, was among the most vociferous in calling for further research in what he called 'a vast field [that] remains as yet untilled'.[34]

On the other hand, however, the question remains as to the ways in which we insert such enhanced knowledge into broader frameworks of interpretation. For example, enhancement of empirical knowledge does not entirely resolve the question of metanarrative (or wilful refusal of it, which in itself constitutes a form of metanarrative). Thus, we may agree with Simon Schama that we need a detailed chronicle, or narrative of individual actions and events; we may also agree with Hunt that we want to know what, historically, emerged through the revolutionary process – and indeed the emphasis in both these camps is precisely on the *emergence* of the new, on developments not pre-given in the 'origins', however the causes or conditions of the revolution may be analysed. But does this agreement really absolve us from taking a view on the wider metanarrative? In both of these accounts, there are in fact alternative metanarratives proposed. For Hunt, a metanarrative about new 'modern' forms of political culture replaces the Marxist emphasis on capitalism or the Tocquevillian emphasis on the state. For Schama, three underlying themes – the relations between patriotism and liberty, beliefs about citizenship and the family, and the centrality of violence – constitute a composite metanarrative. So too, in a way, does Schama's (somewhat self-contradictory) insistence on the 'haphazard', unpatterned character of history, and his resultant decision to present an account which 'opts for chaotic authenticity over the commanding neatness of historical convention'.[35] (Note the 'realism' implied by the phrase 'chaotic authenticity'.) There are interesting ways forward, in which evidence can be brought to bear on these wider issues, and I shall return to this example again in some of the later chapters. But the question of why we should accord primacy to these particular metanarratives, rather than to the classic ones – which, for all the global overstatements, empirical inaccuracies, and required revisions of detail, still draw our attention to the ways in which the French Revolution marked a fundamental historical watershed in both socio-economic and political aspects of 'modernity' – remains for the time being an open one.

Beyond metanarrative?

At first sight, the argument of this chapter may appear to have been rather circular, possibly even self-contradictory: from proclaiming the death of metanarrative in the grand sense to pointing out that all historians work within some general framework of interpretation, some set of supra-historical assumptions (whether about the existence of major historical trends and watersheds, or about the lack of any such patterns) which do in some senses constitute a form of metanarrative, if in more avowedly pluralist terrain. However, it is important to note that the latter are not the same as imposed fictions, creative products of a historian's imagination (whether fevered or otherwise); they are presented in ways which (whatever the 'realistic effects' deployed by historians in their published works) are potentially open to critique and even – in ways we shall explore more fully in the following chapters – disconfirmation. It is true that historians employ literary and other devices to communicate the results of their investigations – on which more in Part III; but this does not mean that historians' 'emplotments' are no more than such literary devices, that the medium is the message (or, to paraphrase Hayden White, the form constitutes the content rather than the other way around). The situation is more complex than such a concentration on literary conventions and cultural forms such as narrative would suggest.

Historical inquiry is, I would contend, more akin to participating in collective 'puzzle-solving' activities than to the individual production of a narrative, however much individual historians take responsibility for their own books, articles, exhibitions, lectures, or other forms of representation. Historical research is an activity carried out within a fairly delimited set of controversies about particular issues, conceived within a wider context of conflicting interpretative frameworks or paradigms.

Individual creativity and imagination will of course enter in through a variety of aspects of the work: from reconceptualisation of ways of approaching problems, to choice of illustrations and style of evocation. Simply 'being human' is a part of the equation through which selected elements of the past are 'translated' to selected audiences in the present. But this does not necessarily mean that history is 'nondisconfirmable' in the same way as works of literature.

The key question is really that of the respects in which competing historical approaches can be evaluated. There are some quite fundamental questions to be asked concerning: the initial choice of paradigm for approaching the past; the conceptual frameworks for inquiry, or categories for analysis; and the assumptions about relations between individual agency and societal (or 'structural') circumstances. There are also issues to do with assumptions about the relationships among the parts, however defined; and to do with choice of methodologies for exploring (demonstrating? discovering?) such relationships. While we can never escape entirely from any kind of baseline of prior assumptions, 'knowledge', and ways of looking at the traces of the past, the key questions have to do with the extent to which alternative or competing historical interpretations can be challenged, revised, amended: in other words, the extent to which they are genuinely open to 'disconfirmation'.

In order to address this question, we need to look more closely at what is an often overlooked but absolutely essential intermediary level of perception and investigation: that of the categories and concepts through which we interrogate the traces of the past. We need to transcend the false dichotomy between 'source-based' empiricism and postmodernist emphasis on rhetoric, and look more seriously at the ways in which we actively construct, select and filter the traces of the past as these play a role in our problem-orientated, puzzle-solving historical investigations. The next chapter turns, then, to the issue of concepts and categories of analysis.

5

LABELLING THE PARTS
Categories and concepts

Paradigms are made up, as indicated, of a number of features. These include, among others, assumptions about what the world is made of. Before looking for 'empirical evidence', or seeking to scour 'the sources', we must have some notion of what it is we are looking at: what, precisely, the past is made of. Whether explicitly aware of it or not, all historians operate in terms of categories and concepts which serve to shape and filter the ways in which they investigate and seek to represent the past. Chapter 6 will look at the ways in which conceptual frameworks affect the collection of evidence, and the ways in which they can be amended or developed; this chapter will first seek to clarify what is at stake when opting for one or another type of historical concept.

The language of history is also the language of everyday life. In this lies part of the problem. Language is loaded with political and moral values; it is never innocent, abstracted or apart from social reality. Historians vary greatly as to their views on whether this is A Good Thing or not; some do not even, apparently, notice the problem.

Historians can never escape the issue of concepts. No historian can simply 'write as it actually was' (to adapt for a moment the Rankean dictum). The language in which the historian writes can be variously located: it can reconstruct the concepts of a previous era (reconstructing in an historicist manner, sometimes known as 'immanence'); it can impose on the past the categories of the present, or employ often heavily loaded concepts of contemporary political and social debates; it can seek to use explicitly defined theoretical categories. But it cannot escape, in one way or another, the use of situated language. A key concern of this chapter will be to begin to determine the extent to which concepts can be 'translated' across different theoretical frameworks or paradigms of inquiry; and the degree to which concepts are open to amendment, refinement and alteration in the light of (conceptually netted) evidence and debate.

A second aim of this chapter is to explore the argument that the solution is to use explicit, consciously defined concepts – what Max Weber called 'ideal types'. I shall argue that *if* the intention is to develop a morally neutral account of the past – an account which can be agreed as a better, closer approximation to the realities of the past than other accounts, on criteria shared across different political and moral perspectives – then the wilful use of relatively neutral, non-contested, theoretical concepts *may* be one way forward. But there are several problems with this proposal. First, there are significant problems with Weber's concepts of ideal types in the first place, since neither questions nor concepts are shared universally by the culture of an age, but rather vary according to world view and/or theoretical paradigm. Secondly, the selection of aspects to be high-lighted in an ideal type is not necessarily morally and politically neutral, and may be, in a variety of respects, quite problematic. Thirdly, as we shall see in later chapters, many historians do not in any event share the view that history is, can, or even should be a morally neutral endeavour; this claim is, rather, one from a particular, situated, viewpoint in the present, and even the very attempt at 'neutrality' may be castigated, from certain perspectives, as an essentially conservative ploy. Historical representations are themselves part of the present, and, on this view, are inevitably political.[1]

I shall argue, nevertheless, that it is important for historians to be explicit about the concepts they are using as interpretive tools. It is also vital to remain open to argument across a range of approaches – even if we can never attain some privileged standpoint outside all interpretive frameworks, whether those of historical actors or of later observers – rather than accepting certain frameworks as acts of faith. This chapter and the next will explore the extent to which (or the conditions under which) there may be some way, if not of arriving at any 'paradigm-independent' or 'theory-neutral' data language, then of providing some form of 'translation' across at least some frameworks of inquiry.

The slipperiness of social concepts

In the natural sciences, categories of description are of course analytic constructs which serve, with greater or lesser degrees of success, to account for observed phenomena: the chemical elements, atoms, neutrons, quarks, and so on, are all constructs imposed on, rather than given in, observed 'reality'. But, as far as sci-entists at any given time are aware, these observed realities exist irrespective of our attempts to name them, and act in the same way under the same conditions whatever we choose to call them.

What we notice about the social and cultural, or human sciences, is that there is precious little agreement among observers about conceptual categories.[2] Although there are continuing disputes in certain areas of natural science, the extent of disagreement seems much less: the Table of the Elements, for example, appears to be universally shared, whether in communist or non-communist regimes, whether the writing around the elements is in Russian, Chinese, French or English. Moreover, the elements in the Table of the Elements really exist, and retain their properties, irrespective of who observes them: hydrogen and oxygen, when mixed in the right proportions, at the appropriate temperatures, under the correct conditions, will always combine accordingly to form ice, water or steam. (The independence of the reality of the natural world from the perception of the observer is nicely caught in the schoolchild's rhyme: 'Peter was a little boy; Peter is no more; for what he thought was H_2O was H_2SO_4'.) This is not the case with the 'elements', or social categories, which form the subject matter of the human sciences.

In the human world, we are dealing with a double set of impositions: not only are there the often highly controversial, mutually conflicting categories imposed by the observer, which will be discussed throughout this chapter; the observed also have their own views, which they are able to express, articulate, and (with qualifications about the one-way traffic of communication with members of past societies) communicate to the observer, as to the nature of their society. Thus, even when analysing the same society, there may be a wide range of views among the observed as well as among the observers. This has led to a problem known as the 'double hermeneutic'.[3]

For example, in twentieth-century Britain perceptions of class among the observed ranged from the two-class 'them-and-us' model prevalent at the bottom of the social heap, through the three-class version of 'we're middle class, and above and below us are the upper and lower classes' to the sophisticated 'multi-strata' or 'we're all classless now' models found in other quarters of the very same society. Similar variations in perceptions of stratification appear to have been prevalent throughout the early modern and modern period.[4] All these are 'working models' of the society current among its participants, even before an anthropologist or historian starts to analyse the society. We shall return to this issue in a moment, when we discuss the question of 'anachronistic concepts'.

There is a significant challenge here to the notion of the historical and social sciences as the pursuit of universally shared, acceptable, truths about the past (or about other societies or our own societies in the present). If we cannot even agree on what it is we are talking about – on categories for labelling the past – it is hardly likely that we will reach agreement on stories constructed in terms of these elements. But, if we are going to continue to investigate the past, we cannot simply agree to leave it like that.

The inescapability of concepts; or, all historians do it anyway

Concepts are crucial to history: a totally inescapable part of addressing, approaching and investigating the past, of searching for 'evidence' (of what?), of summarising 'findings' and describing them in contemporary terms to an audience in the present.

Before the question of concepts is dismissed as abstruse, of no importance to 'real' (that is, empirical, practising) historians who have no time for what they would consider to be theoretical 'jargon', just consider even the way the most non-theoretical historians define their subject matter. Most commonly, the reply will be in terms of a period and/or a theme: to take some classic examples, the bundle of changes in sixteenth-century English high politics interpreted as an alleged 'Tudor revolution in government' (Geoffrey Elton); or the ideas and activities of selected artists and scholars in early modern Italy summarised as a putative 'civilisation of the Renaissance' (Jakob Burckhardt); or the economic, technological and social changes in eighteenth- and nineteenth-century Europe labelled collectively 'the Industrial Revolution' (historians too numerous to attribute); or the far more diverse trends and factors often lumped together in terms such as 'modernisation' (ditto).

Each of these at first sight entirely innocent labels or phrases harbours a multitude of assumptions about periodisation, about the importance of particular aspects or clusters of development, about the selection and shaping of material and the exploration of particular themes. Behind many of them lies a wider historical picture embodying underlying assumptions about origins, patterns of causation, effects, consequences – in other words, many such concepts not only label that which is to be explored, but also insert it into a wider framework of historical knowledge, a larger 'historical picture' of the past. So, for example, the notion of a 'developing country' embodies a bundle of assumptions about a particular path of development previously trodden by western societies, and to be followed, with local variations in pattern and timing, by 'late-comers'; it does not, in contrast to notions of 'under-development', generally allow for the possibility that a relatively 'low' level of economic development may in fact be intimately related to the subordinate position of the 'developing' economy in a wider 'world system' (Immanuel Wallenstein). There is in fact no way of avoiding this question: whether one talks of the 'historical uniqueness' of Nazi Germany, or sees it, variously, as an instance of totalitarianism, fascism, or 'the perversions of modernity *tout court*', one is making a statement about assumptions about what is significant, what 'hangs together': in short, about causation and connotations.

A moment's consideration will thus reveal that any historical concept not only embodies a particular set of presuppositions but can also in principle be countered by a host of counter-arguments, often forcefully self-advertised as 'revisionist', since there is (currently, among western historians) an implicit premium on demonstrating 'originality' in historical interpretation. Thus, for example, the notion of the 'Renaissance' has been unpacked and reconsidered; the supposed 'Tudor Revolution in government' has by no means been widely accepted among English historians; and the dissection of the Industrial Revolution has even gone so far that, in the words of Roy Porter, 'like the Cheshire Cat, the Industrial Revolution has been fading away before our very eyes (alongside other revolutions, such as the English Revolution, or the Scientific Revolution)'.[5]

We are talking here not just of such large concepts (which some might want to follow Berkhofer in calling 'Great Stories'[6], or Lyotard in calling 'narrative substances'); we are talking also about even the smallest constituent elements of those larger contexts, the parts or the social equivalent of 'atoms' of which the wholes are made up. We are talking, in other words, not just about the story's plot, but also about its characters.

As indicated, not everyone would immediately concede the reality or importance of this challenge. From one perspective, the basic elements or categories of historical accounts might seem so self-evident that they appear 'natural', simply the 'way the world is'; on this view, it is perfectly possible to write history which is mutually intelligible irrespective of the differing political standpoints of, say, the historian and various members of his or her readership.

At first sight, this may of course readily appear to be the case. If we are dealing with, for example, individual human beings (Oliver Cromwell, George Washington, Napoleon Bonaparte) we may think we can all readily agree what we are talking about. However, even at this level, all is not as obvious as it might seem. It is clear that historical individuals are, as biological entities, clearly defined in terms of their physical existence and demise (even if we do not in many cases have much factual knowledge about the details of their lives and deaths). But historians are generally interested in features of these individuals which are social, cultural, historical (although biological issues may at times be crucial for political developments, as in the 'madness' of King George III, the ruptured appendix and premature death of the Weimar Republic's first president, Friedrich Ebert, or the assassination of Martin Luther King). Characterisations of individuals are frequently in terms of features – such as political, moral or religious beliefs and opinions – which can only be seen as part of wider collective concepts, operating within given political, economic and social systems.

Consider for example the very first sentence of the introduction to *Politics in the Age of Fox, Pitt and Liverpool* by John W. Derry: 'For half a century British politics were dominated by two men, the Younger Pitt and Lord Liverpool, whose assumptions were derived from the conventional wisdom of the eighteenth century but whose political skills ensured, not only that the country's traditional institutions survived a period of war and domestic change, but that the nation underwent transformation without experiencing revolution or sustained social conflict.'[7] For a book focussing primarily on the detailed analysis of the individual contributions made by a handful of key politicians, this first sentence is densely studded with collective concepts harbouring a host of assumptions about wider patterns of ideological, political and socio-economic structures and change. Indeed, it is precisely the contribution of a book such as this to show how key individuals were able to shape, constrain and transform the field of historical forces in which they operated – which requires analysis in terms of collective concepts which are open to challenge.

To cite another example from a popular biography, the first sentence of the chapter entitled 'The Beginnings of an Extraordinary Man' of Louis Fischer's *Life of Mahatma Gandhi*, reads: 'Gandhi belonged to the Vaisya caste'.[8] All individuals are situated and in deep measure constituted by distinctive historical environments, however much their unique activities may serve to transform these; and historians have to characterise even the most apparently unique individuals in terms of collective concepts, which simply pervade all historical writing, whatever the focus.

There remains huge disagreement about the roles of individuals in terms of what we might wish to call 'historical units of analysis'. As we shall see in the following chapters (particularly Chapter 7 on structure and agency), historians hold widely differing views over whether it is the motives and actions of individuals that should be the focus of explanation, or whether broader mentalities, cultural patterns, social and political structures and conditions should not rather be the focus, given that these both inform and constrain what it is that specific individuals have sought to do, or have succeeded or failed in doing. A very clear example may be found in the work of Lewis Namier on factionalism and personal motives in eighteenth-century English politics. As Penelope Corfield points out, Namier was 'not concerned with persistent or institutional structures, other than as a framework for the personal motivations of the governing elite. His view of society was an atomistic one, stressing the role of individual human nature rather than the structural power of ideology or party, let alone class struggle or economic factors.'[9] This view is somewhat akin to the infamous comment of former British prime minister Mrs Thatcher that 'there is no such thing as society'. Thus even the (often totally unexamined) decision to write in terms purely of atomistically conceived individuals and their motives is to impose some form of 'Great Story' or conceptual framework, even if purely as opposition to other forms of more overtly theoretical conceptualisation.

The problem of concepts is more obvious once we look explicitly at collectivities, or wider social phenomena. Here there are large differences between those who tend to view social realities as 'givens', as essential realities, and those who see them rather as historical constructions. Such apparently innocent and simple concepts as class, nation, or gender can be seen as 'really existing', defined in terms of some 'essence'; or they can be seen, variously, as socially constructed, with an associated range of definitions and explanations. Thus, for example, 'essentialists' with respect to gender tend to view historical differences between sex roles as biological givens. Male and female roles are taken as rooted in biological differences between the sexes, particularly relating to women's reproductive role, but also assuming concomitant tendencies towards nurturing, caring, and communicative relationships rather than aggressive, competitive, individualistic roles. By contrast, a non-essentialist approach would see different constructions of masculinity and femininity as socially and culturally variable. To quote Joan Wallach Scott, one of the most explicit proponents of gender history as distinct from women's history:

> gender is the social organisation of sexual difference. But this does not mean that gender reflects or implements fixed and natural physical differences between women and men; rather gender is the knowledge that establishes meanings for bodily differences. These meanings vary across cultures, social groups and time since nothing about the body, including women's reproductive organs, determines univocally how social divisions will be shaped.[10]

To take another example: the same sort of distinction can be found among historians dealing with concepts such as the nation. For many historians the nation appears to be a historical reality, not only the obvious unit of analysis in terms of which (national) history should be written, but also in many cases as the key actor in history. Historical texts are often peppered with unthinking phrases such as 'it was in France's interest to proceed with caution', 'England had no objection to this plan' and so on. Although such collective agents are almost at the opposite end of the spectrum from the Namierite individuals, this kind of language is also quite characteristic of a certain sort of conservative history of high politics, where the 'nation' is unthinkingly used in place of some notion of a specific governing elite with particular perceptions and interests informed by class, culture and so on. For other historians, the nation is a great deal more problematic: but even among those who agree that concepts of the nation are constructions rather than basic elements of 'the real world out there', there is little agreement over the nature of the construction. For example, while Benedict Anderson posits an 'imagined community' predicated on print capitalism, Eric Hobsbawm points to the capitalist economic system, Ernest Gellner waxes eloquent about assorted features of 'modernity', and Anthony Smith emphasises the importance of a putative 'ethnic core'.[11]

It may be argued that concepts are in fact embedded in specific language communities, some of which are more compatible with one another than others. Clearly, within any language community which accepts certain concepts as 'natural givens', there appears to be little problem of mutual intelligibility; difficulties arise only when attempts are made to communicate with communities which do not share basic assumptions, or to engage in dialogue with theoretical frameworks based on fundamentally different premises.

It is worth emphasising the point that, whether historians like it or not, there is simply no way of escaping the choice (even when apparently refusing to choose) of specific conceptual categories of analysis. The attempt to evade the explicit use of theoretical concepts itself represents a choice of a particular, situated language community, whether or not the historian is aware of this. Those historians who seek to eschew explicitly 'theoretical' language and remain with what seem to them 'common sense' terms, or the language of everyday life, are inevitably prone to represent, thinkingly or unthinkingly, one or another position in the present.

For the most part, this will be entirely unobjectionable for large parts of their readership, who share the same general ground on many issues; it will then suddenly start to appear 'dated', as general assumptions about the world shift, or as fashions change, or even as tidal waves of political correctness sweep the profession and its supposed audience. For example, for a long time the whole of past history appeared, with rare exceptions, to have been populated more or less entirely by males; in the early and mid-twentieth century, it was far more acceptable to talk in terms of reified nations as actors; and the notion of 'races', with some superior and some inferior, was by no means limited to far right circles of Nazis, proponents of Apartheid, or members of the Ku Klux Klan.

Some concepts, however, are problematic even within what might be considered to be 'their own period'. The self-same word can have, not only widely different meanings, but also very different connotations and what might be called emotional weighting. Consider for example the meanings of the words 'democracy' and 'dictatorship'. For a western liberal, some notion of representative democracy (which, at its most basic, allows people at regular intervals to throw out a government of which they disapprove) is the yardstick by which other systems are measured (and found wanting). Against this yardstick, the communist notion of 'democratic centralism' (which seeks to maximise active grassroots participation, but only in the directions set by the 'centre', i.e. the Party) is anything but democratic in the western liberal sense. Conversely, the communist would critique western notions of democracy as a sham, on the grounds that the electorate has no real choice except between one manager of capitalism and another, and that the majority of people are in any event easily hoodwinked by the capitalist-controlled media into thinking one way rather than another. Similarly, the 'dictatorship of the proletariat' is for the Marxist-Leninist a means of ensuring that those suppressed members of the proletariat suffering from false consciousness are led by the far-sighted Party in the essential battle (bloody if need be) for real justice and universal equality against the vested interests of those opposing the loss of their power and privileges; hence, in this sense, 'dictatorship' is A Good Thing. Of course, for the western democrat, dictatorship entails restrictions on what are seen as basic human freedoms and rights, and scorns any notion of majority decisions arrived at by peaceful debate; thus, dictatorship is A Bad Thing.

This example might seem a little polarised, in terms of very specific, explicit views about communism or capitalist democracy. But similar 'political noise' surrounds even concepts which are less obviously rooted in a specific political ideology. Consider for example the notion of 'strong authority' or 'strong leadership', which may be seen by many (conservatives?) as A Good Thing, indeed essential in difficult times – but may also culminate in the constitutional appointment of a dictator commanding a mass following, such as Hitler. Similarly, once we start talking about 'opposition' or 'complicity' we immediately enter a minefield of differing views of whether what was being sustained or opposed was in principle good or bad, and hence whether the underlying criticism implicit in notions such as 'complicity' or 'terrorism' is justified or not. This problem of contested terminology is very evident in discussions, for example, of South African or Irish history; or in relation to the question of whether the communist vision in the GDR was inherently evil or just distorted and repressive in practice because of the peculiarly difficult conditions in which the attempt was made. But an attempt to devise more 'neutral' terminology will not necessarily be any more acceptable, as exemplified by the fierce debates over attempts to 'normalise' the history of the Third Reich, or to write the history of everyday life in Nazi Germany, which provided the backdrop to and precondition for the Holocaust.[12]

To discuss such issues, whether in terms of 'neutrality' or not, is inevitably to

81

raise hackles. And this is precisely the point. Many historical debates are centrally concerned with issues which have mattered, and which continue to matter, and on which people have strong views and take sides.[13] And the language which historians use to write about these questions is not a purely private, personal language of their own, reflecting private personal opinions; it is a shared language, often hotly contested within the communities they inhabit and for which they write. Although in the more extreme cases such loaded language is quite evident and easily discounted, it is often more subtle and pervasive, even un-noticed as part of ordinary speech, as in the case of the so-called 'developing countries', with all that this label implies, referred to above. Conversely, in what may be held to be extreme situations (the Holocaust) the attempt to use 'neutral' or non-loaded language may itself be seen as part of an attempt at sanitising, rendering unproblematic, acceptable, 'normal'.

Thus, the language of everyday life may simply embody very widely shared cultural assumptions, of which large numbers of people within any given community are more or less unaware; or it may more narrowly entail what Gallie called 'essentially contested concepts', which are intrinsically loaded, bearing contested meanings and arousing strong emotions.[14] Even if we can clearly distinguish between language which is wilfully biased and even deliberately designed to deceive, and the more innocent, often unexamined language which is considered to be 'merely descriptive', we cannot escape the situatedness of all language.

If the language of everyday life is often problematic, there is little agreement about how, or indeed whether, it should be qualified, amended, or replaced. Let us look now at a variety of related (and overlapping) conceptual strategies.

'Anachronistic concepts'; or, the problem of immanence

A focus on reconstituting the categories of the past may at first appear to be an easy way into a more uncontentious analysis of the 'worlds we have lost'. We may call those concepts 'anachronistic' which either – in the true sense of the word – are concepts from another time, a different historical world; or which, in the extended sense, are impositions across cultures, not recognised by participants in a different (even if chronologically simultaneous) cultural community. In other words, we are treating the past as a 'foreign country'; and contemporaneous foreign countries as presenting analogous analytical problems of cross-cultural interpretation of the past.

However, the reconstitution of past concepts is not as uncontentious or unproblematic as we might hope. For any 'reconstitution' entails interpretation into the terms of the present. Historians differ as to whether they feel their task is to reconstitute the past 'in its own terms' – or at least in terms which contemporaries would have understood, using concepts which guided their behaviour at the time – or whether it is to explain it in terms which historians believe to be more revealing than those used by contemporaries.

A classic example is provided by the often very heated debates over early modern English history which, in the later twentieth century, raged over such topics as the putative 'rise of the gentry' (Lawrence Stone); whether there was an 'English revolution' related to the 'rise of capitalism' (Christopher Hill); whether there was not rather a 'revolt of the provinces' (John Morrill) or a complex series of splits within a ruling group in what was not a revolution but rather a Civil War among members of the ruling gentry class (Conrad Russell).[15] Without going into the details of these debates here, or discussing the very fruitful empirical research which they spawned, what is of interest for our current analysis is the underlying question of conceptual frameworks.[16] Controversies revolved not only around 'what actually happened where and when' (i.e. the 'classic' historical questions), but rather, or also, around questions such as: what categories do we use to think about what happened, in terms of identification of key social groups, relative weighting of apparent motives and presumed underlying interests, causes and consequences in the light of wider historical changes, and so on; in other words, around the broader conceptual framework we employ, and the roles we accord to participants' perceptions versus our own later interpretive frameworks.

Thus, some revisionists disputed whether Christopher Hill was justified in employing an analysis in terms of class interest and class conflict in what was seen as a period of major historical transition, or changing 'mode of production', when – according to the revisionist historians – what actually seemed to be salient at the time was a struggle for power among competing factions within a broad status group defined by common lifestyle and privileges. To some extent, this may seem to be a purely 'empirical question': we count heads, analyse motives, and then simply redescribe it as we see it in the light of our more detailed inquiries. But precisely which heads we count, and under what categories we count them – and hence the outcome or conclusion of our 'empirical inquiry' – depends precisely on what conceptual framework of analysis we use to investigate the 'evidence'.

Historians do not always argue that we should accept contemporaries' categories as a more adequate conceptual framework, rather than imposing our own 'anachronistic' views about what we presume to be underlying collective entities rooted in common interests or wider social functions of which the historical actors were unaware. Yet they differ widely with respect to ways of navigating this issue, as we shall see. There is the further complication that contemporary perceptions were often no less contested than those of our own day. As Keith Wrightson points out with respect to Tudor and Stuart England:

> no two descriptions of the hierarchy of degrees are quite alike . . . The neatness and fixity of what we conventionally think of as the 'classical' social hierarchy of early modern England is in fact a creation of the interpretive decisions of historians . . . [I]t seems probable that the language of degrees remained very much a vocabulary of the study and the

courts, of the scholar, the herald and the scrivener . . . [T]here is little enough evidence that it enjoyed great currency in the hurly-burly of everyday life.[17]

At the same time, Wrightson argues, the more dichotomous and helpfully vague language of 'sorts' ('the meaner sort', 'the better sort') was in widespread use, allowing a collective identity for notables, including both those who were technically 'gentlemen' and also the more prominent commoners, against those deemed to be socially inferior.

To take a more extreme example of this issue, such a refusal to accept uncritically the mind-set or conceptual framework of a previous age, and to seek for alternative forces presumed to be 'really' at work (jealousy, village tensions and rivalries, and so on), is widespread, if not universal, in historical analyses of early modern witchcraft and magic. This is because a refusal to believe in early modern notions of witchcraft and magic is more generally shared by historians, who therefore start from a prior assumption (common at least to the vast majority of the western scholarly profession) that accusations with respect to the causation of, say, diseases and apparently unnatural deaths, or the failure of crops and harvests, or the milk turning sour, must have some explanation other than one couched in terms of the effects of sorcery. Brian Levack rightly reminds us that at least some of those accused of witchcraft had in fact engaged in some of the magical practices of which they stood accused, and the survival of artifacts for practising maleficent magic (such as dolls for sticking pins in) corroborates the view that some individuals genuinely engaged in practices which could result in not entirely ill-founded accusations.[18] (Physical evidence for making pacts with the Devil is not available.) However, many more people were accused of witchcraft than had apparently engaged in such practices, and despite the fact that tens of thousands were prosecuted for 'maleficium' and 'diabolism', modern historians are inclined to think they were singled out for reasons other than actual practice of witchcraft. There is, in other words, a refusal to accept contemporaries' categories as sufficient. Precisely what the alternative is varies greatly – from 'survivalist' notions about 'superstitious' beliefs, through various forms of social functionalism (as in Keith Thomas' path-breaking analysis of failures in good neighbourliness), to emphases on gender (ranging from sheer misogyny to fear of 'strong women') and/or notions that witchcraft has to be 'understood in psychic terms'.[19] Even the wider phenomenon to be explained is conceived differently from different perspectives. While H. R. Trevor-Roper's classic essay spoke of a singular phenomenon, a putative 'European witch-craze', later historians have preferred rather to think in terms of disparate, often quite isolated 'witch-hunts' requiring a variety of distinct explanations; and the sheer *lack* of persecutions over long periods in many areas is also increasingly the focus of explanation.[20] The point here is to note that historians disagree about what it is that has to be explained (the conceptualisation of the subject matter); and that they are in general unwilling to adopt contemporaries' categories when, from a 'modern' viewpoint, it seems rather obviously absurd to do so, or when 'explanation' cannot remain purely a matter of 'explication'.

There is no simple general position to be adopted on this issue. We may agree with those hermeneutic theorists, following the insights of anthropologists such as Clifford Geertz, who claim that at least one (though not necessarily the only) task of historians must be to seek to understand 'rule-guided behaviour' and hence to redescribe the past 'in its own terms'; to understand alien cultures and mentalities. But, for present purposes, I think we have to take two further steps.

First, we have to remember that, in most societies, both past and present, there is no one universally shared set of concepts for understanding that society. There is not necessarily any single set of 'concepts of the age' which it would be 'anachronistic' not to do justice to. (Note the different social views, for example, of the Levellers, Diggers and Ranters of the mid-seventeenth century, so carefully rescued from obscurity by Christopher Hill, on the one hand, and the contemporaneous views of high church Anglicans under Archbishop Laud on the other.) To claim categorically that we should not use anachronistic concepts presupposes that we know, as unambiguously as possible in the light of the surviving evidence, what would constitute a set of 'non-anachronistic' concepts – which may in turn impose one group's set on another group which did not necessarily share this view of the world. It may be more difficult to do this in the case of largely non-literate societies, when the bulk of surviving evidence tends in the main to articulate the conceptual frameworks of dominant, literate strata. It is much easier when we come to recent or contemporary history. A member of a Christian youth group in 1950s communist East Germany could more easily protest against the official designation as a 'hostile-negative force', a member of an 'illegal organisation' and so on; a 'freedom fighter' in South Africa could protest against designation and treatment as a petty criminal. Much of 'identity politics' is about contesting the meanings of social labels, such that, for example, 'black' does not automatically carry denigratory connotations of second-class status derived from an era of slavery.

We should, in other words, be extremely wary of any over-homogeneous notion of 'the' concepts of an age, which must be employed to redescribe that society; rather, historians need to recognise not only the legitimacy, but indeed even the crucial importance, of employing an external, analytic vantage point. To say this is not necessarily to say that, to return to our earlier example, Christopher Hill got it right when he employed Marxist categories of class to analyse seventeenth-century England; but it is to say that, if he got it wrong, he got it wrong for reasons other than simply the employment of 'anachronistic concepts' as such.

Secondly, we have to remember that we are in the business, not of 'reproducing' the past in its entirety, but of exploring, creatively reconstructing and selectively bringing the past to the present, in the light of current questions to which the worm's eye view of selected past participants might not provide adequate answers. To take a quite extreme example: as an answer to the question of why and how the Holocaust happened, we would hardly be likely to rest content with an account couched in the terms of Nazi ideology and motives, without also trying to explore and explain it in terms which are not necessarily 'immanent' to, or indeed in any way accord with, the world view of the dominant protagonists of the time.

Of course we have to ask how participants – variously, and often in mutually self-contradictory terms at the time – perceived (and possibly also contested other perceptions of) their positions in their society, their motives and goals; but there is no reason in principle – in fact quite the reverse – to argue that historians should not also impose their own later categories and concepts for understanding the past in terms which contemporaries might not have recognised as valid.

Moreover, many of the questions we may want to ask of the past may not even be directly related to the interpretive frameworks of the past: we may want to know, for example, about average distances travelled by different groups in medieval Europe; about differential fertility rates, or patterns of life expectancy; about factors affecting the spread of the Black Death, or the social and economic consequences of Plague at different times and in different places; about the relations between profits and the slave trade. All of these are perfectly legitimate historical questions, which we would hardly expect historians to answer in the terms of the (various) conceptual frameworks of the periods they were exploring. The arguments over anachronistic concepts serve to some extent, it seems to me, as red herrings or camouflage for more serious problems relating to the lack of a shared conceptual vocabulary in the present.

'Theory-drenched' concepts

Another solution might appear to be to develop a vocabulary of analysis that is, very explicitly, at one remove from the language of everyday life – whether that of the present or the past. At its worst, such a vocabulary is what practising historians like to dismiss as 'jargon'. It is also what many think of when they hear the term 'theory': 'using theory' boils down to 'using some concepts taken from elsewhere'; the phrase 'history and theory' tends to mean 'seeing what other disciplines can offer by way of some terminology to help us redescribe the real world less intelligibly'. (I bowdlerise only slightly.) There is an implicit distinction between 'doing history' and 'being interested in and maybe sometimes even using theory', 'theory' here being equated with employing concepts that are not necessarily part of everyday language. This approach is consistent with what, in Chapter 2, I have called 'pidgin paradigms'.

However, it is my contention throughout this book that all history is (whether the historian is conscious of this or not) intrinsically a theoretical enterprise. Historians cannot even begin work, or, more precisely, begin to determine the object of their inquiries, without some form of analytical framework which construes the subject to be investigated. As we have seen above, concepts such as 'the Renaissance', 'revolution', 'dictatorship', are categories for imposing order on disparate and complex historical events, patterns of development, political structures. And constructions of the subject that may seem absolutely 'normal' or a-theoretical to one historian may seem very one-sided or biased to another. Thus, while Namier saw eighteenth-century English politics primarily in terms of the actions of individuals, for E. P. Thompson this was the great era which saw the beginnings of the 'making of the English working class'; and for a gender historian such as Joan Wallach Scott, even E. P. Thompson's radical focus on the construction of a (predominantly male) working class was blind to considerations of gender. In her view, to do justice to gender constructions (male as well as female) would require not simply an 'additive approach' – putting women (back?) into historical accounts – but rather a more fundamental reconceptualisation of the subject.[21] So all that differs with respect to the concepts discussed in this section is that those who have developed them may have been more explicitly self-aware and conscious of what they were doing; and that these concepts may be more firmly embedded in specific systems of thought, frameworks of analysis, or theoretical paradigms.

By 'theory-drenched concept' I mean a concept which is very explicitly defined, and is often rooted in a wider view of the way the world is. It is relatively easy to find clear examples of this kind of concept. Take, for a prime example, Marx's concept of class, which he (ambiguously) defined in terms both of 'objective' features – relationship to the means of production (ownership or non-ownership) – and of the 'subjective' aspect of collective consciousness, of belonging to a group with common interests in opposition to another group or groups. This concept is deeply embedded in a broader – if notoriously self-contradictory – theoretical system, embodying tenets about history as the history of class struggles, about periodisation in terms of 'modes of production' (a combination of class relations and levels of technological development), and so on. This system of thought also entails a large number of metatheoretical assumptions about what is 'really' the case, irrespective of what people think they think (notions of 'ideology' and 'false consciousness'), about primary, conditioning forces ('base/superstructure'), about relations between 'state' and 'society', and about what the underlying factors are which 'really' explain what appears to be the case. Anyone adopting one or another element of this system almost inevitably gets tangled up in debates about how much of the terminology one can employ – often for political or moral reasons of commitment to some notion of 'the Left' – without adopting the whole, sprawling, system of thought. Variants of neo-Marxism in turn spawn their own specific terminologies or conceptual vocabularies, such that anyone reading, say, Nicos Poulantzas or Perry Anderson would need a different dictionary from that required (if one is required at all) for reading Christopher Hill or E. P. Thompson, given the vast gulfs of theoretical disagreement across whatever common Marxist heritage they may claim.

Any given theoretical framework has its own specific definitions of what at first sight appears to be the 'same' word. Thus, if one takes a simple category such as 'power', for example, one can array a selection of alternative conceptions, comparing, say, Marxist, Weberian, Foucauldian and other versions of this term. Each of these deploys different definitions, rooted in different sets of assumptions. The same is true of categories for analysing social inequalities: there is a veritable industry of books on class and social inequality. Equally, we could take examples of concepts relating to social psychology and deriving from Freudian, neo-Freudian or other conceptual frameworks.

It is not my purpose here to enter into any of these debates – such as over the definition and salience of particular concepts of power, or class, or status group – in substantive detail. Rather, I want to raise to attention an often slightly self-contradictory feature of these kinds of concepts. On the one hand, they are very explicitly defined: there is a degree of awareness on the part of the theorist that we require an analytical vocabulary at one remove from the 'way the world at first sight appears'. On the other hand, there is at least an implicit claim that a particular concept can in some way account better for the way the world appears – that it is, in other words, a better means of describing and analysing underlying realities, of making sense of the 'buzzing blooming confusion' of appearances, than other conceptualisations. There is, in other words, some degree of essentialism involved.

This may become clearer if we look at concepts which appear to be derived by a somewhat more inductive process (leaving aside for the moment Karl Popper's strictures on this topic). While some categories clearly appear to derive primarily from the explication of a system of thought (hence their easy dismissal as 'theory', as distinct from 'real history'), others emanate rather from attempting to make sense of substantive material. Those historians who are both theoretically self-aware and also immersed in historical detail may sense in the course of their work that they have 'seen' better how to order that material under some set of conceptual headings or categories, which may then be taken up and played with, deployed, amended and developed by others working in the same or related fields. So, for example, the discussion of the Third Reich moved from notions of a streamlined 'totalitarian' state to more complex ideas concerning a 'polycratic' regime, with multiple, overlapping, competing centres of power: in the eyes of its proponents, such as Hans Mommsen, the latter was not only a superior conceptualisation of the ways in which politics in Nazi Germany operated; it also had major implications for our understanding of Hitler's role (as in Ian Kershaw's interpretation of the structural production of charisma), and for explanations of the genesis of the Holocaust.[22] Similarly, Alf Lüdtke's notion of '*Eigen-Sinn*' was designed to help understand better the complex and often ambivalent ways in which workers related to and protected their interests under different kinds of regime.[23]

Clearly it is particularly helpful if categories can be developed which allow for comparison across periods and cases (as seems to be promised by some notions of social groups, such as the 'peasantry', the 'nobility', and so on). But if different historians actually employ different conceptual vocabularies their analyses will not necessarily be mutually compatible. Part of the problem relates to the degree to which we are prepared to see categories as describing what the world is 'really' like, or as mere 'constructs' for the purposes of inquiry (in other words, we are back, in some respects, to the constructivism/essentialism divide discussed earlier).

We have to return, then, to the basic questions underlying this chapter. Are there any 'theory-neutral' concepts, or are all concepts essentially rooted within different sets of implicit assumptions, explicit theoretical traditions, or paradigms, as described in Chapter 4? It is clear that some concepts are more open to empirical amendment and adoption across different communities of scholars than others, and we shall return to this issue with respect to some specific examples in the next chapter. First, however, we need to look in more detail at what is arguably the most ambitious (and promising?) attempt to develop an explicit way out of these questions: Max Weber's notion of ideal types.

Construction of concepts as 'ideal types'

What of the possibility of developing an explicit theoretical vocabulary which goes beyond the unexamined assumptions of everyday life, and, more particularly, can potentially be shared across different theoretical and political standpoints? Perhaps the most sustained engagement with this sort of endeavour is to be found in the work of Max Weber, and a lengthy discussion of Weber's views may therefore perhaps be forgiven here.[24]

Weber is quite clear that it is not possible to have any description of 'objective facts' without presuppositions (any *'"voraussetzungslose" Abbildung "objectiver" Tatsachen'*); it is inevitable that we work with constructed concepts, and hence essential that we are explicit about these.[25] To this end, Weber elaborated the notion of 'ideal types': wilfully constructed, one-sided constructs accentuating those features which were of importance for any given investigation in the light of particular questions. Such constructs were, for Weber, very decidedly *not* attempts at mimetic redescription of some aspect of the world, but rather an almost wilful distortion of it: an ideal type

> is produced through one-sided *accentuation* of *one* or *several* features, and through the bringing together of a wealth of diffuse and discrete *individual* phenomena, which are present to a greater or lesser extent, and sometimes not at all, and which are accommodated to those one-sided accentuated features, to become one internally unified thought construction . . . For historical work the task arises to establish, in each individual case, how closely or otherwise reality conforms to this ideal picture.[26]

In Weber's view, the beauty of the ideal type method is that it allows the scholar to compare 'reality' against the constructed ideal type. One might quibble that this position is somewhat self-contradictory, in that it presumes that one can in some way independently access and describe 'reality' as something separate from, and to be compared with, the ideal typical concept. Yet at the same time Weber tells us that we can only access 'reality' precisely through a selective analysis of those features which are important for our interests or are of 'cultural relevance' to us.

Weber explicitly eschews any attempt to elaborate a closed, final system of universally acceptable concepts: he comments on 'the pointlessness of a thought which occasionally even grips historians of our discipline that it could be an aim, however distant, of the cultural sciences to develop a closed system of concepts in which reality could be comprehensively grasped in a framework which would in some respects be *final* and out of which reality could then again be deduced'.[27] Yet, although he explicitly denied this, and argued against a 'Chinese ossification' of any conceptual framework, in some senses the extraordinary efforts devoted by Weber to the proliferation of explicit conceptual categories or ideal types amounted to an attempt to develop a social equivalent (admittedly historically variable and ever-changing) of a scientific Table of the Elements, which, in different mixes, produce different complex phenomena in the real world – or, put differently, in terms of combinations of which the real world can be redescribed in an analytical language which allows for comparisons and contrasts across widely separated historical cases.[28]

Thus, for example, Weber elaborated notions of 'mysticism' and 'asceticism', of 'this-worldly' and 'other-worldly' religions, of 'priests' and 'prophets', which together seemed to account for differences in the typical patterns of worldly conduct, and specifically the economic consequences, of the major world religions. The contrast between the activism inherent in ancient Judaism, where religious conduct was conceived as being the 'tool' of the divine, on the one hand, and the more mystical, contemplative belief systems of the East (Hinduism, Buddhism, Confucianism), where religiosity might consist in the exemplification of harmony between heaven and earth, or of religious behaviour as the 'vessel' of the divine, on the other, provided the larger backdrop to more detailed analysis of later, distinctive strands in the western Judeo-Christian tradition: the contrast between medieval Catholicism (where salvation could be achieved by 'good works', and supreme religiosity lay in retreat from the world) and early modern Protestantism (salvation 'by faith alone' combined with a notion of worldly vocation and religious conduct in this-worldly activism); and the further contrast within Protestantism, between the quietist inward-turning Lutheran tradition and the more active, edgy search for signs of salvation among predestinationist Calvinists. It was of course the latter which provided the basis for his 'ideal type' of the 'Protestant ethic' which showed, in Weber's ambiguous analysis, such suggestive 'elective affinities' with what he defined as the ascetic, driven 'spirit of [modern] capitalism'.

Similarly, Weber elaborated sets of concepts for analysing different types of social behaviour, which might be rational in terms of sustaining particular values (*wertrational*), or the pursuit of particular goals (*zweckrational*); for analysing different types of 'legitimate authority' (*Herrschaft*), including 'traditional', 'rational-bureaucratic' and 'charismatic'; and for much else besides. His enor-mously erudite opus on *Economy and Society* is a major compendium of definitional and analytic essays, seeming to promise the assiduous reader (and no one less than assiduous would ever get through this) a well-nigh exhaustive set of tools with which to analyse and understand more or less the whole of world his-tory. And yet, for Weber, the general could only be in service of the particular: concepts at a high level of generality could never tell us as much about the real world as those 'closer to the ground', full of specific detail; generalisations could only assist in particular causal analyses of unique combinations of circumstances, unique chains of actions, events and consequences. It was such unique develop-ments that he explored in his substantive works, including not only the ambitious comparative studies of the world religions but also shorter analyses of disparate topics ranging from the situation of East Elbian agricultural workers to the revolutions in Russia or the conditions for parliamentary democracy in post-war Germany.

An enormous amount has been written on Weber's substantive theses, particu-larly in terms of their historical accuracy (or otherwise), which I have no intention of entering into here. The important points to make in this context are theoretical.

First, Weber's approach has the tremendous advantage of taking us straight out of the swamps of confusion with respect to metanarratives discussed in Chapter 4. By quite explicitly constructing ideal types for the exaggerated, one-sided selection of key aspects of the past from the point of view of questions of interest to us in the present, Weber is able to hold in mind the possibility in principle of innumerable different 'stories' that could be told, and the open-endedness of the diversity of unique patterns of historical development, unique combinations of circumstances, while yet giving us some means of gaining a systematic, controlled overview. Thus for example his contrast between 'priests' (holders of office and bearers of religious tradition) and 'prophets' (who may bring radically new ideas and precepts into the world by claims of direct divine revelation) both helps to make sense of key differences between eastern and western forms of culture, and allows for the emergence of radically new ideas in history. In combination with his focus on the social and political conditions which determine the ways in which such new ideas will be received – depending on whether they fall on stony ground or fertile soil, are taken up or not by specific groups under particular conditions in which they can be historically effective in one way or another – Weber is able to present a much more open, emergent version of history. It is also one which recognises that it is we who are imposing the patterns on the past; but that these patterns are ones which are open to revision, qualification and amendment, in the light of changing current interests, changing conceptual frameworks of analysis, and new material.

There seem to me, however, to be several problems with Weber's theoretical position, notwithstanding the enormous contribution his work has made. Given his explicit views on ideal types, he can always retreat from charges of empirical inaccuracy by appealing to the artificial, constructed character of the concepts ('existing nowhere in reality'). However, this means that one could, in principle, define an ideal type in virtually any way one wanted, not only in order to initiate an investigation, but also, in effect, to make a particular case. In some respects, this is precisely what Weber did with his Protestant Ethic thesis, specifically highlighting those aspects of an artificially constructed conception of Calvinism that seemed in some way to accord with what he held to be crucial cultural aspects of (a similarly artificially constructed concept of) the mentality of at least nascent capitalism, before it developed into a system enclosing (or better: entrapping) its participants in an 'iron cage'. This could be held to be a virtually tautological argument; and yet this 'elective affinity' also was deployed in some senses to imply, but never quite complete, some form of causal argument.

Despite the enormous amount of empirical historical research which this stimulating thesis generated, it has to be said that the theoretical approach is not entirely satisfactory: in fact, precisely because of the ideal type approach, in this case it is far too slippery to be pinned down with any specificity. It is, in other words, perhaps ultra-constructionist, to return to the discussion at the start of this chapter. At other times, however, Weber's approach to concepts verges on being almost essentialist; or at least tends towards what one might call a 'culturally relative essentialism'.

Weber tries to use his conceptual framework as a conscious way of being precise, explicit about comparative method, allowing for wide-ranging thought experiments. Yet oddly, his ideal types do embody very specific assumptions about the way the world is, or at least the way it more or less universally appears to be, at any given time. Weber frequently implies that, while concepts are not 'natural givens', universal categories, neither are they very restricted (in the limiting case, purely individual) inventions: rather, constructed concepts are far more generally shared across a given culture at a given time. While culturally given values (or *Wertideen*) will determine what is of interest and the way it is investigated, purely personal – political or moral – views should not necessarily affect either the choice of concepts, or the pursuit of research within a given conceptual framework (although they might affect the degree of interest, or lack of it, with which an individual might greet particular bodies of research). By the conscious construction of an explicit theoretical vocabulary, it should, according to Weber, be possible to agree on at least the logical correctness and factual accuracy of scholarly historical analysis and conclusions, whatever lessons for action one might subsequently draw – as an active and committed human being – from this analysis.[29] Weber thought that, for all the differences in political opinion between, say, a Marxist and an anti-Marxist, it should be possible for both to agree on the important concepts of the age, or categories of analysis. Thus, for both those opposed to, and those in favour of, modern capitalism, it would be important to arrive at a shared and 'correct' analysis of its workings – whether the aim was to sustain or to overthrow it. Thus, in Weber's view, capitalism pro-

vided a set of questions for the modern age which transcended political and theoretical boundaries (although there might be other questions of more interest for
those holding one world view than another).

Weber's views are, however, again just a shade self-contradictory. On the one
hand, he suggests that all investigations are, in both objectives and methods,
shaped by the cultural values and interests of the 'investigator and his age': 'precisely *what* becomes the object of the inquiry, and the extent to which this inquiry
extends itself into the endless possible causal connections, is determined by the
values (*Wertideen*) governing the investigator and his times . . .'[30] On the other
hand, in Weber's view the findings should be universally valid, irrespective of cultural values, standpoint and interests: 'Since it is and remains true that a
methodologically correct scientific proof in the area of the social sciences, if it is to
have achieved its aim, must also be recognised as correct by a Chinese person.'[31]

This view is barely more tenable than that of the essentialist position. If we
return for a moment to the concept of 'nation', it is abundantly clear that this is a
historically emergent construct rather than something which is, and always has
been, simply 'given', a constituent element or part of the 'real world out there'.
But it is also quite clear that even among those taking a constructionist approach,
and living in an 'age of nationalism' where explaining the emergence and historical importance of 'nations' was widely seen as important, there are large
differences even in conceptual definition. Nor, for that matter, would Marx necessarily have agreed with Weber's particular, ideal typical, construction of the
'spirit of modern capitalism' (which should itself of course not be confused with
the concept of capitalism as a social and economic system). The problem is, in
other words, not entirely resolved by an appeal to culturally specific 'concepts of
an age'.

Ideal types are hence inevitably imbued with very particular assumptions
about what is important, what sets of factors should be grouped together or seen
as a coherent bundle making up a historically significant whole; and these sets are
chosen on the basis of particular interests, which may be more or less contentious, more or less generally shared within 'the culture of an age'. They have
the great advantage of being explicit, and hence open for discussion; but this discussion may not end in any consensus.

Let us return to an example which was not one discussed by Weber, but which
relates to a period of history he did not live to experience or analyse in its
entirety: the dictatorships of the mid-twentieth century, and their conceptualisations under the headings of totalitarianism or fascism. These examples illustrate
how easy it is to slide from the appearance of scientific objectivity as defined by
Weber to something which is very much more problematic in terms of political
and moral loading – a slide which is not necessarily excluded by Weber's own
explicit approach, but which, in these cases, has certainly acquired more political
noise, and arguably less analytical purchase, than might be thought appropriate.

Among those who treat the concept of totalitarianism very explicitly as an
ideal type, there is very detailed discussion of precisely what aspects constitute

defining features of 'totalitarianism', ranging from Hannah Arendt's views to those of Friedrich and Brzezinski, and subsequent discussions.[32] According to the way in which the ideal type is defined, different historical cases can be put into some sort of order as 'more' or 'less' 'totalitarian'. But this is, in whatever definition, a template which filters out all manner of other aspects of the historical cases thus examined.[33] And it does so from a particular political point of view: that of critique from a democratic perspective. It thus lumps together that which, say, capitalist Nazi Germany has in common with the communist state which succeeded it in East Germany, the GDR; and, by an often only implicit process of guilt by association, makes the Soviet satellite state of the GDR appear 'as bad as' the expansionist and genocidal Third Reich. Dictatorships of the Left and the Right are united under this heading.

Quite the opposite is the case with the Marxist notion of 'fascism', which focusses on the economic system. However, this concept, too, lumps together different historical cases (of which proponents of the concept disapprove) on the basis of what, from a certain political perspective, appears salient: in this case, the fact of a dictatorship within a particular form of capitalist state. The contrast, in this case, is not with 'democracy' (as in totalitarianism) but with 'communism'. The ordering framework is thus quite different.

What we have here are, in principle, simply two ideal types constructed or defined on the basis of what is 'culturally significant' or 'salient' from the perspective of a particular inquiry. But, contrary to the spirit of the Weberian methodology, they are anything but neutral, innocent: indeed, they are as much 'theory drenched' and indeed 'essentially contested' as anything we have considered in previous sections of this chapter. The fact that we can treat them as constructs to be analysed and argued over, rather than essential 'elements of reality', or 'the way the world is', is of some value. But it does rather serve to underline the problems we encounter in historical analysis of finding any shared set of analytical constructs, any vocabulary beyond a very specifically rooted, substantive and descriptive terminology, denoting purely individual cases.

Concepts, evidence, and the emergence of new interpretations

Thus, current assumptions shape the categories and concepts through which we interrogate the past. Categories of analysis have been likened to a fishing net; however murky and impenetrable the depths of water into which we cast our nets, the fineness of the mesh, or the size of the holes in the net, will strongly influence the size of fish we are capable of netting – and thus influence the way we imagine and describe the unseen world beneath the waves.

This might, at first glance, appear to give considerable succour to the relativist case of the postmodernists. We seem to be trapped in a vicious circle of endless discourses; the texts-commenting-upon-texts syndrome. All modes of inquiry seem deeply rooted in metatheoretical assumptions which play a major role in determining what will be seen and how it will be interpreted and re-presented.

It also seems to run completely counter to the apparent straightforwardness of most practical historical research. There is a very widespread view among practising historians that to do history means to engage in the systematic search for empirical evidence – the surviving traces of the past – which will provide the raw material to reconstruct a previously unexamined topic, or to revise previously received interpretations of a particular question 'in the light of new evidence'. Whether presented explicitly, or whether unconsciously sustained as an implicit operating principle in historical investigations, this pursuit of the evidence is an essential feature of historical practice (discussed further in the next chapter). A good historian, on this view, is one who honestly, faithfully, with as open a mind as possible, earnestly endeavours to cover as much of the relevant source material as possible (whether through comprehensive coverage where sources are scarce, or sensible and consciously designed sampling procedures where sources are abundant) in pursuit of 'the truth'. The 'sources' are the fount of all knowledge; 'source criticism' is the basis of all 'methodology'.

This unthinkingly presupposes that we have a common conceptual apparatus for netting the 'evidence', the 'facts'. But as we have seen, there is no such simple analytical vocabulary shared by all historians. Conceptual categories for analysing the past are, moreover, not simply a matter, on the one hand, of personal, individual views and motives; nor, on the other, are they universally shared within any given age. Neither personal bias nor general historical period simply determine the selection of categories of analysis. Rather, these vary across theoretical paradigms and language communities, both within any given period and across time.

How then – if at all – can widespread faith in the reality of the past and the importance of the sources be reconciled with the theoretical argument presented above? To put the question differently: given the importance of the prior conceptual framework for the ways in which the past is netted, how can 'empirical evidence' assist in the development of new, different – better(?) – interpretations? How can we say with any confidence that we are dealing with a form of knowledge that is not in large measure the effect of prior assumptions but is amenable to revision in the light of extra-theoretical material – irrespective of the conceptual net in which it is caught? Indeed, in what ways can 'evidence' serve to amend at least some, if not all, types of conceptual net?

As with everything else, there seems to me to be a spectrum here. From the perspective of some paradigms, there possibly is little or no chance of escape from what one might want to call a circle of self-confirmation. Nevertheless, outside such limiting perspectives, I would argue that – to a point, and with certain qualifications – there is a way through this apparent impasse. When paradigms – and the associated conceptual language – are particularly restricted to a limited community of scholars (bound, for example, by common political values and assumptions) then there is a degree of self-reinforcement at play when analysing 'reality'. When, however, there is a broader language community there can be a greater degree of openness. Even when paradigms are not shared, there may be many 'paradigm-independent' – or perhaps better, 'cross-paradigm' – shared words and concepts with a very or at least relatively closely defined and widely shared meaning (such as, for example, widespread disbelief among at least a majority of modern western historians in the reality of magic as the genuine cause of certain apparent effects; acceptance of common definitions of concepts such as the church or political parties and organisations – but not necessarily of 'religion', 'generation', 'gender', 'power'). Even so, we shall run into what may be redefined as methodological (rather than theoretical) problems with respect to the different ways in which phenomena are captured under what may appear to be common analytical headings in different social and historical contexts.[34]

These more neutral, or broadly shared, categories of analysis will, I would suggest, tend to be at a more restricted level of empirical attribution: in other words, they will not refer to historical wholes (concepts such as feudalism, totalitarianism, fascism) or obviously labile cultural constructs, but rather to more specific, delimited features or institutions. Rather than bundling together a large number of factors, and attributing, implicitly or explicitly, patterns of development, causes and consequences, they will tend to remain at the level of the more restricted and concrete. They will of course also be constructs – we cannot escape that – but they may be concepts which can be more broadly shared across different theoretical and political paradigms.

What then becomes essential is that larger, more holistic concepts are 'unpacked' to determine the peculiar combination of defining elements or features out of which they are constructed; and examined for their associations and connotations, and for any broader historical interpretations or *Geschichtsbilder* which they carry with them, into which they insert the specific case study. This allows for a reasoned – and empirically rooted – critique, on the basis of rather more than simple political likes or dislikes, or of 'guilt by association' with any particular scholarly community and its presumed identity and politics. Let me propose the following tenets:

1   There can never be a universally accepted equivalent of the 'Table of the Elements' for the social world.
2   Nevertheless, we can be very precise about the meanings or definitions of the terms we are employing; there can be a relatively broad community which can agree on the use of this particular vocabulary.
3   The broad community of common conceptual vocabulary will, however, not be coterminous with the general 'culture of the age'. Rather, it will be one or another of the stronger or more loosely defined paradigm communities. With care, this can be a very broad (democratic) community, where openness of debate and rational agreement over interpretations of the past are possible, irrespective of differences in political and moral commitments in the present (but see further Chapter 9).
4   Concepts may be more or less closely tied to a particular theoretical

paradigm, or a political position, or a wider historical picture. The broader, and the more loosely defined, the community of scholars, and the 'lower' (more specific) the level of the concept, the more open any interpretation is likely to be.

5   There can be a degree of translation across different theoretical language communities; but this will to some extent depend on the degree to which the broader paradigm is or is not deeply rooted in particular extra-theoretical presuppositions which are essentially matters of faith.

6   To proceed astutely will require a degree of willingness to learn new theoretical languages, and to engage in dialogue between the kinds of 'realities' that are caught through different conceptual spectacles. Some may appear to lead down ever less fruitful blind alleys; others may suddenly appear to open up new worlds of interpretation, accounting for more elements of perceived reality (for example, viewing the Third Reich as a 'racial state' rather than analysing the question of its 'social revolution' in purely class or socio-economic terms; or seeing the Third Reich as a case of 'polycraty' rather than an instance of 'totalitarianism').

We face a conundrum: 'facts' alone are not enough; there is not and arguably cannot be any such thing as a universal vocabulary for analysing and redescribing the past. But at the same time we want to participate in an intersubjective conversation about salient, selected aspects of the past, and this is a conversation which demands a shared vocabulary.

Perhaps the best we can do is to make a qualified statement along the following lines: One can, if one operates with a relatively open conceptual apparatus, both be theoretically aware, conscious of the constructed, culturally and politically situated, character of conceptual frameworks, and yet at the same time proceed on the basis of a belief that interpretations and concepts can be open to revision – within a broad language community – in the light of the *conceptually netted* evidence. We need now to turn more directly to questions of evidence and the uses of the sources.

6

LOOKING FOR CLUES

The question of evidence

In Salem, New England, in 1692, nineteen individuals were hanged and one was pressed to death for witchcraft; over one hundred others were tried and imprisoned for suspected witchcraft. According to Increase Mather, the then President of Harvard College, that renowned seat of learning in the New World, the 'preternatural' actions of the Devil were clearly to be seen in the evidence of the bite marks, pinching, bruising, fits, twisting, bodily contortions and strange half-closed eyes of the victims, as well as the clear evidence of the existence of the witches' Familiars and Black Men.[1] Some three centuries later, a medical framework of interpretation appears more plausible: far from being evidence, as Increase Mather argued, of the 'preternatural' work of the Devil, the fits, pinching and pricking sensations, swollen throats, hallucinations and other afflictions of the alleged victims of witchcraft are interpreted by one late twentieth-century scholar as the symptoms of *encephelitis lethargica*, an epidemic of which also had swept Europe in the period 1916–30 with patients displaying very similar symptoms.[2] Similarly, while in seventeenth-century England there were earnest discussions of precisely what physical 'proofs' there might be of having entered a pact with the Devil, by the mid-nineteenth century such 'proofs' were no longer as convincing, and rather more 'naturalistic' explanations appeared more plausible in accounting for precisely the same 'evidence'. As Charles Upham put it in 1867:

> It was believed that the Devil affixed his mark to the bodies of those in alliance with him, and that the point where his mark was made became callous and dead . . . [I]f, as might have been expected, particularly in aged persons, any spot could be found insensible to torture [usually pricking with a pin by a member of the jury – MF], or any excrescence, induration or fixed discoloration, it was looked upon as visible evidence and demonstration of guilt.[3]

There is obviously enormous scope for interpreting the 'same' evidence very differently, depending on one's broader framework of interpretation.

One might think from this example that paradigms are extremely broad, covering a wide spectrum of background assumptions characteristic of a particular

time and place. In some respects of course this is true, although at least two qualifications are needed. First, such agreement on background assumptions varies
with the subject matter of investigation. Most – probably all – late twentieth-
century and early twenty-first-century western (Anglo-American?) historians are
highly unlikely to believe in the reality of witchcraft or magic. They will thus
more or less all treat participants' perceptions (witchcraft accusations and so on)
as requiring explanation in terms of something other than those of contemporaries. However, if the topic were to do with persisting religious traditions rather
than discredited magical beliefs, the reality or otherwise of the existence of God,
for example, might simply be bracketed out of a historical account, such that historians of various religious faiths or none could in principle agree on an
explanation of, say, the role of Puritanism in early seventeenth-century England.
However, here enters the second qualification. Even within a broad paradigm 'of
the age', as in the case of witchcraft, there are specific paradigms which (often
only implicitly) introduce enormous scope for looking at the 'evidence' very differently, depending on one's theoretical framework – functionalist, feminist,
psychoanalytic, and so on.

The question of evidence as intermediary between past facts and present
understandings is thus not as simple as it may sometimes appear; and the difficulties are not all related to methodological problems of 'source criticism', on the
one hand, or theoretical problems premised on the assumption of indeterminate
multiple readings of a 'discourse', on the other. It seems to me that the real question hinges on the extent to which conceptually netted (and hence theoretically
contaminated) evidence can be used not merely to 'fill in gaps' within any one
body of knowledge, but also to mediate between, qualify and amend a range of
different conceptual and theoretical frameworks or paradigms of inquiry. This is
a question which is inadequately addressed in the existing theoretical literature
on the nature of history.

There are a number of issues to be addressed in this chapter. First we need to
cast a look at the nature of 'sources' and at debates over their evaluation and
interpretation. We will then turn to questions concerning the relations between
sources, concepts, theories, and more general images of the past. While many
practising historians develop great expertise in the relevant sources for any given
field, and lay great emphasis on the discovery of new sources as a means of
advancement of historical understanding, postmodernist philosophers of history
often argue that there is some form of illicit leap from the individual sources,
mined for factual evidence, to the wider images of a historical totality presented
by the historian. Despite the fact that, as we have seen, there can be no 'theory-
neutral data language', and that 'evidence' can be gathered only within the
context of wider sets of assumptions and associated conceptual frameworks, I
shall argue that the latter are not completely 'water-tight', impermeable, totally
resistant to refinement and change in principle (although the personal commitments of some historians associated with certain approaches may be so in
practice). Analysis of key historical controversies reveals that there are good

reasons for thinking we can develop enhanced, wider and more detailed knowledge of certain areas of investigation, and produce explanatory and interpretive accounts which are more congruent with the available evidence than previous approaches may have been. Thus, while cautioning against any naïve inductive empiricism (and one would be hard put to find many practising historians willing to admit to being guilty of this), I argue against the postmodernist temptation, following Roland Barthes, to see the sources as primarily serving the purpose of lending an air of verisimilitude to a would-be realist piece of historical fiction.[4]

The source of all wisdom?

'Source criticism' plays a major role in most accounts of 'historical method', or even 'theory' in historical research. Among German academics, indeed, *Quellenkritik* holds an almost sacred place. It is of course part of the most basic historical training in secondary and higher education (even ensconced in the British secondary school National Curriculum for history for 11- to 14-year-olds, who may in practice end up with more 'skill' in source criticism than factual knowledge about any given period or topic). A primary focus on the sources is summarised by Dominick LaCapra in what he calls 'the documentary model', in which 'the historical imagination is limited to plausibly filling gaps in the record, and "throwing new light" on a phenomenon requires the discovery of hitherto unknown information . . . Indeed, all sources tend to be treated in narrowly documentary terms, that is, in terms of factual or referential propositions that may be derived from them to provide information about specific times and places'.[5] Another rather denigratory term for this kind of approach is what is often called 'archive positivism'. Before focussing on criticisms, we need to be aware that not all practising historians are quite as naïve in their practice as may be made out by postmodernist critics.

First of all, it has to be said that there is extraordinarily widespread agreement that sources are the crucial bedrock of historical research. Many works on the 'nature of history' pay a great deal of attention to the question of sources. In Geoffrey Elton's view, 'what matters are the sources, that is to say the physical survivals from the events to be studied. And here the first demand of sound historical scholarship must be stressed: it must rest on a broad-fronted attack upon all the relevant material.'[6] Or as John Tosh puts it, embarking on his own account of methodological issues relating to sources: 'Whether the historian's main concern is with re-creation or explanation, with the past for its own sake or for the light it can shed on the present, what he or she can actually achieve is determined in the first instance by the extent and character of the surviving sources. Accordingly, it is with the sources that any account of the historian's work must begin.'[7] Ludmilla Jordanova's work on *History in Practice* similarly provides thoughtful short discussions on points to be aware of in evaluating both sources and historians' uses of sources.[8] For all that he goes on to say in subsequent chapters about the imposition of narrative, even the generally sceptical Neville Morley, in his highly readable book on *Writing Ancient History*, includes a lucid and intelligent exposition of 'the use and abuse of sources' (particularly when there is a serious paucity of material, as in his example of C. Vibius Postumous).[9] And, despite his wide theoretical reading, Richard J. Evans' characteristically pugnacious encounter with postmodernism essentially comes to rest on the simple assertion that 'The past does speak through the sources, and is recoverable through them.'[10]

But, from whatever quarter they come, such historians are scarcely what could be caricatured as naïve empiricists. There is a quite remarkable degree of 'craft' agreement among most practising historians, whatever their varied theoretical orientations, that certain searching questions must be put to and about the sources. In view of extensive discussions elsewhere, such questions may be summarised fairly briefly here.

Clearly, the first set of issues must relate to the nature of the topic for investigation, the questions being asked, and thus the overall research design. One of the reasons for the proliferation of new areas of historical inquiry in the later twentieth century was that historians became more imaginative about potential sources for topics for which it was previously thought there was insufficient source material, such as the beliefs and culture of the vast masses of the illiterate in the middle ages and early modern period. Once a wider range of sources were addressed (and not merely state papers, the letters of the literate, or published works on religion and philosophy) it became possible – as for example in the pioneering works of Keith Thomas and Peter Burke – to explore in more depth aspects of popular culture and social history which had previously been ignored or deemed inaccessible.[11] Similarly, the lives, beliefs and practices of medieval and early modern women, so long written out of history, could be retrieved by imaginative use of a wide range of sources, as illustrated in the survey by Henrietta Leyser.[12] General accounts or 'national histories' need no longer be limited to the kinds of 'traditional' narratives of kings, queens, and battles lampooned in *1066 and All That*, but could seek, with greater or lesser degrees of success, to evoke the experiences of the poor and dispossessed, to give a sense of place, of fashion and customs, and to insert more into the historical imagination than merely the imputed motives and actions of great historical figures.[13] Family structures, sex, emotions, attitudes towards death, changes in habits and manners, all became the subject of legitimate historical inquiry.[14] Modern and contemporary history was opened up with the use of visual sources such as film and photographic records, and through the active 'production' of sources through oral history techniques – all of which was accompanied by quite sophisticated discussion of the potential, limits and pitfalls of such 'evidence'.[15]

Professional historians are not (always) fools. Anyone interested in exploring some lost aspect of the past will inevitably first pose questions about the general character and availability of relevant sources. What sorts of potential sources were produced at the time – not only written sources such as state papers, court records, memoirs, correspondence, diaries, but also material artefacts, art and visual culture, architecture, music, field patterns, and so on?[16] What intended and unintended processes of destruction, differential survival and preservation (not least the selective actions of contemporaries and later archivists with respect to potential paper sources, and of 'modernisers' of one sort or another across the ages with respect to material remains) have led to the destruction, neglect, or continued existence of different sorts of evidence? Thus, documents and other pieces of evidence from previous eras have to be evaluated in the light of 'external' considerations, such as the variable 'sedimentation' in some surviving material form of different types of social experience and human activity. Then more 'internal' questions need to be asked. For example, with respect to written sources: who wrote this document, when, for what purpose, with what audience and intended effects in mind? What other contemporary or later sources can be brought to bear in assessing the reliability and validity of any given source? Is it, indeed, of much use in trying to answer the question put? Or does it perhaps lead to further and hitherto unsuspected questions?

Far from uncritical use of the sources as an accurate record of aspects of the past, practising historians are highly aware of at least certain issues concerning what is actively done with the sources, depending on their range, scope and sufficiency. How, in the light of wider knowledge and assumptions, should any given source be 'read'? In what ways are we justified in bridging gaps in the evidence by means of plausible surmise, imaginative re-enactment, intelligent argument on the basis of contextual evidence or 'triangulation'? What is the extent of the gap between what we feel we can reliably 'know' on the basis of the sources available, and the broader arguments we want to explore? How do our background assumptions (whether or not these are justified) and our pre-existing 'knowledge' affect the ways in which we 'read' the sources? When the source base is apparently too vast, what sensible and intelligent sampling procedures can be devised? What, in short, is added by the historian's active manipulation and interpretation of surviving material? If the facts do not actually 'speak for themselves', how much is added by the role of the historian, and what does this imply for the degree of plausibility or provisional character of the resulting account?

The treatment of the sources is very often a major criterion for evaluating a given historian's work. All manner of 'fallacies' in selection, treatment and evaluation of sources are covered in David Hackett Fischer's book on *Historians' Fallacies* (which is revealing subtitled *Toward a Logic of Historical Thought*, on the assumption that showing where historians have gone wrong can somehow begin to reveal the contours of how to do it right).[17] In his highly imaginative but somewhat controversial interpretation of the 'Great Cat Massacre', Robert Darnton seeks to explain the story of some Paris apprentices who, in the late 1730s, slaughtered and held a ritual trial and execution on the gallows of several sack-loads of cats, including the favourite cat of their mistress, and not content with the initial hilarity of this escapade, re-enacted it in mime on many subsequent occasions.[18] On some views, Darnton's essay exemplifies the illuminating use of very diverse sources to make intelligible to modern readers an apparently inexplicable and indeed rebarbative 'practical joke'; on other views, it stretches the imagination beyond permissible bounds, deploying sources from too far afield to sustain the interpretation. In the context of his attempted rebuttal of postmodernist scepticism, Richard J. Evans deploys the example of David Abraham's controversial use of sources, including many self-confessed 'errors' in transcribing or translating or selectively quoting from sources, to sustain a schematic Marxist interpretation of the collapse of the Weimar Republic.[19] In all these cases, critiques are premised on the underlying assumption that there are correct or appropriate procedures for using sources, and that while each particular case must be viewed on its own merits, sometimes the limits of historical practice have been transgressed. In Evans' summary, whatever the differences between historians' methods, 'the vast majority of the historian's efforts are devoted to ascertaining [the facts] and establishing them as firmly as possible in the light of the historical evidence . . . [Footnotes] are not mere rhetorical devices designed to produce a spurious "reality effect".'[20]

Western historical practice is thus not merely remarkably focussed on the sources, to which much explicit methodological discussion is devoted; it is also, through the social processes of education, apprenticeship and professional critiques, remarkably sophisticated in actively sustaining a set of assumptions about appropriate questions and procedures in the comprehensive and critical use of relevant sources. Systems of examination, the award of degrees, the professional peer review of books and articles, the building (or destruction) of reputations, ensure that there is a great deal more sophistication in the critical use of sources than might be assumed from those theorists who critique 'archive positivism'.

The trouble, however, is that a reiteration of the importance of a critical and intelligent evaluation of the sources – and a reminder about the possibility of getting things *wrong* – does not really meet some of the points being made by at least certain postmodernists. There are two points in particular which are often raised, which are not necessarily intrinsically related to each other, and which need to be dealt with in turn. One has to do with post-structuralist notions of indeterminacy of meaning, and a related scepticism about the possibility in principle of any one 'reading' being better than another. The other has to do, not so much with the interpretation or truth value of individual statements made about the past (which may be accepted as possible), but rather with the way they are placed in wider historical pictures or stories (whether narratives in the conventional sense of story-telling, or in the extended sense of placing selected evidence within a larger synthesis, even if presented in, for example, a structural, non-event-orientated style of historical writing). This is rooted in a view that there is no 'past as such', no stories waiting out there to be found rather than constructed. It seems to me that these points can relatively readily be addressed, but not simply by a return to the bald assertion that the truth lies in (properly and sensitively evaluated) sources. Sources may not be the source of all wisdom; but this does not mean that there is no means of constructing any real knowledge about the past that is more than a random collection of individually true facts.

Extra-textual realities? Or, sources do not speak
for themselves

Those historians influenced by literary and particularly post-structuralist theory tend to focus not so much (or not only, or not at all) on the 'contextual' types of questions generally addressed by practising historians, but also more directly on alternative 'readings' of a given text itself, paying attention to 'ruptures', 'absences', multiple possible readings. By seeking to 'destabilise' the perspective of viewer/object of perception, they seek to shed new light on 'illusions' and 'reality effects'.[21] Although perhaps taken to extremes in some cases, this insistence on re-evaluating and reinterpreting written and visual sources, being attentive to issues of language or 'discourse' as well as 'factual information', is perhaps not as far from at least some historians' practice as might on occasion be supposed (although it may well be more or less irrelevant to the practices of historians interested in topics such as trade figures or death rates). Many 'traditional' historians would probably concede at least some mileage to the point about openness to a variety of interpretations of utterances, artefacts, and other remains of the past. Although some postmodernists seem to have great difficulty in realising that (probably the vast majority of) practising historians do not simply think the sources 'speak for themselves' or provide an unmediated window on some past reality, in fact historians spend a great deal of time worrying about how to interpret or 'read' particular sources.

The question really is what conclusion one should draw from the fact that humans inhabit webs of signification and significance, and that to enter into past webs of significance requires some 'reading' of what is a 'pre-interpreted reality'. This is scarcely a new problem or insight (depending on the way one looks at it). It was central to the hermeneutic tradition which prioritised interpretation of meanings, and reconstructions of the rules guiding social action. Nor is this sort of inquiry at all incompatible with attempts at causal explanation. The possibility of 'interpretive understanding', which seems to be an essential and intrinsic feature of being a human, social animal capable of highly sophisticated levels of inter-subjective communication should, as Max Weber pointed out, make for easier, not more difficult, explanation of past human actions and events – and by extension, of historical sources. To raise issues about 'discourse analysis' could thus be seen as merely adding a dimension (and some not always very helpful vocabulary) to controversies over specific stages in some forms of historical practice. Perhaps the major question here is whether or not one can see criteria for preferring one interpretation over another, or whether – as post-structuralists would prefer – meaning has to be 'endlessly deferred', with no absolute fixity. Yet even postmodernists tend to write as though what they say is 'right' (and even buttress their arguments with appropriate scholarly footnotes). And while extreme postmodernists such as Keith Jenkins draw the conclusion that all historical knowledge of any 'real' past is therefore impossible – premised on a confused notion of what is 'real' in the human past as being in some way not implicated in webs of signification? – most postmodernists probably live their lives on the basis of assumptions about the possibility of rational adjudication between competing interpretations of salient aspects of the recent past.

Even inter-subjective communication in the present relies on 'readings' of what others have told us, evaluated in the light of a wide range of criteria beyond the immediate 'source' at hand. Humans simply do not (for the most part) live in an entirely immediate and instantaneous present: they generally act in the light of what they did yesterday, what they plan to do tomorrow, what others around them are doing and thinking – and in the light of their own shifting interpretations of all these things. All 'reality', present or past, entails 'pre-interpreted texts' (as well as a lot more than texts, whatever the discourse used to describe them – such as physical illness, death, severe weather conditions, plane crashes) which are enshrined in wider webs of signification. These may sometimes be difficult to evaluate; but such evaluation is an essential part of human social existence on an everyday basis.

Let me illustrate this with an example from everyday life. Take for example a simple incident: children coming home from school. Even the brief moment of 'present' will – if there is any kind of communication between parent and child on being reunited at the end of the day – involve wider reference to past and future, or 'extended present' (= the 'present as such'?). It will also involve what one might grandiosely want to call the skills of deconstruction. Any parent will instantly concede that an account of the day at school – incidents with teachers, other pupils – can only be 'pre-interpreted' (in the light not least of how their child feels about the others in the story, or about the parent to whom the account is given). The parent's response to this account is 'pre-interpreted' (in the light of how the parent feels about the child, his or her own state of mind at the time, general knowledge of protagonists at school, views on whether any particular incident should be explored further, as might be the case with bullying, or whether the point of the conversation is to 'unwind' and then turn to other pursuits, and so on). 'Texts' about the same day produced at school will have other purposes and formats: for example, incident sheets ready for school reports, disciplinary procedures, even exclusions. A school inspector might have yet another version of the events on this particular day, as might – in quite other words – the teachers on their return to their respective homes. In short: human beings are social, communicative creatures, who daily exercise their capacity to interpret particular 'texts' in the light of wider frameworks of knowledge and purposes. And there is no more any given 'reality as such' for the present than there is for the past. But this does not prevent us from, for example, having fairly rational views on whose account to trust in the case of an accusation of bullying, in the light of other relevant evidence and 'knowledge' (previous behaviour, 'character', the coherence or otherwise of independent witness reports, the existence of bruises or more serious injuries, other physical evidence). And when it matters – say, as a parent of a bullied child – it seems unlikely that postmodernist scruples about the 'pre-interpreted nature of the texts' or the allegedly illicit construction of a putative 'present as such' would prevent intervention in the light of what is taken as the most adequate or plausible among competing interpretations of events.

There are of course important differences between this example, in which we assume we have particular insider knowledge and personal interests at stake, and the problems involved in investigating a more disembodied or distant past in which we were not (usually) in any real sense active participants – although very often there may indeed be strong personal, political or moral interests at stake. But the problems do not lie in the supposed lack of unmediated access to 'reality', and lack of a 'past as such' against which to assess such 'non-unmediated' interpretations. Rather, they lie in the processes of historical thinking, research, and interpretation – which is precisely why practising historians need to develop highly aware theoretical antennae.

There are, however, some rather different problems involved, which have to do, not with the interpretation of any given 'text' taken on its own, but rather with the ways in which these texts are inserted into a wider framework of interpretation. Take for example a case concerning the relations between the East German Protestant Church and the GDR State Security Police, the Stasi. We know from large numbers of reports by the Stasi that Manfred Stolpe, a senior figure in the East German Protestant Church hierarchy, informed regularly on confidential church matters to the hated secret police.[22] The 'fact' that Stolpe was a Stasi informer or IM (*inoffizielle Mitarbeiter*) is beyond question; and Stolpe himself has admitted it. This, however, does not tell us very much. Interpretation of individual documents is not the major problem; interpretation in the context of a wider framework of knowledge is what actually proves to be far more contentious.

Any one of these Stasi documents, as such, can be 'read' with more or less sophistication; for example, the regular Stasi language of 'hostile-negative forces' (*feindlich-negative Kräfte*) and the like has to be translated into what I would like for the moment, naïvely, to call 'our own' terminology. (This of course begs a number of questions.) The crucial issue, however, does not so much concern the interpretation or 'translation' of these 'pre-interpreted texts', but rather how the now undoubted fact of Stolpe's activities as an informant to the Stasi should be interpreted in relation to the role of the church in the destabilisation of the GDR in the 1980s. In the context of these wider controversies, should one interpret the significance of a whole stream of such documents as showing that Stolpe was but part of the larger story of relatively successful state and secret police infiltration of the church? Or that Stolpe – as he himself claimed – was actually serving the interests of the church, and protecting individual dissidents from worse fates at the hands of the state authorities by ensuring, by complicity with the Stasi, that dissident pastors would be subjected only to internal church disciplinary procedures? Or should this latter claim be dismissed as purely a post-1989 self-justification? Quite separately from the issue of motives and short-term consequences, how should this be woven into the longer story of the 'gentle revolution'? Did Stolpe's complicity essentially serve to sustain the state, or rather to 'buy time' for oppositional groups in the GDR, such that, when the opportunity came in 1989, they were sufficiently well organised to make an effective protest? How, in short, should individual Stasi documents recording Stolpe's discussions and revelations of confidential internal church affairs to the East German secret police be written in to the larger story of the stabilisation or decline and collapse of the GDR? The answers, of course, lie not only in the documents, but also (*not* rather) in the organising and inquiring mind of the historian.

Here we come perhaps to the key issue raised by postmodernists, which is not successfully answered by an appeal to the sources: the question about the ways in which the stories told by historians relate to individually true facts about the past; or, to use the Hayden White term, the question of emplotment. Far more problematic than the question of indeterminacy of meaning is the question of what is done with sources: the question of their relation to the wider images of the past, and alleged notions of a 'past as such' which is presented by historians.

Sources and the 'past as such': the particles and the whole

We need now to pick up again some of the themes about emplotment and meta-narrative introduced in Chapter 4. Hans Kellner provides a nice summary of what is at stake. For traditional historians, the sources are 'those particles of reality from which an image of the past is made':

> While few historians object to the idea that histories are produced, most will assert that the guarantee of adequacy in the historical account is found in the sources. If the sources are available, scrupulously and comprehensively examined according to the rules of evidence, and compiled in good faith by a reasonably mature professional, the resulting work will more or less 'image' reality.[23]

In Kellner's view, however (as we have seen above), 'history is not "about" the past as such, but rather about our ways of creating meanings from the scattered, and profoundly meaning*less* debris we find around us.'[24] Thus bits may be true, but Kellner concurs with Hayden White that the stories are not simply out there, waiting to be found, but rather are products of our cultural conventions. In a slightly different vein but reaching comparable conclusions about the status of history, Ankersmit argues that there is simply no means to access a 'past as such' which could be used as an independent arbiter of any given interpretation. There are simply texts and more texts, with no 'past as a complex referent of the historical text as a whole'.[25]

This argument hinges on a lack of any necessary relationship between the individual facts about aspects of the past, and the coherent narratives formed out of those discrete facts. What is at stake here is the question of where the coherence of the latter comes from. For Kellner, it is a coherence derived from rhetoric rather than representation:

> There is no story *there* to be gotten straight; any story must arise from the act of contemplation. To understand history in this way is not to reject those works which make claims to realistic representation based upon the authenticity of documentary sources; it is rather to read them in a way that their authenticity is a creation effected with other sources, essentially rhetorical in character.[26]

By contrast, Kellner suggests, 'traditional' historians are mistakenly committed to a set of five assumptions and associated anxieties, relating to: the existence of a 'totality'; of a 'fundamental unity' in written texts; the possibility of coherence rather than simply collation of the 'scattered relics of the past'; the possibility in principle of reaching ever better accounts of 'what actually happened'; and an alleged 'anxiety about closure'.[27]

This contrast is premised on a mistake. Kellner is committing a classic case of a false dichotomy. I need not hold the views imputed to 'traditional' historians as the sole alternative to insistence on rhetoric as the only means of giving (spurious, aesthetically produced) coherence to a historical account. If we accept the argument developed in Chapter 4, about history as puzzle-solving, and about many possible 'end-points' of history depending on questions in the present, we can say that even without any notion of unity, totality, coherence, and so on, we can explore real relationships among elements in the past and give an account of them in the present which is based on more than rhetorical coherence. Conceding that there is no single, unified 'past as such', and that many stories are possible, does not logically entail accepting that there is no way of saying whether or not some stories are more plausible than others, or that all 'readings' may be equally valid.

Clearly there are issues of indeterminacy here; the historian plays an active role in shaping, interpreting, contextualising, and even ultimately 'emplotting' the story: but this story is developed as a series of answers to specific questions, for which there may be better or worse means of testing ideas (or hypotheses, to use a more formal term), discarding those which do not seem to work and rigorously exploring those which seem to fit the evidence better. It is this process of investigation – of looking for and rationally using 'clues' – which allows the development of bridges between lost aspects of the past and diverse accounts in the present. The ultimate 'emplotment' may be presented in a wide variety of ways (on which more in Chapter 8); but it is crucial that the form of eventual representation includes some guide as to how the bridges were constructed, and the types of material from which they were built, so that others can retrace the steps, check for adequacy, and look at alternative routes over the chasm separating the present from the non-revisitable past.

The really crucial issue has to do with what, for want of a better way of describing it, I shall call the operations of the intermediate layer between the sources, on the one hand, and the historians' account, on the other. This is a layer which is often missed both by postmodernists and by their 'traditional' opponents. While the former seem largely to see some form of almost random emplotment, the latter tend simply to divide historical work into 'research' and 'writing'. I mean, however, something slightly different here. I mean the processes by which the kinds of concepts and categories we have looked at in Chapter 5 are deployed (or, to use social science terminology, 'operationalised'); and the ways in which, if at all, empirical evidence netted in this way can be used to amend and revise both conceptual categories and more general interpretive or explanatory frameworks or specific theories. It seems to me that this intermediate level provides the crucial basis for being able to argue that historians' accounts are neither simple write-ups of 'what the sources say', nor invented images of the past constructed out of 'random debris'.

Simply appealing to the 'facts', as we have seen, is not sufficient. The really crucial question revolves around the ways in which, or the extent to which, narratives and theories (which implicitly underlie any kind of narrative) are open to amendment and revision in the light of empirical evidence; or, to put it slightly differently, the extent to which 'emplotment' is not merely some arbitrary, essentially stylistic choice of an individual historian, but is rather a collective endeavour, rooted in a determination to test imputed relationships among elements.

We can never escape from paradigms, and from some form of conceptual framework though which the evidence is netted. But a brief survey of any given area of historical controversy will reveal that some (not all) aspects of some (not all) paradigms are indeed open to amendment and revision in the light of empirical evidence. If we look at the way in which historical interpretations and controversies actually develop (rather than positing some lone scholar plucking a few titbits from the archives almost at random and stringing them together into a neat story line), this will soon become apparent.

The interplay between theories, concepts and evidence can be illustrated by way of some substantive examples covering a range of historical approaches and interests: first, the development of the historiography of the French Revolution; secondly, Ian Kershaw's biography of Hitler in relation to wider debates about the Holocaust; and thirdly, some wider comparative historical investigations into the formation of the modern world. These examples – however briefly each area will necessarily have to be treated – serve to demonstrate the use of conceptually netted evidence in the context of wider debates, allowing for amendments and revisions to the theoretical approaches and substantive explanations which are offered. They illustrate the ways in which historical practice is not a matter of lonely scholars plucking at remnants from the historical debris, interpreting them more or less as they please, and weaving them into individualised plots; rather, they demonstrate the ways in which the collective endeavours of historians over time serve to move forward both the terms and the contents of rational (if sometimes emotionally highly charged) collective conversations about specific questions to do with the past.

The French Revolution

The French Revolution, as indicated previously, provides an excellent example of competing explanatory frameworks applied to a highly complex, and potentially emotive, cataclysmic historical event. Even a very brief survey of selected aspects of its historiography reveals clearly the interplay of theory and evidence.

The French Revolution was one of the major events of modern history, with an impact across Europe and the world. Opinions of contemporaries and of later historians were polarised by this dramatic and violent upheaval. In the classic Marxist interpretation (Soboul, Lefebvre, Hobsbawm – and in an updated version, Gwynne Lewis), the French Revolution was interpreted largely in class terms. It was seen as the revolt of a rising bourgeoisie against the rule of the old feudal nobility, bringing about the abolition of feudalism and the conditions for the development of modern capitalism. On this view, while in the early stages of the revolution the bourgeoisie relied on the popular support of the *sans-culottes* and the peasantry to topple the old order, once the common goal had been achieved the bourgeoisie then suppressed the popular classes. This interpretation is no longer widely accepted, at least in the simple form in which classes appear to act almost automatically in terms of presumed long-term class interests. It spawned a major reaction and a much more complex picture has now emerged.[28]

The Marxist view was initially challenged by revisionists such as Alfred Cobban, who argued first, that by 1789, 'feudalism' in its pure form no longer existed; and secondly, that the class system was much more complex, the 'nobility' and 'bourgeoisie' were internally far more differentiated and had much more in common than had previously been supposed.[29] Cobban unpacked each Marxist concept in turn, and showed that it did not exist as such, or play the role allotted to it by Marxist historians. Revisionist historians then went out to find all sorts of evidence of complexities in class structure (on which more in a moment). While effectively demolishing any simplistic Marxist interpretation in terms of clearly definable class actors, revisionists did not replace the Marxist view with any new overall explanatory framework.

Historians who might loosely be called 'post-revisionists' have paid much more attention to culture and 'discourse'. They emphasise the importance of the Enlightenment context, the emergence of a 'public sphere', and the development of revolutionary consciousness through political processes, events, symbols, as for example in the work of Lynn Hunt.[30] So, for example, they might emphasise the differences between the collapse of the *ancien régime* and the emergence of revolutionary processes as a separate and subsequent set of developments: hence, revolutionary consciousness was not so much a cause of the collapse of the *ancien régime*, but rather more an effect of it. Others emphasise structural questions, particularly the importance of the international state system and the impact of warfare on the finances and hence the internal politics of the state. Skocpol, for example, emphasises the strains imposed on the French state by involvement in the American War of Independence; Blanning emphasises the importance of warfare on the European continent, and dates the origins of the 'French revolutionary wars' (or the impact of warfare on French domestic politics) from 1787, with the Dutch Civil War and the invasion of Holland by Prussian troops, posing a threat to France's northern border.[31] Although there are major differences between these two (not least that Theda Skocpol is influenced by neo-Marxism), both have in common that they do not seek purely for *domestic* factors in explaining the outbreak of revolution. That is, neither is content with an explanation purely in terms of domestic class conflict (as in the classic Marxist account) or Enlightenment thinking (as in one version of the cultural story) but both stress that such factors must be combined with analysis of external 'structural' factors – location of the state in a wider international context.

The question thus arises as to whether more detailed research and investigation of the evidence has led to any kind of new consensus. There remain major differences on specific questions, such as whether terror was an integral feature of the revolution from the outset, or emerged as a response to extraordinary circumstance in 1792–4; or how one should evaluate the roles of Louis XVI or Robespierre.[32] Analysis of either of these questions depends on an interplay between evidence and wider presuppositions about the role of the individual in history which we shall consider further in the following chapter. But at a broader level, there is now a general consensus that there were at least two separate processes which cannot be subsumed under a common explanatory framework (as in the original Marxist account): on the one hand, the collapse of the *ancien régime*; and on the other hand, the emergence of a revolutionary chain of events. Both have to be examined in some detail to tease out the relative importance of different factors at different times, including aspects of socio-economic and political structure, the impact of certain events, and the roles of individuals, in a given international and cultural context.

Thus we can see an interesting interplay between theories, concepts and evidence, leading to the movement of specific controversies onto new terrain. If we take, for example, the Marxist concept of class as one element in this set of controversies, the arguments of historians have revolved around issues of which contemporaries themselves were somewhat aware (and which indeed played a key role in the unfolding of events in 1788–9). Should the concept of class relate to 'notables' as an emerging social group defined by wealth and privilege, or rather to the older notion of the three 'estates' defined by functions (clerical, noble and commoner – those who pray, those who fight and those who work)? While many revisionist historians initially devoted much effort to showing that the revolution did not correlate neatly with class in any Marxist sense, such studies (which were often primarily local in focus) often had difficulty in suggesting any plausible new general framework of interpretation. Perhaps the most important point to make here is that, unless one is committed for irrelevant extraneous reasons to trying to preserve one or another kind of theoretical approach, one can examine both simultaneously. Both sets of concepts are empirically open; one can simultaneously count under both headings, and explore the fluidity of change in eighteenth-century French society. In this light, one can explore the intertwining of two 'stories' about social change and concepts of stratification in French society: namely that, until the fiscal crises of the 1780s, the sense of belonging to a class of 'notables' may have become increasingly salient; but the calling of the Estates General in 1789 (which had not met since 1614) highlighted the formal continuance of the older notion of estates, which was now felt by many of the more privileged and well-to-do members of the Third Estate of commoners to be quite inappropriate, and which constituted a major precipitant of the revolutionary events in the early summer of 1789. Thus a historian can operate with several sets of conceptual categories, and can look at both objective and subjective criteria and changes over time (for example, Tim Blanning points out that 25 per cent of the French nobility in the eighteenth century were newly ennobled *noblesse de robe*, with certain consequences); it is possible to count heads and see what consequences there are for looking at the material under different headings and from different angles. Similarly, one can analyse cross-cutting loyalties and the effects these may have had on political sympathies at the time of the Tennis Court Oath. Revisionist critiques thus served to reveal that eighteenth-century French society could not appropriately be conceived simply in terms of classes as composite actors with common material interests driving their collective actions. Research spawned by such critiques produced a wealth of empirical detail and possibilities for enhanced understanding of the historical dynamics of the collapse of the *ancien régime* and the emergence of a revolutionary process.

There is a slightly deeper issue here, however, which has to do with underlying assumptions about connections between different factors. Paradigms tend to entail deeper assumptions about inter-connections between different factors and the relative importance of any given area. One of the key issues on which different paradigms differ, for example, is the question of whether what groups of people have in common (such as common material interests as a class) is deemed to be more important in explanatory analysis than are the respects in which people differ and hence make unique historical contributions. For example, does one prioritise the motives of the bourgeoisie, as excluded from their proper place in political discussions, or of the *sans-culottes* as an underprivileged class serving to radicalise revolution; or does one play up the actions of unique individuals within these circumstances (the personality and roles of Louis XVI, Marie Antoinette, Lafayette, Robespierre)? Does one prioritise some notion of, for example, the allegedly intrinsic violence of all revolution; or is terror rather a contingent factor which is largely explicable in terms of seeking to achieve difficult ends in problematic circumstances; or in terms of a conjunction of the latter and the roles of key individuals, paying due regard to their unique motives and possibly ideology (Robespierre being influenced both by Rousseau's ideas and by the momentum of popular terror)?[33] Underlying assumptions on such questions arguably make a quite major difference in the ways in which historians choose to write about the French Revolution (contrast Albert Soboul with Simon Schama, for example), even if, in principle, many differences of emphasis could be empirically resolved through close argument. It is important to be clear about where the residue of differences rests; it appears to me to have to do in part with underlying philosophical assumptions, and the question of what satisfies curiosity, questions to which we shall return in the next chapter.

Without going into any further substantive detail on this example (where the debates are by no means resolved), there is an important general point to be made with respect to the relationships between sources and stories. Historians do not proceed by making more or less arbitrary decisions, based purely on aesthetic grounds, political sympathies or the 'language community' in which they have been trained, as to what concepts to employ; whatever conceptual or theoretical approach they choose to take, they necessarily now have to take account of the empirical findings of other bodies of research. And while such findings may have been netted under certain conceptual categories, the latter too are (to a greater or lesser extent, as we have seen in Chapter 5) open to critique and revision. There is a reasoned interplay of arguments at a level mediating between the sources and the stories which means that our constructed pictures of the 'past as such' are neither merely the product of personal presuppositions nor more or less arbitrarily plucked out of the ether.

Hitler and the Holocaust

The debates over the French Revolution have been treated, however cursorily, as a collective endeavour reaching over a relatively long period of time. The same point can as readily be made if we consider, for a second example, the work of a single historian, Ian Kershaw. Kershaw's work is situated, quite explicitly, within the wider context of the 'intentionalist/ functionalist' controversy about the origins of genocide in Nazi Germany. For all the arcane academic prose to which this debate initially gave rise, it circled fundamentally around the question of blame. Put very simply: on the basis of the evidence, is the transition from racism to genocide better explained by reference to Hitler's morbid intentions, or as a product of the chaotic functioning and cumulative radicalisation of the regime? Where should explanatory weight be laid? And which broader interpretive framework better accounts for the evidence?

Clearly we have to be careful in respect of speaking about 'the evidence', a term which, as we have seen, is fraught with conceptual shoals. However, I am here presupposing that even postmodernists who dispute the accessibility of the past 'as it really was' will accept the possibility of more or less accurate, if isolated, individual statements about, for example, the numbers of civilian women, children, old people murdered in any one massacre carried out by one of the Einsatzgruppen who followed the German Army into the Soviet Union in the summer of 1941; or patterns of functioning of the gas chambers at Auschwitz over a more extended period of time. If we now consider the details of the way in which the intentionalist/functionalist debate developed over the past two decades of the twentieth century, we find that the weight of research tended to shift away from the search for a definitive moment of decision from above, or written 'Hitler order', to a focus on initiatives on the ground and a focus on the perpetrators of murder. With growing knowledge of the details of the chaotic, relatively uncoordinated mass killings, with a massive escalation in scale and momentum from late June to early September 1941, came new ways of groping with how to describe – and in the process, 'explain' – this escalation. Narratives which laid major explanatory emphasis on Hitler's intentions (positing a straight line from *Mein Kampf* to the gas chambers of Auschwitz, delayed only by Hitler's opportunism and capacity to wait for the appropriate conditions to carry out his murderous plans) seemed to many no longer – if ever – sufficient to account for the haphazard way in which relatively uncoordinated acts of violence developed apparently without a guiding hand on high into what became eventually known as the 'final solution of the Jewish question'. Equally, the curiously disembodied language of the 'functionalist' approach, which almost seemed to anthropomorphise the 'functioning of structures' or to reify the process of 'cumulative radicalisation', as if redescription in these terms amounted to explanation, seemed to cry out for real agents, human beings to populate the structural positions. Puzzling over what was known (and not known), Kershaw's reconceptualisation in terms of 'working towards the Führer' managed to present an account which fitted the accumulating evidence better.

Of interest here is not so much the detail and outcome of the historical controversy (which is of a scale and importance to which justice cannot be done here), but rather the way in which this particular controversy illustrates the possibility of interplay between competing approaches, the search for 'new evidence', and ways in which a sudden flash of reconceptualisation can serve to move a debate forwards.

Kershaw is not concerned to exemplify a particular paradigm or defend a particular entrenched theoretical position; nor is he concerned to 'emplot' from on high, stringing together a plausible narrative on the basis of historical titbits selected almost arbitrarily from the records. Rather, Kershaw's concern is to solve a historical puzzle: to make better sense of the evidence. Thus, for example, he reasons:

> Some Einsatzgruppen claimed after the war that Heydrich had conveyed to them in his briefings the Führer's order to exterminate the Jews in the Soviet Union. But the actual variation in the scale of the killing operations in the first weeks, and the sharp escalation from around August onwards, strongly suggests that, in fact, no general mandate to exterminate Soviet Jewry in its entirety had been issued before 'Barbarossa' began.[34]

In his exploration of the events of the autumn of 1941, both deploying his wider knowledge and understanding of Hitler's personality and habits, as well as piecing together specific findings from exhaustive research into the course of events during these 'fateful months', Kershaw is able both to emphasise Hitler's own fanatical hatred of the Jews, and to take due account of the structural dynamism rooted in the internal rivalries and tensions within the Nazi state. Hitler's role had, in Kershaw's interpretation, 'consisted more of authorising than directing'; and the transition from what could still be considered as primarily military killings, to massacres of civilians, to a notion of a 'final solution' as the efficiently organised murder of millions, was one which was faltering, relatively unplanned in advance, lurching from one ghastly stage to an even more ghastly one, which in turn provided, as in a ratchet, the step up to the next and yet more unthinkable stage in an irreversible process of ever-escalating violence and brutality. Kershaw's notion of 'working towards the Führer' thus nicely provides a means of resolving the intentionalist/functionalist controversy – or at least shifting the fronts and moving research and debate into new waters.

It is perhaps worth reminding ourselves just how far our understanding of Hitler's role in the Holocaust has come. The treatment of this topic in Kershaw's biography is a far cry indeed from the inadequate few sentences (cumulatively totalling all of two paragraphs) devoted to it in Bullock's biography of Hitler, first published in 1952:

> It has been widely denied in Germany since the war that any but a handful of Germans at the head of the SS knew of the scope or savagery of these measures against the Jews. One man certainly knew. For one man they were the logical realisation of views which he had held since his twenties, the necessary preliminary to the plans he had formed for the resettlement of Europe on solid racial foundations. That man was Adolf Hitler . . . There are few more ghastly pages in history than this attempt to eliminate a whole race, the consequence of the 'discovery' made by a young down-and-out in a Vienna slum in the 1900s that the Jews were the authors of everything he most hated in the world.[35]

The state of play on interpretations of the Holocaust at the start of the twenty-first century is dramatically different even from that of a mere ten or twenty years earlier.[36]

In the case of the intentionalist/functionalist debate, we have two competing paradigms, one of which emphasises individual agency and the other structural dynamics; we have the search for new evidence which would help to resolve the issues; we have an accumulation of studies; and we have a new framework of interpretation, combining both agency and structure, and appearing better to account for the evidence. The postmodernist presumption of almost arbitrary emplotment or imposition of narrative by an individual historian does not adequately capture the processes of puzzle-solving in the context of broader controversies exemplified by this set of debates. Although one can argue that, by virtue of its almost unimaginable nature, entailing as it does the transgression of almost every norm of humanity (if for once such a phrase can be used in a more absolute sense, without the kinds of qualifications attached in other contexts), we can never have a completely satisfactory explanation of the origins of the Holocaust, it would at the same time be hard to argue sensibly that our understanding has not been immeasurably enlarged by the debates and research of the past half century.

Comparative history

The same kinds of questions with respect to concepts and frameworks of inquiry arise when the focus is on comparative historical investigations, which we may take as a final set of examples.

Why did a uniquely dynamic form of capitalism, associated with scientific, technological and industrial revolutions, arise in western Europe and not elsewhere, not earlier? Why did some countries experience major, dramatic, revolutionary political and social upheavals, while others appear to have had slower, more evolutionary patterns of political change in the course of 'modernisation'? Why did some twentieth-century states fall prey to dictatorships of left and right while others retained some form of democracy? Are there general patterns which explain the rise and fall of empires, or does each case need to be looked at as a unique set of specific, unrepeatable historical events? What explains different patterns of 'nation-building', different assumptions about entitlement to citizenship? As soon as one begins to wonder about 'large questions' such as these, major issues of conceptual categories that are fruitful for exploring more than one case arise.

What one needs, clearly, are concepts which are at a sufficient level of abstraction to allow for comparison across historically different cases; and a reasoned set of principles for selecting cases for comparison and contrast, in order to set up rigorous tests of any general hypotheses about possible explanations. Both the conceptual framework and the specific hypotheses will to a considerable extent depend on underlying assumptions about the ways in which societies work, the essential causes of change (or 'motors of history'), and what it might be worth looking at or for in greater detail.

For example, as we have seen in the preceding chapter, in his classic comparative studies of the world religions Max Weber set up a conceptual grid of contrasting concepts – this-worldly versus other-worldly, priest versus prophet, mysticism versus asceticism – in the light of which he contrasted the religions of China, India, ancient Judaism and Christianity, and, within the latter, the contrasts between Catholicism and varieties of modern Protestantism. This allowed Weber to identify what he thought were uniquely activist, this-worldly aspects of western civilisation in contrast to the mystic, other-worldly orientations of eastern world views; and to highlight in great detail what he held to be the 'elective affinities' between the peculiarly ascetic, this-worldly activism of Calvinism, on the one hand, and the 'spirit of modern capitalism', with its focus on hard work and the reinvestment of profit in pursuit of forever renewed profit, creating the modern 'iron cage', on the other. Far from writing an idealist account of world history, Weber took great care to examine the social roots of the different types of religiosity, and to explore the unique combinations of historical circumstances – economic, political, social – in which particular religious orientations were able to take root and achieve certain secular effects.[37] While much of the substantive detail of Weber's work has been open to debate and challenge, this extraordinarily wide-ranging oeuvre illustrates a remarkable clarity of thought and mastery of material, consistently controlled by guiding questions and concepts.

Where do such concepts come from, and what are their implications for the way in which a particular investigation is carried out and the kinds of answers which are produced? There is clearly an active role here for the organising mind of the historian, proceeding on the basis of hunches, hypotheses, assumptions about 'things to look for'. These assumptions depend in part on the kind of background paradigm or theoretical tradition within which the historian is working. For example, both Barrington Moore and his erstwhile pupil Theda Skocpol worked within the loose penumbra of a neo-Marxist theoretical tradition emphasising the importance of social classes and class conflict, rather than the roles of different belief systems, as key factors in historical change. Thus Barrington Moore's *Social Origins of Dictatorship and Democracy* is set up to examine 'the varied political roles played by the landed upper classes and the peasantry in the transformation from agrarian societies . . . to modern industrial ones'.[38] His wide-ranging historical comparisons allow him to develop historically grounded generalisations about different patterns, or 'routes' to modernity, depending on factors such as the interactions between historically constituted agrarian classes in the context of social structures with different degrees of segmentation, bureaucratisation or political centralisation. Skocpol (as indicated above) sets up a comparison drawing attention not only to the inter-relations of specific social classes (in Marxist vein), but also (in Tocquevillian and Leninist traditions) to the relative degrees of strength or weakness of the central state apparatus, the state's location within a wider international system, and the character of revolutionary leadership.[39] Her comparative analysis of the successful social revolutions in France, Russia and China, in contrast to unsuccessful revolutions at other times (Russia in 1905) or in other places (for example, Germany in 1848), allows her to identify what appear to be key factors explaining revolutionary eruptions and outcomes. There are other ways too of doing comparative history, with different implications for the kinds of answers which are offered.[40]

Not all comparative history operates on the grand world-historical scale of the examples just given. Comparisons may be quite local and delimited in both geographical and temporal scope, as, for example, in Marcel Faucheux's comparison of the counter-revolutionary uprisings in the Vendée and neighbouring Brittany during the French Revolution, or Marc Bloch's very detailed analysis of changes in agrarian conditions in different parts of France in the eighteenth century.[41] Comparisons may be achieved by juxtaposing the works of more than one historian, each analysing cases with which they are familiar under the rubric of common questions and headings, as in the various works on Enlightenment and absolutism, or the peasantry and the nobility, in eighteenth-century Europe.[42] Comparisons may be designed, not to develop or test hypotheses which are to have the status of abstract generalisations, but rather to identify what is unique, distinctive, new, as in contrasts between the Italian and the 'northern' Renaissance. There may be many more 'cases' of a particular historical phenomenon under investigation – popular festivals, *rites de passage*, youth rebellions, terrorist attacks, marriage and divorce rates, crimes against property and persons – which may be more readily susceptible to comparative analysis and correlation with other factors under certain conditions. And, at the other extreme, even the most stridently apparently anti-comparative history (as in the case of those historians emphasising the absolute uniqueness of the Holocaust) is implicitly comparative, in selecting and highlighting certain features of a particular case which supposedly render it distinctive from all other possibly comparable cases (other instances of atrocities and mass murders, such as those perpetrated by the Stalin and Pol Pot regimes).

These works illustrate the influence of theoretical assumptions about what kinds of factors it might be important to be attentive to, among the possible myriad ways of looking at highly complex unique historical developments. Some investigations are premised on a quasi-experimental view of historical method: since no artificial laboratory experiments can be set up (which would ideally hold certain factors constant and make comparisons among other variables within a carefully controlled environment), the best that historians can do is try to be as open and attentive as possible to the range of factors which might be of significance, and as rigorous as possible in choosing useful cases against which to test (not merely to exemplify) their hypotheses. As C. Behan McCullagh points out, to some extent the conceptual apparatus which is deployed to analyse selected cases depends on prior assumptions: in Skocpol's case, for example, 'the analysis is plausible because it is based upon theories which are already accepted as probably true, and because the cases which Skocpol has examined support and do not invalidate those theories'.[43] Given the very large number of possible variables in individual historical cases (including both contingent events and the motives and actions of unique individual personalities), as well as the relative paucity of multiple instances of certain major historical developments (such as 'successful modern revolutions'), such methods can hardly aspire to attain scientific levels of exactitude. Nevertheless, they can prove extraordinarily fruitful and stimulating ways of making sense of historical patterns and variations over long stretches of time.

In principle, the two ends of the spectrum – from those explicitly looking at large historical comparisons to those emphasising the uniqueness of individual historical cases – are operating from different poles within a field which still requires the organising mind of the historian to marshal and deploy the evidence which is held to be relevant to the question being asked. For all that has been said about the slipperiness of social concepts in contrast to those of the natural sciences, issues to do with research design – the clear framing of questions, rigorous thought about ways in which to test hypotheses, look for evidence, rethink hunches in the light of new findings – are as important in historical investigation as in any of the natural sciences. Sources do not 'speak for themselves'. They stand as clues, as proxies for wider issues and questions. And this is true whatever type of historical investigation is being undertaken, irrespective of whether the historian is setting about writing a single historical narrative, or more explicitly setting up frameworks or strategies for testing hypotheses or investigating hunches (depending on how formal the historian wants to sound about what he or she is doing). It cannot be emphasised too strongly that the key issues have to do, not only with the character and interpretation of the sources, but also with the purposes of investigation. Clear strategic thinking is really crucial to any inquiry, whether the goal is the reconstruction of a unique set of developments, a single case, or a larger comparative investigation of similarities and differences.

Between the sources and the stories

The evidence can answer back; but only up to a point. There remain major issues with respect to the ways in which we choose to look for the evidence. Any historical investigation into the past selects aspects relevant to the question posed, and gathers evidence under conceptual categories which derive in part from paradigms or theoretical traditions which suggest hunches about the way the world works, and what sorts of evidence should be looked for.

The big question then arises: if interpretation of the sources is to some extent rooted in wider frameworks and assumptions, to what extent can the sources be used to critique these? Are we trapped in self-confirming circles, or can theories be genuinely tested, historical interpretations 'disconfirmed'?

I would suggest that, as we have seen above, in certain cases both the concepts used to investigate the past, and the specific substantive explanations offered with respect to parts of the reconstructed past, can be tested, found wanting, qualified, discarded, replaced. There can be some degree of translation across paradigms, some advance in both knowledge and understanding of certain questions. Even granted that sources do not provide translucent 'windows on' a 'real' past, and that there is no unitary, coherent 'past as such'; even granted that it is possible to engage in debates over interpretation of particular sources, which may be difficult or even impossible to resolve in any definitive way; even granted that we bring prior assumptions and associated theoretical frameworks to the inquiry; we can nevertheless seek to test our assumptions, to provide evidence and grounded reasons for rejecting certain views and developing others. These processes of inquiry and debate are not premised on any absurd notion of mimesis; nor on the simplistic assumption that all we need is commitment to the 'agreed rules of historical method' and an honest, comprehensive approach to 'the sources'. Rather, they entail awareness of a theoretical level *between* the sources and the story.

Not everything can necessarily be easily resolved, for a whole variety of reasons. Some conceptual frameworks may be, as indicated in previous chapters, far less open to empirical qualification and amendment, or translatability, than others. 'Large concepts' which are made up of multiple disparate elements, for example, may actually be more in the way of theories, although they are used as a means of labelling rather than in an attempt at explaining interconnections. Notions such as 'feudalism', 'transitions to democracy', 'civil war', 'revolution' and so on often provoke major disagreements among scholars about both definitions and explanations. 'Smaller' and arguably less loaded concepts (such as 'landed classes', peasantry, nobility and so on) may be easier to define and look for variations. But even at this level it is possible to assume widely varying contents to the 'same' concept, as in different understandings of the term 'popular culture'. Other reasons might include too little evidence and too overpowering a commitment to particular paradigms of interpretation. A very nice – spoof – example of this is to be found in Leszek Kolakowski's essay on the 'Emperor Kennedy Legend: A New Anthropological Debate', parodying and showing how badly we can get a few snippets wrong from the perspective of different paradigms proper.[44] In this case, the imagined example was based on extremely little evidence, which was then woven up into quite different frameworks of interpretation. In the 'real world', it would be likely that at some stage further evidence would be sought in order to try to resolve the differences; but this might not necessarily be achievable where there is a mismatch between what is known and what interpretive edifices are constructed upon it. The point here is that such an example is possible; not that it is what always happens.

Sources are important; and there is the possibility of advancement of understanding, not only within given frameworks of interpretation, but indeed even across these. Some commentators have suggested the possibility of a purely sociological reading of Kuhn's notion of paradigms, where paradigm shifts come about primarily for reasons to do with changing language communities. Others have pointed out that there are also – or instead – rational, logical, and evidential reasons for paradigm shifts, and that the sociological interpretation is merely one element in any comprehensive history of classical science. Kuhn himself lays emphasis on the accumulation of 'anomalies', findings which cannot be accounted for within any given paradigm. There are also technical and practical aspects to some paradigm shifts: at least with respect to the application of certain scientific theories, there is the key requirement that they *work*. Whether or not we know why (and apparently we do not), aspirin is widely recognised as an effective means of pain relief; whatever a feminist may think of 'male dominated medical discourse', she is likely to accept a diagnostic mammography, a recommendation of invasive surgery or course of chemotherapy for the treatment of breast cancer; and most people embarking on a plane journey are prepared to believe, whether or not they understand the underlying science, that properly designed and equipped aircraft are capable of effective flight under the appropriate conditions. It is clear that this notion of practical efficacy is less helpful (if it helps at all) with respect to historical interpretations and explanations. Nevertheless, there are grounds for thinking that there is more to paradigm shifts in historical interpretation than purely sociological, political or aesthetic criteria; in other words, there are grounds for suggesting that the evidence can, with certain qualifications, 'answer back' and render some interpretations more plausible than others.

There are, to put it slightly differently, definite constraints on the kinds of interpretations or explanations which historians can offer; and there are reasons rooted in empirical evidence for putting forward new concepts and interpretations, or preferring one explanation to another. Yet, while empirical evidence does have an important role to play, there remain certain indeterminacies, and preferences for one type of explanatory or interpretive 'landing place' rather than another which are rooted in metatheoretical assumptions about the nature of being human and the character of social worlds. Hence there are what might be called paradigmatic restrictions on the ways in which sources are or can be used as evidence.

Thus we find ourselves in an interesting situation. I have argued above against both postmodernist attempts to rupture (if I may for a moment borrow a favourite postmodernist word) all sensible or necessary links between the sources we find and the stories we tell; and also against the generally implicit assumption attributed to traditional empiricist historians that the sources, if treated sensitively, will more or less 'speak for themselves'. I have suggested that we need to be highly aware of the intermediate processes, the intervening conceptual and investigative strategies which allow us to build explanatory bridges whose structure and constituent materials can be re-examined and amended by others, within the context of certain traditions of inquiry and debate. Nevertheless, despite all that has been said in this chapter about the intelligent use of the sources in resolving or transforming conceptual and explanatory debates, there do sometimes remain bedrocks of fundamental difference as to where the balance of explanatory or interpretive weight should be laid. It is to the question of what serves to satisfy curiosity that we now turn.

7

SATISFYING CURIOSITY

Structure, agency and underlying assumptions

'Men make their own history, but they do not make it just as they please; they do not make it under circumstances chosen by themselves, but under circumstances directly encountered, given, and transmitted from the past.' In stark contrast to this succinct formulation by Karl Marx, his close contemporary, Thomas Carlyle, was the classic exponent of the 'Great Men' theory of history:

> Universal History, the history of what man has accomplished in this world, is at bottom the History of the Great Men who have worked here . . . [A]ll things we see standing accomplished in the world are properly the outer material result, the practical realisation and embodiment, of Thoughts that dwelt in the Great Men sent into the world; the soul of the whole world's history, it may justly be considered, were the history of these.

And, a little later: 'The History of the World . . . [is] the Biography of Great Men.'[1]

This laid the foundation for much of what Peter Burke has dubbed 'traditional history', characterised by, among other things, a focus on 'the great deeds of great men, statesmen, generals, or occasionally churchmen'.[2] And it is precisely against this focus on 'Great Men' that many of the supposedly 'new perspectives' (with, actually, long and distinguished heritages themselves) have been developed.[3] The issue of structural determination or constraint versus individual agency has continued both to perplex and to divide historians, with some tending to emphasise the former, others the latter.

Questions about the individual in history may be found across a relatively wide range of substantive areas. There are the classic political histories focussing on great statesmen, generals, revolutionaries, which have come to be viewed as 'traditional history', and against which 'new' types of political history have been written. Some of these have been largely 'perspectival' corrections, emphasising 'new perspectives' by exploring history from below, social and labour history; others have come from radically different paradigms proper, suggesting that it is not the actions of individuals, but rather the structural circumstances of action, that actually explain outcomes. There are comparable counterparts to these debates in intellectual history and art history. The 'traditional' focus was primarily on great thinkers (the great names of the Enlightenment, or disembodied intellectual histories leaping from one text to the next), or on great painters, sculptors and so on. 'New perspectives' sought to broaden the field of cultural history, to widen the purview from the isolated examples of outstanding texts or creations to the more typical and commonplace; while, from the point of view of new 'paradigms proper' there was a major shift in underlying assumptions, as in some variants of New Historicism which held that texts could be explained only as products of a particular age or context.[4]

Differences relate in part to variations in what serves to satisfy curiosity; and this in turn may be dependent on deeply held underlying metatheoretical assumptions. It may for some historians and their readers be far easier to get absorbed in, and empathise with, the life of real (if dead) human beings, than it is to follow and get excited by an argument couched in abstract language, examining structural contexts or general trends.[5] But for others, there is a sense in which 'one-damn-thing-after-another' history leaves a feeling of not having 'really explained' a major event in the way in which a history setting the tales in a wider context of broader patterns may do. Similarly, while some might simply accept certain ideas at face value and treat them as adequate causes, others would seek for 'deeper', even subconscious and unacknowledged motivations, or suggest that the ideas could be more or less ignored altogether in explanatory accounts of particular developments. In some versions, the structure/agency antinomy echoes that between, on the one hand, 'history as science', uncovering the 'real causes' or developing wider generalisations and, on the other, 'history as storytelling' or traditional narrative histories of unique developments.

The antinomy between those emphasising the actions of individuals (with reasons, motives and behaviour constituting the main explanatory elements in the story) and those emphasising structural or collective features (political and economic organisation, institutional arrangements, collective 'mentalities', social circumstances) has run deep among historians. At its heart lies the question of the extent to which human beings – their beliefs, their actions, and the consequences of these – are conditioned and shaped by aspects of their environment; and the extent to which, or conditions under which, in turn, humans can alter the world into which they were born. In very old-fashioned terms, we are back in the terrain which used to be discussed in terms of 'free will' and 'determinism', although the sophistication and terminology of this debate has developed dramatically since the two poles were seen as mutually exclusive, diametrically opposed. The underlying issues have in fact been played out in a variety of theoretical terms.

There have been debates over the question of 'methodological individualism' or 'ontological individualism', versus 'holism', 'social organicism', or 'collectivism'; in other words, over whether all explanations should not ultimately be reduced to answers in terms of the intentions and actions of individual human beings, or whether they can remain at the level of social practices, general trends, attributes of institutions, structural contexts and constraints, or even, at the extreme, structural determination of individual action.[6] There is the contrast between Collingwood's view of history as the imaginative re-enactment in the historian's mind of past thoughts, on the one hand, and Émile Durkheim's injunction to 'treat social facts as things', on the other, arguing that the explanation of social action requires more than reference to individual motives.[7] The individual/society and agency/structure antinomies are further cross-cut by the questions of the role allotted to ideas or mentalities on the one hand, and material circumstances or other 'objective' factors, on the other (the idealism/materialism antinomy); and by the contrast between 'structural history' and 'the history of events'. Further complexities are introduced by debates over what is sometimes termed the 'idiographic/nomothetic' divide: over the question of whether historians can seek only to reconstruct unique chains of events, or whether it is possible to uncover more general 'patterns' in history – which need not be conceived of as 'universal laws', but rather as statistical regularities, or conditional within particular specified circumstances.

My purpose in this chapter is not to review in any detail these theoretical debates which have been widely and often admirably covered elsewhere – but rather to explore, or to make more explicit, the ways in which different paradigms may be premised on deeper underlying assumptions with respect to these theoretical axes, which are not s0 readily capable of rational resolution. Philosophers of history and theorists of the social sciences may well be able to argue for one case or another, or to refute particular standpoints in principle; but the practice of historians appears to be premised not only (and in some cases, not at all) on explicit views on these philosophical debates, but rather on what seem to be deeper assumptions about the character of the human world over time. Returning to the discussion of paradigms in Chapter 3, what we are concerned with here is the question of what, within any given paradigm, serves to satisfy curiosity or count as an answer to a given question or puzzle. This may be a relatively loosely held matter, depending on what is of substantive interest at any given time (as in the case of mutually compatible perspectival paradigms, or 'filling gaps' in knowledge within a given framework); or it may be a matter of fundamentally irresolvable differences in underlying assumptions about, for example, social conditioning, the relations between ideas or cultural attributes and material circumstances, and the question of wider patterns in human history.

Paradigms, agency and structure

Variations on the question of 'structure and agency' or 'individual and society' have long been a focus of explicit theoretical controversy. There have, for example, been several attempts to formulate in relatively abstract terms a theory of 'structuration', which would overcome some of the polarities of 'structure/agency' debates. Drawing on the example of language, in which speakers are born into a particular community, the rules of whose language they learn, internalise, and subsequently deploy and develop creatively, contributing to processes of change, Giddens and others have sought to explicate the ways in which, over time, human beings both experience and alter the structures in which they live their lives.[8] Similarly, there have been detailed engagements with the issue of whether all explanations must ultimately be reduced to the level of the motives and actions of individuals through whom social change cumulatively occurs; or whether some explanations can remain couched at the level of institutional collectivities, social trends and the like. The proverbial example has been adduced of the Martian arriving on earth and inquiring into the meaning of a transaction with a small piece of paper (or, in the up-dated version, no doubt an even smaller piece of plastic), who would need an explanation couched in terms of 'social facts' pre-existing individual transactions: namely, banks, paper money, cheques and credit. Methodological individualism has been further refuted very successfully by reference, for example, to statistical regularities in relations between rising unemployment and rising crime rates, which vary together in ways not explicable simply in terms of the millions of different individual reasons for committing a crime; or to the ways in which relationships between organisations or between them and the state may be explained in terms of attributes (political power, legal status, command over physical and material resources) not shared by the individuals who work within them and thus in some sense collectively constitute them.[9]

Nevertheless, for all the abstract discussions of theorists who appear to have achieved some resolution of the issues in principle, historians are still deeply divided in their practice. And there are, in fact, much deeper implications: for differences in emphasis have far wider connotations in terms of the kind of historical explanation proposed for any given phenomenon, and the assumptions about the nature of human behaviour and social being. We need therefore to distinguish here between the (often unthinking) practice of historians who tend not to worry too much about whether or not they are committed to a doctrine of 'methodological individualism', and the more explicit discussions of philosophers on this issue.

It is very often precisely those historians who 'have no time for theory' who are most committed to some implicit version of methodological individualism, or at least to a scepticism towards anything that might be called 'social causes' or, perhaps worse, explanatory 'factors'. Debates phrased in terms of the 'individual versus society' have also to some extent been coloured by differences between conservative and radical perspectives on the world.[10] This has been further muddied by a degree of partly professional, and perhaps also partly political, irritation on the part of 'traditional' historians – who believe that history should properly focus on, in Geoffrey Elton's formulation, 'everything men [sic] have said, thought, done or suffered' – with what they dismiss as ill-informed, theory-driven 'sociological' approaches and their emphasis on general social categories.[11]

Let us look then at the ways in which these differences have been played out in practice. Some of the most popular historical works are works which seek to 'bring to life' some historical individual and his or her acts.[12] The focus on individual agency appears in some ways to be the easiest or most accessible approach to understand. After all, our own lives are predicated on a belief in our own individuality, as we daily go about our business thinking what appear to us to be private thoughts, taking decisions and acting on them. It is exceedingly easy to 'tell stories' – to narrate and account for our own biographies in terms centred on the individual as agent; and it appears, for some historians, 'only natural' to generalise this approach to explaining the past.

There are also respectable philosophical traditions on which to draw. R. G. Collingwood was one of the foremost proponents of the focus on individual purposes as causes.[13] Despite considerable disagreement about the validity of Collingwood's approach, it nevertheless is still called upon when a 'traditional' historian feels this kind of history is coming under threat. Geoffrey Roberts, for example, adduces it to come to Arthur Marwick's aid, when the latter appears to be flailing helplessly, wildly bashing all available objects of his theoretical dislike (lumped together under a confused and general notion of 'metaphysical history'), but wielding only the blunt bat of 'common sense'.[14] Roberts provides a helpful list of philosophical foundations for the 'human action approach', including 'ontological individualism' and Collingwood's view that 'history is the history of human thought and human action'.[15] In passing, it might be noted that Collingwood can be held to have adopted an approach compatible with an emphasis on social action, where individual motives and purposes are defined by social roles; but the point remains that Collingwood's primary injunction to the historian is to 're-enact the past in his own mind', in order to understand particular motives, purposes, and attempts at realising those purposes (whether political, military, artistic, scientific, religious). The truly 'historical' explanation, for Collingwood, can only be arrived at when we have re-enacted or re-thought those past thoughts in our own minds, and thus got behind the words and the documents to the realities of the minds that created and left them. Without this, 'names and dates, and ready-made descriptive phrases . . . may well be useful, but not because they are history . . . [but rather] dry bones, which may some day become history, when someone is able to clothe them with the flesh and blood of a thought which is both his own and theirs'.[16] Whether viewed in terms of private purposes and motives, or as attributes of social actors, individual intentionality is a key in the Collingwood notion of history.

The range of approaches which tend towards the 'structure' end of the explanatory spectrum is very broad. We have already considered some theoretical approaches which appeal to 'structure' (whether apparent or 'deep') and, in particular, a multitude of sins is often deemed to be lurking under the rather specific heading of 'structuralism'. For all their differences, the same basic, very general, principle may be shared across quite diverse approaches. This is the view that – however important they may be – the reasons, intentions and actions of individuals do not constitute sufficient explanations of many phenomena which interest us in the human past.

Structural approaches vary greatly, however, as to the extent to which they reject intentions and actions as important explanatory factors. The most radical structuralists virtually write human action out of history entirely. Thus we have, for example, the search for the universal 'deep structures' of the human mind on the part of Claude Lévi-Strauss, or, in more extreme terms, the wilful 'anti-humanism' of Louis Althusser.[17] Drawing on the work of the later Marx, Althusser argues that modes of production determine what classes are found in relation to other classes, together constituting the mode of production. Taking Marx's views on the materialist determination of consciousness to (what appear to the unconverted to be absurd) extremes, Althusser sees human action as but a product of the underlying structures, whatever the supposed self-delusions about their own autonomy of those who are acting. This, in Althusser's view, allows for a 'scientific' approach to history, examining underlying laws and dynamics irrespective of participants' views and allowing next to no autonomy for human action.

With relatively rare exceptions, such as Nicos Poulantzas and others influenced by structural Marxism in the 1970s, this form of radically structuralist Marxism had little influence on historical practice. The versions of Marxism which did become influential among practising historians, at least in the Anglo-American world, were in general more humanistic in tone, taking their general inspiration from Marx's political commitment and vision; and on occasion more specifically also from the somewhat fragmentary and elliptic interpretations of Marx provided by Gramsci and Lukacs.[18] Perhaps the British Marxist historians, Christopher Hill, E. P. Thompson, and E. J. Hobsbawm are among the best-known exponents of a version of Marxism which managed to combine an emphasis on underlying socio-economic structures and their modes of transformation with a real concern to listen to the voices and visions, however apparently crazy, of previous generations. In the substantive historical works particularly of Christopher Hill and E. P. Thompson, there is a determination to 'rescue from the condescension of posterity' the voices and actions of previously marginalised groups – and even, in the case of some of Hill's work, of exceedingly prominent individuals.[19] An explicit theoretical commitment to the importance of human agency, and respect for the ideas and actions of real human beings, also came out very strongly in E. P. Thompson's angry debate with Perry Anderson.[20]

Proponents of more moderate structural explanations may simply insist that the explanatory focus has to be shifted to the conditions under which certain intentions could or could not be realised – although even here there are differences in the extent to which ideas and intentions play a role in an account focussing primarily on structural conditions as the key explanatory variable. Thus Theda Skocpol, for example, in her structural theory of social revolutions, argues that the motives of the poor and oppressed remain more or less constant throughout history, and cannot therefore be called upon to explain the

differences between successful and unsuccessful revolutions.[21] The key explanatory variables, therefore, relate not to motives for rebelling, but rather to the
conditions under which such revolts can be successful in instituting a new social
order, and hence translate (relatively frequent, unsuccessful) rebellions into (rare,
successful) historical social revolutions. It is essential, in other words, to examine
features such as splits within ruling elites, which provide space to be exploited
and opportunity for rebellion from below, and weaknesses in the state's capacity
to suppress revolt (often as a result of being overstretched in the international
arena), which allow the rebellions of the previously oppressed to have some
chance of success against more powerful classes and institutionalised systems of
repression.[22]

Not all structural explanations are self-professedly Marxist, important though
this background may have been for many. Other historians, while underlining the
importance of structural conditions in explaining the outcome of individual
actions and motives, have allowed a greater role for ideologies, cultures, and
beliefs. Perhaps this is the biggest difference between those coming from the
Marxist heritage and those outside it; the latter would accord far greater autonomy to the power of ideas, which need not be reduced to presumed class
interests or the experience of certain material conditions. Class interests may
have some plausibility (though not always – this is an empirical question) when
analysing the motives for action in revolutions, but this is far from always the
case. If there is no prior commitment to the whole set of Marxist assumptions (or
the 'paradigm proper'), including the notions of 'ideology' and 'false consciousness', then ideas can be taken more seriously as important factors in their own
right, even in the context of an explanation which is couched in terms of the
structural conditions explaining the outcomes of human action.[23]

Max Weber, famously, asserted an essentially individualist mode of explanation and yet practised this form of structural approach.[24] While he explicitly
asserted that explanation of social action should be in terms of motives for
action, in his substantive works Weber in fact diverged from this approach in two
crucial respects. First of all, insofar as Weber looked at motives (or the ideas,
goals, values, which lay at the root of action), he in fact focussed not on purely
private, individual motives but rather on collective beliefs or systems of thought
and values, which were 'carried' by particular social groups and professional
classes (such as priests and prophets) in particular institutional contexts, and
which might be challenged by others. While there might be what Weber called
'elective affinities' between particular sets of ideas and certain forms of social
experience, the former could not be reduced to or explained by the latter. Secondly, individual motives and beliefs were in themselves not a sufficient
explanation, or cause, for the observed historical effects or consequences of
action. Rather, Weber always pointed to the specific conditions, or historical circumstances, under which particular idea systems or values could be successful, in
what he elsewhere saw quite explicitly as a titanic battle of competing values on a
power political stage. In a sense, what Weber emphasises here is a notion of

'elective interests', or many wills working together in a common direction based on common interests.

Very occasionally an individual can make a major difference; but even this is dependent on historical circumstances. Weber's concept of charisma allows for the extraordinary power of unique human beings to expound new ideas ('. . . but I say unto you . . .') while at the same time indicating that such ideas will take root and prove historically significant only if they fall on receptive soil; no individual can become a charismatic leader without acquiring, and constantly actively sustaining, a faithful following. This depends on the particular conditions in which the individual seeks to propagate the message, and on the capacity of that individual repeatedly to reassert, in whatever way, the power and relevance of that message. Yet charismatic authority is inherently unstable, tending either to disintegrate or to become institutionalised (in some form, in Weber's view, of what he called bureaucratic or rational-legal authority). Weber's concept of charisma has proved particularly helpful for those historians who are highly aware of the importance of structures and yet at the same time deal with individuals whose historical role has seemed of indisputable, overwhelming importance. To take a notable recent example: one of the founding fathers of the West German 'Bielefeld School' of societal history, Hans-Ulrich Wehler, managed to provide a social history of modern Germany, couched within a 'modernisation' framework, which was extraordinarily lacking in individual agency until Wehler reached Bismarck; at this point, Weber's concept of charisma had to be summonsed and deployed to account for the apparently crucial historical role of one individual.

Motives, mentalities and historical circumstances

This leads us quite directly to the question of the relations between the topic or focus of interest, on the one hand, and the importance of the background assumptions or prior theoretical framework of the historian on the other.

Sometimes the reason given for a difference in explanatory focus is simply that the topic of interest may just have (or not have) to do with human motives. For some historians it may go without question that, while narratives of 'high politics' inevitably require analysis of individual motives, analysis of long-term economic trends may require reference to quite different factors (although it might be noted in passing that really committed methodological individualists might want to argue that even long-term economic trends are but the product of a myriad disparate individual decisions and actions). Peter Burke gives the example of price rises in sixteenth-century Spain, which may require answers about silver imports or population growth that are not easily susceptible to treatment of individual motives on Collingwood's model.[25] Similarly, the focus of interest in some of the classic works of the *Annales* School of French historians was on the *longue durée*, on aspects of climate and historical geography, and on collective mentalities over long stretches of time. We could go on to elaborate other examples of historical topics of legitimate interest, where we might not feel entirely satisfied by explanations couched primarily in terms of individual intentions, such as the history of life expectancy and mortality, or the demographic consequences of bubonic plague. And even though the social and economic consequences for the bargaining power of peasants after the Black Death might be susceptible to analysis in terms of individual motives, this would not necessarily be the most useful avenue of approach to general trends of interest.

The fact that some areas of legitimate historical inquiry are less easily dealt with in terms of individual motives and actions than others is to some extent banal. It can readily be mapped onto what in Chapter 3 I have called 'perspectival paradigms': that is, looking at a different segment of reality entails adopting a somewhat different approach.

But to rest content with the notion that the subject matter simply determines the most appropriate level of analysis actually misses the point: very often the same subject matter can be looked at in quite different ways. There are several different issues at play here. One could, for example, argue that it is only under certain historical circumstances that specific individuals find themselves in a position to (appear to) 'make history'; under more constraining conditions, there is either less leeway for action, or less likelihood that certain actions will have particular effects. This issue is, however, slightly distinct from another one: namely, the extent to which, even if we agree that we need to highlight individual motives and actions as causes, these have in turn to be seen as to some considerable degree informed or constituted by given historical contexts and cultures or mentalities.

It may be helpful at this point not to rehearse further what are by now rather familiar theoretical debates, the lineages of which have been traced often enough, but rather to focus more closely on what is at stake in historical explanations. Under some historical circumstances, does individual agency actually have more *Handlungsspielraum* or freedom of manoeuvre than others? Are some circumstances more compatible with 'great men' than others? How far, indeed, are 'great men' actually 'produced' by structures? Or can we not reach any consensus on these questions? If not, why not? These questions can be more clearly addressed by looking at some substantive examples.

At first blush, the records of history are spattered with the actions of 'great men'. Consider, for example, the roles of some of the so-called absolutist monarchs or rulers of early modern Europe: say, Charles I of England, the kings of France from Louis XIV to Louis XVI, or Frederick I, Frederick William I and Frederick II of Prussia. Consider too the 'great' twentieth-century dictators: Hitler, Mussolini, Stalin. Or we could consider some somewhat more uplifting examples of individuals who appear to have made a dramatic mark on history: Martin Luther King and Mahatma Gandhi. Clearly all of these were, in very different ways, individuals of considerable power, and it is vital to emphasise their unique personalities and beliefs, the quality of their commitment, the impact of their decisions and the resonance of their actions at particular times.

But a moment's thought will indicate that, however fascinating, such a focus on the individual alone is not enough. For one thing, even such highly visible historical individuals were, in important ways, in large measure 'products' of their historical circumstances. And, just as importantly, their historical impact can also be explained only by a focus on what one might quite legitimately want to call the structural circumstances – and some quite accidental features – of the worlds in which they lived. Even more strongly: for those historians prepared to look at this sort of thing, there are patterns which can be discerned once one begins to compare structures.

First of all, individual motives and aspirations are at least in part (even largely?) historically conditioned. For example, it is clear that all the early modern rulers mentioned above shared certain assumptions and imperatives. They lived in a world of competing states, perceived at that time rather as dynastic possessions than as fixed expressions of a 'nation', whose ever-moving boundaries had constantly to be protected (even expanded) by the use of diplomacy and force. The maintenance of personal power and military might depended crucially on raising of revenue. In the seventeenth and eighteenth centuries taxation was no more popular than it is in the twenty-first; hence, if parliaments were unwilling to vote through revenues, rulers would seek to do without their aid. In other words, features of domestic politics (the assumption of rulership over a state as a hereditary, dynastic possession) and of the international situation (a more or less constant state of warfare between states, both over land within Europe and, increasingly, also over colonies overseas) gave rise to repeated financial crises for rulers. Seeking to centralise and enhance monarchical power through the attraction of a loyal, court-oriented nobility and dispensation with parliaments was not just what one might consider to be a unique attribute of an individual ruler, but was in large measure a feature of a specific world-historical situation.

Secondly, explanations of the outcomes of individual aspirations *can* be developed purely by narrating unique chains of circumstances. Nevertheless, in a comparative framework it is quite striking to notice the extent to which the success or otherwise of such attempts (two monarchs lost their heads in the process) depended on a variety of specific historical conditions in each case. These include, for example, the relative strengths of and interrelations among different social classes and their representative institutions: contrast, on the one hand, the relatively wealthy seventeenth-century English gentry with its intermingling of landed and urban interests and successful defence of parliamentary institutions, with, on the other hand, the impoverished Prussian nobility of the later seventeenth and eighteenth centuries, easily cut off from alliance with the towns, who were unable to defend representative institutions against absolutist rule. Similarly, one can compare the importance of 'conjunctural' factors ranging from sheer male longevity, fertility and associated lack of disputed successions (Prussia) to the challenges and opportunities presented by involvement in warfare (English involvement with the Scottish and Irish; longstanding rivalries between the English and French; French involvement in the American War of Independence;

Prussian rivalry with Austria; and so on).[26] Here, one might argue that the apparent powers of these absolutist rulers, or their failures in attempts at power, had – almost ironically – a great deal more to do with 'structural' circumstances than epithets such as 'the Great', slogans to do with the 'divine right of kings' or '*l'État, c'est moi*' might suggest. These early modern 'great men' could be readily cast as both products and sources of power in a particular historical context.

We could pursue a comparable line of general argument for the twentieth-century 'great men', surveying a wider range of political and institutional settings. Ian Kershaw's analysis of Hitler, to take an example already discussed at some length, has shown just how much the notion of Hitler as charismatic leader was not, as one might at first expect, simply the source, fount and origin of a strong, streamlined dictatorship, but rather in increasing measure the structural product of an increasingly chaotic, multi-centred system of power (sometimes termed 'polycratic').[27] With the proliferation of overlapping and competing spheres of competence within the Third Reich, there was increasingly no ultimate authority to which appeal could be made other than 'Hitler's will'; the *Führer-Befehl* came to displace the role of normal governmental decision-making, as the latter disintegrated and disappeared. Kershaw developed the notion (taken from a contemporary source) of 'working towards the Führer' to explicate the ways in which satraps and underlings might compete with one another to 'fulfil' the Führer's will even without explicit orders on specific issues. Thus, in setting a general tone and direction of policy (ridding Europe of Jews), Hitler's intentions were clearly central; but it was the peculiarities of a chaotic power structure, riddled with personal rivalries and competition for power, prestige and personal favour, which explained the way in which Hitler's murderous intentions were transformed into brutal reality. Similarly, historians differ in the role which they allot to Soviet leader Mikhail Gorbachev when explaining the series of 'gentle revolutions' or 'velvet revolutions' which brought about the end of communist rule in eastern Europe in 1989–90. For some, Gorbachev appears as, in effect, the equivalent of a dramatic 'deus ex machina' who leaps onto the stage to produce a denouement just in time for the play to end, when the plot was not going in any particular direction. For others, Gorbachev was himself the product of cumulative economic and associated political crises in the Soviet Union, which was incapable of sustaining military expenditure in the context of a reinvigorated Cold War in the 1980s, which help to explain his own rise to power and the restructuring strategies and reforming forces he unleashed.

What of those charismatic individuals who seemed to break the historical mould entirely; whose fervently held beliefs made a fundamental difference to the histories of their countries and indeed the world: who appeared to be challengers to, rather than products of, particular systems of power? It would be impossible to write about Mahatma Gandhi or Martin Luther King without acknowledging – with all due humility – the immense contributions made by their respective religious faiths and their personal capacity to put the cause in which they believed above any concern for their own personal well-being or safety. But it would also do them little justice to engage in a form of totally decontextualised hagiography. The struggle for independence in India was but one among many movements for decolonisation in the twentieth century; an explanation of its success must appeal to more than the figure of Gandhi, however much of a model and a pattern he set for subsequent non-violent demonstrations. And the civil rights movement of America in the 1950s and 1960s owed an immense amount in its form and culture to the integrity and inspirational leadership of Martin Luther King (and indirectly, in turn, to his hero Gandhi); yet a wider explanation must appeal to factors such as the impact of the Second World War, the emerging post-war consumer society, the new cultural and social (and musical) movements of the 1950s and 1960s, and the cataclysmic conjunction of the Blues and Beat generations with US involvement in Vietnam.

The question arises, perhaps, as to whether these patterns are 'made' rather than 'found'. There are, interestingly, similar debates within the sphere of natural sciences (are mathematical relationships intrinsic properties of the world as it is, or imposed on it by a particular framework of categories and assumptions?). Whatever the resolution of the debates in the natural sciences, which are not our concern here, there are some interesting historical regularities to ponder in relation to this question. I have suggested, above, some generalisations or regularities which may be observed within a given set of conditions – for example, early modern European absolutist states. Interestingly, it is also possible to pursue or explore patterns across quite different historical contexts. So, for example, it is possible to use general thematic headings under which to analyse striking similarities – as well as obvious differences – between the revolutionary events of France in 1789 and those of the GDR in 1989. These might include: weaknesses of political leadership at the top (Louis XVI, the ageing Honecker); acute financial problems for the state and impending economic collapse; growing discussions among political elites not only about the need for specific reforms, but also more generally about the nature of the political system, opening up spaces and scope for popular involvement; an international situation posing challenges to continued stability; and so on. In different ways, this is what Skocpol does for her comparison of France, Russia and China; the ready extension to the case of the GDR is quite striking.

To some extent, of course, such patterns are 'imposed'. The historian plays an active role in choosing cases and constituting the object of inquiry (early modern absolutist states; revolutions; and so on); in deciding on analytical categories or headings under which to compare and contrast (concepts and assumptions about what it is worth looking for); in 'seeing' patterns which might be missed by historians who are focussing rather on the mass of individual details and differences. Yet it is clearly worth pausing to think about the extent to which it is possible to observe regularities of one sort or another in the historical record, whether these have to do with demographic patterns, crime rates, trade relations, patterns of economic development (relationships between levels of literacy or education, industrialisation and urbanisation) or wider regularities in massive sociopolitical upheavals.

There is, in short, a lot more to historical explanation than the motives and actions of individuals, however important these may sometimes be in affecting the course of historical development. And it is not easy to provide or write any easy historical recipe for deciding how best to mix the variety of (what, *pace* Elton, I shall continue to call) factors involved: social and economic conditions, political institutions and developments, collective beliefs and mentalities, inter-relations among states at given world historical stages, as well as the unique ideas and behaviour at crucial junctures of particular individuals, born into positions high and low, likely and unlikely. Nor is there any easy formula for constructing any given framework of interpretation, even conceding such a mix.

It seems to me that some more general points come out of these examples. First, it is foolish indeed to argue for a purely 'individual' or 'agency' approach to history; even the most determinedly 'narrative' approach, couching the account in terms of individual motives and actions, necessarily has recourse to collective cultural features (informing motives) and structural features (permitting, encouraging or constraining actions). Conversely, however, the role of (historically formed) individuals cannot be denied, although there is wide disagreement about the extent to which apparently individual attributes and aspirations are shaped by historical circumstances.

Secondly, there are certain wider historical patternings. These may be specific to any particular historical case, amounting to the (institutional, social, cultural) 'circumstances of action'; or they may, in different patterns, be visible across a number of cases. The way to resolve the issue of 'structure' and 'agency' is thus not to adopt some easy theoretical slogan (such as appealing to an abstract notion of 'structuration') but rather to examine in more detail, and historically, the forms and varieties of what we might call anthropological mediation, or the sociocultural construction of historical individuals – their beliefs, actions, and the consequences of their individual and collective actions – in different historical circumstances. Where the spotlight is thrown will depend to some extent on the precise question being asked, and the ways in which particular sorts of curiosity will be satisfied.

Underlying assumptions; or, the satisfaction of curiosity

How do historians come to the view that they have adequately explained or interpreted a given set of developments, a period, a problem? When do readers feel they have grasped 'what it was about', 'how it was like', 'why this and not that occurred'? What satisfies curiosity for different producers and consumers of historical investigations?

What counts as an 'answer' to a particular puzzle, or fills the gaps in relation to a feeling of ignorance, varies dramatically across different paradigms. There is nothing intrinsically problematic about this if what we are talking about is merely a matter of what I have called a 'perspectival paradigm', focussing on a particular topic of interest. While wandering around the sumptuous palace at Versailles, visitors may simply be curious to 'find out more' about the religious piety, familial fidelity, and prodigious appetite of King Louis XVI, or the frivolity, fashions and court intrigues of his wife Marie Antoinette. They may not want, at that moment, an account of why France fell prey to a social and political revolution at that time, whereas Germany in 1848 or Russia in 1905 did not. These are simply different questions, designed to satisfy different sorts of curiosity. Any visitor to Florence may well wish to 'know more' about, say, the Medicis, Michelangelo, Leonardo da Vinci, or Machiavelli, and hence seek out historians' works which are informative on these particular individuals. Or our mythical visitors to France and Italy may wish to know more about medieval and early modern popular beliefs and superstitions, and hence seek out the work of social and cultural historians instead. It is in this case simply a question of what serves to satisfy curiosity about some specific aspect of the past at a particular time. (Here, the difference between 'knowledge' or 'information', on the one hand, and 'explanation' or 'interpretation' on the other, may become an issue: a Dorling Kindersley guide or an encyclopaedia reference may be all that is needed in the former case.)

However, there are also deeper issues at stake, particularly when there is a question, not of perspectival paradigms which may in principle be mutually compatible, but rather of differing assumptions across conflicting paradigms proper. Such assumptions might give radically different answers about the relative weighting of, for example, individual versus collective actions, or ideas versus structures. Thus some differences may actually, when examined a little more closely, be rooted in approaches which are not intrinsically incompatible; others rest on bedrock, irresolvable differences with respect to underlying assumptions about the nature of being human. Such differences are found as much among consumers as among producers of historical interpretations: what serves to satisfy curiosity for one historian and his or her audience may not do so for another.

To revert to the example of witchcraft: is a particular woman assumed to have been put to death for witchcraft because she actually committed an act of *maleficium*; or because there had been some unacknowledged failure of neighbourly obligations towards her; or because of the unconscious effects of childhood experiences and guilt associated with aspects of mothering; or as a function of maintaining village cohesion? The answer which is held to be an adequate explanation can vary widely according to assumptions which are not always readily open to empirical test or the evidence of the sources (as in the case of the psychoanalytic interpretation), although it may be possible to design research strategies, such as the comparison of a wide number of cases, to test some of the others (for example, the relations between ideas of neighbourliness and village cohesion in early modern Europe). Or, to take as another example the Lutheran Reformation: a perspectival paradigm rooted in intellectual history might choose to focus on Martin Luther's theology in the context of traditions of Augustinian piety, and late medieval scholasticism and humanism, without denying the importance of the wider social and political context of early sixteenth-century Germany for ensuring that Luther did not simply get burnt at the stake as many 'heretics' before him had done. From a Marxist perspective, however, Luther's ideas and their historical impact would be subordinated to or explained in terms of 'deeper' forces, rooted in changing social relations in late medieval feudalism, and the kinds of associated social conflicts evident in the Peasants' War of 1525–6.

In respect of substantive historical investigation, we may well wonder why it is that, in practice, narrative approaches focussing on individuals have (at least recently) tended to be associated with 'conservative' or 'atheoretical' historians, while those focussing on more general trends or 'structures' have often been held to be in some sense 'left-wing'. (Perhaps one should add that there are of course exceptions. Simon Schama, whose wilfully anecdotal 'chronicle' of the French Revolution, *Citizens*, is constructed as a narrative of individual illustrative events, can scarcely be accused of theoretical naïvety.[28] And those Third Reich historians of the *Volk* who served as precursors to some of West German societal history can hardly be held up as left-wing sympathisers.[29]) As far as politics goes, there are obviously some affinities between approaches influenced by variants of Marxism and an awareness of huge social forces, trends and constraints beyond individual action; there are also affinities between conservative delusions of an individual's capacity to act effectively in and on the world, and freedom from undue social and political constraints and economic burdens.

Underlying political and other differences in approach there are also deeper differences on philosophical issues. Here we find ourselves swimming in the large, inchoate sea of more or less eternal questions about what it is to be human, and how it is that we become as we are, or act in the ways in which we do. Views on these matters are often articles of faith. It is notable just how often proponents of particular theoretical positions make absolute statements founded in little more than assertion about the relations between, for example, texts and contexts, or conscious ideas and 'underlying forces' or material circumstances.

Thus radical structuralists and post-structuralists hold extreme views, as indicated earlier. Thus those theorists positing 'deep structures' essentially write off individual ideas, desires, actions as but surface epiphenomena; and post-structuralist followers of Lacanian psychology start from a denial of any stable identity rooted in an autonomous subject. Conversely, those (generally far less theoretically explicit) historians who prioritise narratives of individual action, while recognising that combinations of circumstances may foil intentions or displace the effects of actions, often fail openly to acknowledge just how far the individual motives and actions are themselves historically conditioned.

Between these extremes lies a broad band in which historical disagreements often appear to be about something substantive, but in fact are rooted in, or at least somewhat complicated by, prior convictions of which participants may be only dimly aware. If we take, for example, analyses of race and racism in American history, we find that efforts to understand racism – that is, scholarly efforts that are rooted in a fundamental rejection of the biologistic ideas of racism itself – may appeal to a variety of explanatory paradigms. Thomas Holt's analysis of what he calls the idealist, economistic, psychological and cultural paradigms for explaining racist phenomena lead him to the view that there is 'a fundamental discontinuity between most behavioural explanations sited at the individual level of human experience and those at the level of society and social forces'.[30] What any given analyst of racism seems to think is '*really*' or 'fundamentally' at stake – the legacies of slavery, class oppression, psychological motivation, the impact of an explicit ideology, the prevalence of a broader cultural discourse – varies widely. And while psychologistic approaches focus on explanation at the level of individual anxieties and their expression in aggression against a visible Other, racism is clearly one area where the social or collective must take analytical priority; the problem is to determine precisely where to lay the burden of explanation.

Gender studies too provide an illuminating example of fundamental disagreement about the relations between society and the construction of the individual. Most (contemporary western) people would probably hold the view that a clear distinction can be drawn between biological sex as naturally given, and socially constructed gender roles which are historically variable (although the latitude of the latter is far from undisputed, and it certainly took a considerable time before the legitimacy of studying such variation was conceded in the western historical profession). But while practitioners of women's history might argue how best to explain the diversity of women's roles and experiences in different types of society, some feminists would go even further and argue that sex itself is not a 'naturally given' but rather a social construction. Let me quote from one of the chief protagonists in this debate, Judith Butler:

> the internal stability and binary frame for sex is effectively secured . . . by casting the duality of sex in a prediscursive domain. This production of sex *as* the prediscursive ought to be understood as the effect of the apparatus of cultural construction designed by gender.
>
> As a result, gender is not to culture as sex is to nature; gender is also the discursive/cultural means by which 'sexed nature' or a 'natural sex' is produced and established as 'prediscursive', prior to culture, a politically neutral surface *on which* culture acts.[31]

In Butler's view, 'feminist critique ought . . . to understand how the category of "women", the subject of feminism, is produced and restrained by the very structures of power through which emancipation is sought'.[32] It would, on this approach, be more or less pointless to start engaging in a would-be 'scientific' discussion of chromosomal differences, since even the terms of this scientific 'discourse' are themselves (contaminated) cultural constructs. Without even beginning to enter into debates on sex and gender in substantive detail, it will immediately be apparent that this particular version of feminism entails a quite different conception of biological difference than is widely prevalent. Readers will no doubt already have had their own reactions to these quotations, in terms of their own prior assumptions about sex and gender. This example may be seen as blatantly 'theoretical': the 'underlying' assumptions are all too obvious, and too easily rejected by those mainstream historians who hold assumptions about the difference between 'biological sex' and 'culturally constructed gender' which are currently seen as 'self-evident' or 'common-sense'; but it is merely an extreme case of a phenomenon which is far more prevalent than is often acknowledged.

A final example may be taken from the clearly by now somewhat hoary, but actually fundamental, debates over social classes and presumed material interests. When we analyse the work of some historians in the light of the question 'who acts?', the answer is collective actors, or classes. Thus Hobsbawm, for example, couches his analysis of the French Revolution very clearly in the classic Marxist terms of collective class interests, as did Christopher Hill on the English Revolution.[33] Or consider the following fairly typical paragraph from the Marxist historian Albert Soboul:

> If the French Revolution was the most outstanding bourgeois revolution ever, overshadowing all preceding revolutions through the dramatic nature of its class struggle, it owes it both to the obstinacy of the aristocracy, which remained firmly attached to its feudal privileges and rejected all concessions, and to the passionate opposition of the popular masses to any form of privilege or class distinction. Originally, the bourgeoisie had not sought the total downfall of the aristocracy, but the aristocracy's refusal to compromise and the dangers of counter-revolution forced the bourgeoisie to press for the destruction of the old order. It achieved this only by forming an alliance with the great mass of the urban and rural populations and they in turn demanded that their own needs be satisfied. Popular revolution and the Terror swept the board, the feudal system was irrevocably destroyed and democracy established.[34]

Note that each class appears to be a singular actor, conscious of 'its' own interests, and developing appropriate political strategies in pursuit of these interests. This is a far cry from those works which concentrate on the background of the French Enlightenment, or the contingent character of particular trains of events, and the unique characters and roles of particular individuals, from Lafayette to Robespierre.

It is of course easy enough to poke fun at Marxist notions of 'false consciousness', or at the idea that classes in some way are capable of collectively acting in their own unrecognised long-term interests; or even at the need to rewrite the theory in terms of consequences rather than causes. Thus, on the revised Marxist interpretation (or what cynics might dismiss as a salvage operation), the English Revolution became 'bourgeois', not because of its (non-bourgeois) origins in a split among members of the English ruling classes, but rather because the political system for which it paved the way opened up some of the prerequisites for the subsequent development of classic, full-blown bourgeois capitalism; similar arguments have been developed in face of 'revisionist' approaches to the French Revolution. Yet, however much subsequent empirical research has unpicked these particular overviews couched in terms of presumed class interests, there still remain important questions about the ways in which certain sorts of collective social experience (which may be rooted as much in 'race' or 'gender' as in 'class' in the traditional definition) tend to shape sets of ideas (or patterns of 'culture') which are widely shared across members of that group under particular circumstances; and at the ways in which, conversely, people from quite disparate social backgrounds can come to feel they are members of a cohesive grouping through the power of common experiences, ideas and symbols, as embodied in, for example, constructions of the 'nation'.[35]

The outer parameters of historical paradigms

What is of interest here is the interplay between (socially and historically constituted) individuals and the circumstances in which they live their lives. Here, historians often tend simply to prioritise one or other end of the spectrum because of prior assumptions, rooted either in what I have called 'implicit paradigms', with respect to often unacknowledged beliefs about the nature of being human, or more explicitly in 'paradigms proper', entailing certain tenets of faith about 'reality' and what should be 'reduced' to what else in order to satisfy curiosity. If we are clear about these issues, it will be easier to be clear about where there are areas of disagreement which can legitimately be resolved – or which one could in principle seek to resolve – by appeal to 'the facts', and where there are simply competing interpretations rooted in irresolvable differences in metaphysical presuppositions. In other words, we can better define the complex parameters and boundaries of historical interpretation.

Is there any means of resolving these questions, without having to take a view, or make a statement of faith – outside the sphere of historical scholarship proper – on the question of what it is to be human? Sometimes there may be: we can, for example, develop historical analyses of the conditions under which groups of humans come together with common values and goals – which may be rooted in common religious, moral, political or material interests, or based in conceptions of gender, ethnicity, nationality – and construct or maintain a powerful sense of collective identity; and we can analyse the struggles, the interrelations with other groups, the differences made by a particular individual in certain circumstances. We can to an extent bracket out our own views on the ideas or beliefs involved (as indeed, in contrast to Marx, Weber argued we should do with respect to religious beliefs, looking only at 'elective affinities' between belief systems and social experience, and analysing the consequences for social action).[36] But there are other respects in which specific analyses will be rooted in broader philosophies of history, and assumptions about what it is to be human, which cannot be subjected to empirical analysis. Thus, the development of human societies, with their repeated struggles between changing conceptions of good and evil, their attempts at producing the 'good society' or combating whatever is variably seen as the workings of the Devil, may be viewed in the light of all manner of wider religious certainties or philosophical doubts. These largely remain outside the scope of what professional historians do, at least in the widely accepted contemporary western senses (American/European) of what history is supposed to do; but in some ways such wider philosophies creep in at the edges, whether in the form of conceptions of the role of historical knowledge in the present – preserving memories, keeping a torch of faith alive, flying a particular political flag – or in the form of denying (with equal lack of possible proof) all pattern or meaning in human history.

Part III

REPRESENTATIONS: THE PAST IN THE PRESENT

8

REPRESENTING THE PAST

Historical traces are all around us: we inhabit a world full of signs of the past, of survivals, reconstructions, commemorations. We are born into worlds which were previously lived in; we grow up with degrees of awareness of different aspects of the past. Historical consciousness is an inevitable part of the human condition; we are intrinsically beings who live within some conception of time, some knowledge that certain things have gone before, are changing, and will change in the future. Every human society inhabits landscapes of memory: from the surrounding hills in which the Gods created humanity, where the evil demons lived, where famous battles were fought, to the urban jungles counter-posing mock Gothic railway stations, fragments of ancient walls, modernist architecture, medieval churches, council house slums, street plans following ancient sheeptracks or eighteenth-century grids or multi-lane highways. The traces of the activities of previous inhabitants of this planet are all around, from old stone chipping tools found by the seashore through medieval strip field patterns still waving through the field grass, to disused railway lines and rusting car dumps, although some traces will be more wilfully preserved than others. Physical representations of past activities are everywhere, however jumbled and lacking in organisation.

So too are points of symbolic reference to the past in our collective mental universes. As I wrote the first paragraph of this chapter (though I was still unaware of it at the time of writing) the twin towers of the World Trade Center in New York and a wing of the Pentagon in Washington were being destroyed by terrorist attacks in suicidal plane crashes. Within even the first few hours of disbelief, shock, horror and confused commentary, comparisons were being drawn with Pearl Harbor. This historical reference point – the Japanese attack in December 1941 on the American naval base which precipitated the decisive involvement of the previously isolationist United States in the Second World War – provided an instant, evocative, highly condensed short-hand for discussion of the possible meanings and implications of the terrorist attacks on mainland America on 11 September 2001. Under the news slogan 'America Under Attack', commentators raised questions of similarity and difference with Pearl Harbor: what difference did it make that there were thousands of civilian casualties in the heart of the symbolic centres of American commercial, financial, military and governmental life; were the 2001 attacks the works of an isolated terrorist organisation, or officially backed by some government; would it mean 'retaliation' against a group of individual terrorists, or major international warfare? In comparison with Pearl Harbor, what did these attacks mean? More immediate historical questions were also posed. Which groups might come into the frame of reference; what had US and international intelligence services known or not known; how had security on domestic flights been sufficiently lax to allow three of the four hijacked flights to succeed in their deadly missions?

This (literally) explosive event illustrates the myriad ways in which we inevitably think historically – by posing questions, seeking historical parallels and clues, trying to make sense of a disturbing event and place it in wider contexts of explanation and understanding. It also (sadly) illustrates the sensitivities and difficulties of historical representation: from my own unease, writing as events unfold, about whether even to discuss, in an analytic and distanced manner, this very immediate tragedy; through the difficulties of the 'instant historians', the commentators, journalists and television teams piecing together camera footage, interviews and commentaries; to the potentially far more inflammatory consequences of the interpretations and rhetoric deployed by major politicians, including US President George W. Bush (with his loaded and inaccurate statement that 'this is the first war of the twenty-first century') and other international leaders.

There are clearly differences in a variety of respects between representations of this very contemporary history – the denouement of which has, at the time of writing, yet to come – and of events and developments in remoter pasts, such as the eruption of the volcanic Mount Vesuvius in AD 79, burying the people of Pompeii, or the death by drowning in the river at Nantes of the hundreds of victims of a particularly vicious perpetrator of the Terror in the French Revolution, which no longer affect us as directly and personally. In the latter two cases, the emotional involvement of most of us is likely to be very much less of an issue, even if our sympathies, rooted in a common humanity, are aroused in one way or another by the shock and horror of these stories, particularly when well told. In this last phrase, however, lies the nub of some of the questions we need to address in this chapter. How, to whom, and for what purposes, are historical stories (in whatever format) told? How do historians seek to achieve what effects in their historical representations? And what are the implications of different ways of representing the past?

I have argued in previous chapters, against the views of a variety of postmodernists, that the 'form' does not determine the 'content': that there is more to historical investigation and argument than 'emplotment' or the 'imposition' of a narrative as a cultural convention which uses, but is not intrinsically rooted in, the realities of the past. I have suggested that historical puzzle-solving can produce arguments and interpretations which are open to rational debate and amendment in the light of theoretically netted evidence, and that there are general causal relationships between disparate events in the past which can be explored (rather than being more or less invented) by historians in the present. Nevertheless, the ways in which the results of historical investigations are presented are far more important than many practising historians realise. Modes of representation play a major role in the impact (or lack of it) of historical work among different groups or 'audiences'; and questions of representation are also crucial to a topic we shall also look at from a different perspective in the next chapter, that of value-freedom or objectivity.

The production of systematic representations, the bringing together of disparate pieces of evidence, in the writings of academic historians constitutes merely one specific strand – or perhaps rather several variations and types of strand – within what is, as indicated, a far wider field of historical traces, whether or not these are 'read' as such, and of symbolic universes of historical reference, or collective consciousness of living within a changing world. In this chapter, we shall be particularly concerned with the varieties of representation designed to achieve a more sophisticated historical understanding of selected aspects of the past in the present. What constitutes 'more sophisticated' of course varies massively, depending on the target audience and purposes of presentation of the past. But there can be no historical knowledge at all without some form of systematic investigation and bringing together of disparate traces, placing them in a wider context of interpretation, and some attempt at effective communication of the results.

The choice of mode of representation will necessarily intrinsically affect the type of history which is being 'written' (in the broadest sense of the word). There are two major points which must be made here. First, an attempt at representation of selected aspects of the past emphatically does not mean the pursuit of the unattainable goal of mimesis, or the attempt to provide some form of exact copy in the present of aspects of a lost past. (Some postmodernists thus target a straw man here.) There are choices to be made about the forms and purposes of representation, and these will affect the ways in which the results of inquiry are filtered or translated to different audiences in the present. Secondly, however – and equally emphatically – such variation in modes of emplotment does not logically entail an inevitably fictitious quality to that which is being represented. Shifts in meaning, ambiguities, additions and losses will of course be entailed by the processes of selection and translation, and no two historical accounts will be identical; but this does not mean that there are no criteria for distinguishing relative degrees of adequacy in different accounts for different purposes. There is a wide range of modes of representation: varieties of academic or 'scholarly' history writing, popular historical works targeted at a wider audience, textbooks, exhibitions, reconstructions, commemorations and sites of memory, historical documentaries and other visual representations.

There is also a great variety of purposes of historical reconstruction: from entertainment to argument, from information and understanding to empathy and emotive arousal. Thus historical knowledge – which is arguably an inevitable element in all human social existence – may take many different forms and face in many different directions in the present. For this reason – and for reasons explored further in the next chapter, on history and partisanship – it is all the more important to be able to ground the claim that historical knowledge is of a different order from the truths and insights of fiction or myth.

Forms and aims

Most historical works will have, simultaneously, a variety of purposes: not only to inform or instruct, but also to arouse emotional involvement or invoke sympathy, to entertain, to persuade. It is unlikely that the first and most didactic of these could be achieved without at least a degree of input from one or more of the others. But it is worth distinguishing between modes of historical representation which have one or another of these latter purposes as the primary, if not the sole aim, before coming back to look in more detail at historical texts which are primarily designed to inform or instruct.

For centuries, a primary purpose of public historical reconstruction and commemoration has been emotive: to elicit a sense of sympathy with high ideals, former heroes, the glorious past, in order to engender a sense of common collective community and purpose, a common set of goals and willingness to fight the good fight in the future. Thus representations of (very various) creation stories, statues of heroes and cultural icons, paintings of great battles, war memorials, commemorative services and occasions, all form part of the construction of public collective memories, of emplotment of the past in particular ways. Different states have their 'sacred sites'– the Statue of Liberty, the Lincoln Memorial – symbolising key moments in the country's history, myths of foundation or liberation. Such sacred sites rise and fall in significance over time: in stark contrast to London's Westminster Abbey, the Parisian Basilica of St Denis, which holds the mortal remains of a nearly unbroken line of France's kings from Dagobert I in 639, through the decapitated Louis XVI and Marie Antoinette of the French Revolution, to Louis XVIII in 1824, remains remarkably off the tourist track in the modern French Republic. Many memorials are scattered across the landscapes of everyday life, passed daily by people with barely a notice: from the unofficial roadside crosses or dedicated park benches inscribed with the name of a loved one, known only to immediate family and friends, through the battle sites and key stages of the American War of Independence or the Civil War in the United States, to the ubiquitous war memorials and plaques commemorating the names of those from a particular community who 'gave their lives' in the First World War in schools, town halls and village squares, across Britain, France and Canada.

Such manifold forms of representation do not necessarily have to be 'official' or state-sustaining (though, given the material resources required for some of them, including control of physical public space, many are). Courbet's realist paintings of common peasants, some of the First World War poetry of Wilfred

Owen or Siegfried Sassoon, Picasso's *Guernica*, the anti-Vietnam War songs of the 1960s (deploying not only lyrics but even the sounds of war as in the wailing guitar and regular rapid-fire clashing of drums in Jimi Hendrix's *Machine Gun*) – all provide, in different ways, forms of historical representation against the dominant or official views in a distinctively emotive manner. Nevertheless, given the aesthetic and emotive qualities of works which are primarily conceived as works of art and expression, rather than some notion of 'straight' representation, 'reading' or interpreting such visual and musical representations is open to considerable range and ambiguity. Different media have different means for presenting ambiguities for the reflections of the audience. It will be apparent to anyone who has watched different renderings of plays by Shakespeare or Brecht, or read the works of Irmtraud Morgner or Christa Wolf, that historical novels and drama are often as much about a particular present, or about supposedly timeless dilemmas of the 'human condition', as they are about the specific past which is conveyed.

Some historical representations appear to be designed almost entirely for the purposes of popular entertainment (in the terms of the brochures, a 'great day out for all the family'). If mad King Ludwig II of Bavaria designed his mock-medieval castles for his own private entertainment, then Disneyland took over the caricatures for the paying masses; a similar point can be made about blockbuster quasi-historical films, the quality of which varies enormously (from *Ben Hur* or *Gandhi* to a wide range of second-rate films about allegedly heroic escapades of American or British participants in the Second World War). Others may (also) be more didactic. One can argue about the position of the fine line between historical drama and documentary, comparing, say, the would-be authenticity of Holocaust representation in Spielberg's *Schindler's List* with the extraordinary capacity to evoke the past found in some of the slow, almost deadpan interviews of former victims, witnesses and perpetrators in Lanzmann's *Shoah*. Both contrast with the more determinedly active historical presence in the television series *The Nazis – A Warning from History*, which seeks not only to convey a sense of atmosphere and to provoke thought, but also to analyse, to explore interrelations. In an era of visual images, the lines between entertainment and education begin to blur for the less discerning viewer – a point which is as true for the printed word as for the visual image, but where differences in degrees of accessibility may prove effective deterrents. The position remains, however, riddled with ambiguities.

There are many different national and subcultural modes of re-presenting selected aspects of the past, which are constantly contested and changing. The mid-twentieth-century English (and I do not now mean British) notion of 'national heritage', with its preservation of stately homes, for decades contrasted with the relative lack of interest in the past in a forward-facing America; then in the later twentieth century the 'search for identity' and 'roots' became an all-consuming passion for many Americans. For two decades or so after the Second World War, West Germans ignored, re-used, or virtually obliterated traces of the

Nazi past; then, in the 1970s and 1980s, a spate of controversial forms of commemoration, memorialisation, reconstruction, rendered the Nazi legacy an integral part of the cataclysms of contemporary politics. The fissures of French resistance and compromise under Nazism led to comparable debates over the ambiguous past, as did the memories of war in Japan. 'Overcoming' the communist past in Eastern Europe after 1990 has led to new ghosts and reworking of memories.[1]

While genuinely – and intentionally – imaginative treatment of historical themes for creative purposes can provide all manner of insights, the growth of the 'history business' as part of tourism can also produce the most banal, moralising (and also in many ways inaccurate) representations. Thus for example while Arthur Miller's play *The Crucible* ostensibly deals with the late seventeenth-century witch-trials in Salem, Massachusetts, it has to be understood in the context of the McCarthyite witch-hunt of communists in 1950s America; on both counts, it achieves great insights. By contrast, the supposedly educational 'representation' of the Salem witch-hunt in the Salem Witch Museum enjoins visitors to 'dispel the myths and separate reality from fiction in our new exhibit'. It makes great claims: 'You Are There. Witness the testimony of the hysterical girls, the suffering of the blameless victims, and the decisions of the fanatical judges who sent innocent people to their deaths.' Its brochure unashamedly tells the prospective visitor that the 'gift shop contains a variety of souvenir and gift items', and the museum is an 'ideal destination for field trips and motorcoach tours'. Without the extraordinarily overblown cashing in on the miserable events of three centuries ago, it is highly dubious whether this otherwise entirely ordinary little town would enjoy the thriving tourist industry that it does. History – especially of the sort that can use slogans such as 'Lies. Suspicion. Ignorance. Murder. When the Witch Hunt began, no one was safe from being accused' – can be highly profitable. The London Dungeon is a similar example, exploiting as it does a certain lust for gory stories and hideous sights (and smells) in an authentic, dark and dank atmosphere. To note this is not necessarily to condemn it. Such historical representations may nevertheless feed a historical imagination which is open to further investigation and perhaps (even hopefully) adjustment in the light of growing knowledge. Historical interest may be aroused by representations such as these which can then lead to further and more serious exploration of the topic thus introduced – and may even be helpfully encouraged by the range of books, from children's colouring books to serious monographs, on display in the gift shops.

There are also far more slick and professional popular representations, which combine commercial acumen with real educational intent, such as the increasing number of 're-creations' of houses, even whole villages and towns, in different periods in the past. The re-creation at Plimoth Plantation of the settlement of the original settlers who came over to the 'New World' in the *Mayflower*, or of a slave plantation owner's home at Stone Mountain, Atlanta, Georgia, or of an early nineteenth-century village at Old Sturbridge Village in Massachusetts, are all good examples, as are the 'living museums' in the disused mines of South Wales, or the re-created village in Ironbridge, 'cradle of the industrial revolution', in England, or the Swiss collection of ancient dwellings at Ballenberg. Nevertheless, with their sometimes stilted and obviously artificial devices, such as in some cases dressing the 'residents' (= staff) in period costume, coaching them to speak in whatever is deemed to be a period accent and pretending that they know only what could be known at that time, these historical representations – with their occasionally jarring failures and disjunctures – can have quite odd effects for the modern-day visitor.

Such effects are not simply rooted in the momentary lapses of slick presenta-tion (as when a 'native Indian' at Plimoth Plantation, sitting picturesquely in his supposedly authentic tipi to illustrate the good neighbourly relations between *Mayflower* settlers and indigenous peoples, informs visitors that at the end of the day he gets changed into shorts and drives back to his suburban home in his air-conditioned car) but rather run deeper. The problem perhaps lies in the pretence of authenticity while not providing sufficient 'immersion' in the alien culture to be able really to 'speak its language' or be drenched in it; yet at the same time removing the possibility of recognition of this difficulty and open translation to and from the securely known present.

In her discussion of a similar situation at the manor house of Llancaiach Fawr, in the Rhymney valley on the way to Merthyr Tydfil in South Wales, Catherine Belsey puts it thus:

> Llancaiach Fawr invites us to cross a boundary between present and past, between one historical moment and another, into a vanished epoch . . . to encounter cultural history as participant observers, by sus-pending our own interests, identities, commitments and convictions . . . [Yet] what I found most unforgettable was my own acute embarrass-ment . . . The problem was . . . that I was asked to cross the boundary in one direction, and irreversibly for the duration, to enter the past in a dialogue where, deprived of any intelligible reference to the present, I had no secure place to speak from . . . When the familiar present ceases to be a secure foothold, the past becomes more remote, not less, harder to read, because the only frame of interpretation to a modern visitor is relegated to a distance, out of reach.[2]

In this sense, while the moment of pretence may be both enjoyable and educa-tional, it remains an experience rooted in distinctively different aims from those of most historians. It artificially portrays a frozen moment in time, rather than facilitating enhanced understanding of both difference and change; and it does this in ways with which neither the staff/actors, nor the visitors, necessarily feel entirely comfortable. Unlike what might be thought to be a comparable situa-tion, that of visiting anthropologist in an alien culture, the 'natives' are not really so; and the 'visiting anthropologists' are not genuinely forced to make their lives among the 'natives', but remain well aware that they have paid for a brief tour as visitors, not as participant observers who have to learn how to cope with different attitudes and behaviours (nor can they be even very certain about the authenticity of the latter). Again, we have an experience which may be prior to and stimulate subsequent historical investigation, but which is of a rather different order.

Part of the problem of such reconstructions is that they at least implicitly present to the visitor an assumption of the 'known-ness' of the past, and the 'unknown-ness' of the 'present' which is still in the mythical future of the presented past. The approach of historical museums is much more firmly rooted in a known present, presenting selected aspects of what is admittedly only a partially known past, interpretations of which are to a greater or lesser degree controversial. The variety – within certain limits – of possible interpretations may be highlighted; or an exhibition may determinedly present a particular type of interpretive narrative, presenting a message congruent with a distinctive political context (contrast, for example, the Holocaust Museum in Washington DC with the very differently slanted presentations of the Holocaust in the former communist states). Being less geared towards commercial success and hence financial self-sufficiency than the public entertainment forms of representation and reconstruction discussed above, museums and exhibitions tend too to be more dependent on grants, benefactors, public funding bodies, which may affect the range of representations possible.[3]

As far as the mode of historical representation itself is concerned, primarily didactic exhibitions have certain distinctive features. Take, for example, the Holocaust Exhibition at London's Imperial War Museum (whose Director is alleged to have quipped that the title consisted solely of the three most unpopular words in the English language). This exhibition consists of a selection of artefacts, contemporary texts, photos and video footage, contemporary eyewitness accounts and later recollections, and other types of representation (such as a model of a part of Auschwitz-Birkenau), accompanied by historians' overviews and brief commentaries. The exhibition has immense immediate impact, in part because of key juxtapositions of the general and the personal: the global numbers of Jews murdered in a particular incident or killing operation, alongside a photo with the name and details of a particular individual or individuals which serves to personalise it, to evoke feelings of immediate empathy and a sense of common humanity (such as the photograph of one small boy walking wide-eyed, plump-cheeked, to his death at the Babi Yar massacre). This kind of representation cannot make the detailed historical argument of, say, a contribution by Hans Mommsen to the intentionalist/functionalist debate; but it can be far more powerful in evoking emotions, prompting questions and active exploration of the topic. And cumulatively, such an exhibition can present a kind of argument or moral and political message. The contrast between this and, for example, the representations of the Holocaust in the historical museum on Unter den Linden, in the centre of (East) Berlin, first under the former communist regime and then under democratic auspices after reunification, could hardly be starker.

The relationship of an audience to an exhibition is also different. Unlike a book, there is not the implicit imperative to start at the beginning, work through precisely as the author laid it out, covering every word to the end. (Though how many readers actually read books in that way? But at least the intention of the author may be to present one coherent, sustained argument in a logical order, to be read 'from start to finish'.) In an exhibition, people wander, linger over one exhibit, skip others, pass quickly, miss out whole sections, deeply ponder others. While exhibitions do present an implicit metanarrative, it is in some ways harder to ensure a sustained argument, to ensure that the 'reader' follows the 'story'. And the intention may in any event be primarily to document and to preserve, and not necessarily to present a clear (or strong) explanation. While the impact may be more immediate, more compelling, possibly provoking a more immediate personal response, the form of representation may be less geared towards intellectual engagement with controversies over interpretation and explanation. Nevertheless, implicitly or explicitly, through decisions about selection and omission, contextualisation and interpretation, emphasis and marginalisation, exhibitions inevitably embed or present one interpretation more firmly than other possible 'readings'.

Active engagement with and varied forms of representation of the past have been ubiquitous and enduring features of at least western societies for centuries, from Renaissance notions of creative reworking of ancient genius to the more didactic nineteenth- and twentieth-century conceptions of preservation and distanced admiration. As David Lowenthal has put it:

> the past is not dead . . . it is not even sleeping. A mass of memories and records, or relics and replicas, of monuments and memorabilia, lives at the core of our being. And as we remake it, the past remakes us. We kick over the traces of tradition to assert our autonomy and expunge our errors, but we cannot banish the past, for it is inherent in all we do and think.[4]

Both as individuals and as members of different forms of collective community, humans think and act in ways patterned and conditioned by selective perceptions and reappropriations of multiple pasts.

The shaping of the form: historians' texts

It is not entirely clear why the 'reconstructedness' of the forms of representation considered above should appear more obvious than is the case with the written word on its own, as in books and articles. After all, total immersion in atmosphere and period is perhaps more easily achieved when more senses are involved, as in evocative historical films making use of visual and musical effects as well as language (think of Steven Spielberg's *Schindler's List* compared with an average historical textbook account). Perhaps the difference is that in many self-confessedly artistic, aesthetic or entertaining forms of representation, the constructedness is on display, the creativity of the producer explicitly demonstrable, whether for praise or critique: we are precisely invited to admire the artistry of the film director, the painter, the musician. The medium is as important as, if not more important than, the message; the latter does not necessarily have to be 'right' (although this may be an aim, as in certain forms of realism), other than in the sense of some sort of artistic authenticity. (Even expressionism and surrealism strive for an authenticity of expression of inner experience.) Historical texts usually, however, lay greater emphasis on claims to provide an accurate account. Competent readers of words on the page may well get easily immersed, their imaginations brought into play; but they may not. And historical representations in forms such as articles in the specialist press, or monographs, may not prioritise stimulation of the historical imagination over making a particular argument in the context of a specific historical debate, for example. Although the purposes of scholarly historical representation through the written word may be quite varied, not getting the story wrong is generally an underlying constant.

As we have seen, the very possibility in principle of this aim has been challenged. As discussed in previous chapters, postmodernists query the very possibility of 'finding' rather than 'imposing' stories. Hans Kellner, for example, has suggested that the very constructedness of written history in some ways prevents the possibility of what he calls 'getting the story straight'.[5] In his view,

> Rhetoric, representation, and reality . . . cannot be separated from one another. To do so is to repress that part of human reality that accounts for our understandings, convictions, and values. The moral high ground of the historical realists . . . is always won at the expense of language and its imperatives, the 'other' sources of historical representation.[6]

Similarly, Roland Barthes has pointed to the ways in which it may simply be the conventions of historical discourse that present the spurious sense that such writings are a reliable record of what actually happened, in contrast to more obviously constructed representations.[7]

It is possible to concede the point to Kellner that the form of representation does entail both the addition of certain elements, and also associated losses: historical representations are just that – representations of selected features, not attempted reproductions of some mythical and unattainable totality. But, as I have argued in preceding chapters, this does not preclude a simultaneous commitment to 'getting the story right', at least in the sense that historians have a duty to try not to 'get anything wrong'. The latter applies both to individual statements of fact, and to presumptions about relationships among these statements which, as suggested in preceding chapters, are often very much more open to processes of 'disconfirmation' than writers such as Hayden White would have us suppose.

Nevertheless, writing is also important: historians should be more aware of the choices they face in seeking means of representation which are appropriate to different purposes. It is difficult to know with any certainty whether most (or even many) practising academic historians think as hard about the ways in which they present their work as they do about the questions, the research, the evaluation of the evidence, the relationships of their findings to debates in the existing literature.[8] Perhaps more than the historians who actually write the books, publishers are certainly conscious of intended audience and hence the pitch and register of a given historical work. So too are those who have ulterior purposes, whether to instil a sense of 'national pride', or to evoke sympathy for certain groups and condemn others, or to put across particular messages to particular groups. The writer of popular work for the 'general reader', or a textbook targeted at a particular age group of schoolchildren following a particular syllabus or curriculum, will write in a different way from one seeking to arouse sympathy for a particular political cause, religious movement, forgotten hero or oppressed group. While academic historians may profess to be merely following the Rankean dictum of 'telling it like it was', even this requires a determination (however unconscious) to engage in interpretation across cultures, from one world to another, from one culture to a possibly quite different set of audiences or groups in the present, with as little intrusion as possible of the writer's own views and prejudices. Not everyone would agree that this either can or should be the aim of history.

Those writing historical texts inevitably face certain choices beyond those concerned with 'not getting it wrong' (if this is conceded as an important task of history). There are a number of aspects on which historical texts, even those treating ostensibly the 'same' object of inquiry, will differ according to wider assumptions, scholarly conventions and theoretical paradigms as well as the individual creativity and imagination (or otherwise) of the author. It seems to me that one can pick out certain features common to professional historical texts, whether written as traditional narrative or in more explicitly argumentative or analytical styles, which may help to cross-cut the debates of the later twentieth century about realism and about a putative 'revival of narrative' in historical writing.[9]

The unreliable narrator?

Whether the form of the historical account is one of narrative realism, or of a more stringently argued analytical approach, in the vast majority of historical texts readers are repeatedly made aware of the movement between present and past, between what is known with a degree of certainty, what is being presented as argument, what must remain mere surmise. Readers, in the conventions of western scholarship at least, are also more often than not made aware of the existence of alternative interpretations – not least, very often, in order to present the author's interpretation as in some sense 'original', innovative, and so on. What most historians seek through their texts to present is not some 'reproduction of a story which is assumed to be found or given in the past' but rather an argument presenting an answer to a puzzle, satisfying some form of curiosity, about selected periods, places, elements, problems in the past as seen from a particular standpoint in the present.

The conventional apparatus of a scholarly work is of course to some extent, as Barthes reminds us, designed to produce a 'reality effect'. Quotations from primary sources may well be deployed to evoke a sense of atmosphere, of time and place, of arguably spurious authenticity. They may also be deployed to establish scholarly credentials: to display the wide range of that which has been scoured to produce the necessarily selective account. They may or may not be abused to serve extraneous purposes in establishing a reputation, laying proprietorial claims to privileged knowledge of a particular field, and so on. But this does not logically preclude them from *also* being an effective means of communicating with an audience an insight based on extensive research in the sources, on the basis of which certain generalisations and arguments may be made with a degree of plausibility, even certainty, that what is being said is in some sense 'adequate' as a description or explanation, or at least the most likely interpretation, of a salient aspect of the past. Moreover, there is an important further aspect here: that of the nearest the historian can get to the scientist's notion of replicability. The use of the footnote – and associated scholarly apparatuses, such as appendices, lists of archives consulted, bibliographies – should in principle allow other scholars, if they are so minded, to retread the author's footsteps and take an independent view of the argument presented.[10]

Historians vary quite widely with respect to the presence or otherwise of their own voice in the text. It is true that, reading some narratives, one gains the impression that the historian as active intermediary is nowhere evident except on the title page; and that the record of what happened is essentially unproblematic. The naïve reader of such a text may then be left unaware of alternative possible accounts, of controversies in the specialist literature and so on. The events are recounted as simply 'what happened next'. But, leaving aside how many readers are so naïve as never to be aware of possible slant (on which more in a moment), irrespective of the visible presence or otherwise of the authorial voice, this is a far from universal practice.

Many historians, as indicated in previous chapters, explicitly seek to establish the importance and innovative character of their own accounts by locating them within a wider field of historical controversy. Even within a relatively unproblematic narrative, the historian's mind is often visibly present, actively weighing up the evidence and assessing the plausibility of one or another interpretation in the light of wider knowledge and assumptions. Where there are gaps in the evidence, or problems of interpretation, the lay reader is most inclined to view the professional historian as the person who has been most engaged, most immersed in the material and whose judgement is thus perhaps most to be trusted; and it is precisely in this respect that the historian may explicitly insert his or her voice, rather than trying to smooth over gaps or massage the evidence into a realist and unbroken account.

This is as true of historians who are not explicitly interested in 'theory' as it is of those claiming that their approach is in some way new, innovatory. It is indeed part of the western convention of being a 'good' historian, one who has carefully considered and tried to make sense of all the available evidence. One could select any number of illustrations of this procedure. There is, for example, John Hardman's assessment of Robespierre's agonised smashing of his jaw in the confused hours before his final execution at the scaffold:

> Though it would be more elegant to have Robespierre, having denounced so many false attempts to assassinate him, finally succumbing to a real one, I prefer the suicide explanation and take the increasingly belligerent measures discussed at the end by the Robespierrists as evidence not of confidence but of despair.[11]

Or consider Michael Crawford's authoritative account of *The Roman Republic*, which repeatedly makes use of intelligent surmise on the basis of fragmentary surviving evidence, wider knowledge, and possible historical parallels, as in the following passage:

> the native cults of the different foreign nationalities probably provided an elementary principle of organisation. Certainly numerous foreign religions were represented in Rome in the first century BC and were apparently perceived . . . as a threat . . . At the same time unofficial books of prophecy circulated widely, perhaps a symptom of a propensity to insurrection, as they were in seventeenth-century England . . . Overall it is hard not to suppose that the difficulties of the ruling oligarchy were compounded by the composition and the wretchedness of the population of the city of Rome . . . The violence of politics in Rome . . . was also, I believe, a factor in the slackening of political scruple which eventually allowed Caesar and Pompeius to fight for the possession of a *res publica* . . .[12]

At no time is the reader given to understand that there is an omniscient narrator presenting the past 'as it really was'; the very position of 'authority' rests on the display of a combination of extensive knowledge and intelligent synthesis and supposition.

Postmodernists have sometimes focussed on the issue of 'closure', critiquing an artificial imposition of coherence on the past. It is thus all the more important to emphasise that quite the opposite is very often the case. Far from presenting a closed and 'final' narrative as though it were actually thus given in the archives or the past, for many historians the written word allows for a greater discussion of ambiguity, of what is not known, of gaps. This is, tellingly, admitted by Natalie Zemon Davies in her introduction to what is, unusually for a historian, a book of a film: *The Return of Martin Guerre*. She starts by commenting (ironically, in the light of Kellner's views) that 'rarely does a historian find so perfect a narrative structure in the events of the past or one with such popular dramatic appeal'; but goes on rapidly to concede some doubts about the concessions the film version was having to make, 'departing from the historical record':

> These changes may have helped to give the film the powerful simplicity that had allowed the Martin Guerre story to become a legend in the first place, but they also made it hard to explain what actually happened [sic!]. Where was there room in this beautiful and compelling cinemato-graphic recreation of a village for the uncertainties, the 'perhapses', the 'may-have-beens', to which the historian has recourse when the evidence is inadequate or perplexing? Our film was an exciting suspense story that kept the audience as unsure of the outcome as the original villagers and judges had been. But where was there room to reflect upon the significance of identity in the sixteenth century?[13]

There could hardly be a better summary of what historians are able to do by way of discursive analysis and critical reflection in the written text which goes way beyond the kinds of simple or singular narrative emplotment or naïve realism which sometimes seems to be assumed.

Plot, character and voice

Of course historians play an active role in shaping what stories they choose to 'make' of the material which is at their disposal at the time of writing. (It is also perhaps worth remembering that research and writing are not such discrete, separate, activities as many commentators appear to assume: seeking to make sense of material requires organising and shaping it, often by producing a preliminary written account of it, sensing that it may fit certain patterns, realising that there are gaps which if filled might confirm or otherwise such patterns; there is a constant interaction between processes of research and writing.) There are very definite decisions made by historians in the present which 'pre-shape' the accounts of the past which are finally produced.

There is of course emplotment in the sense of the pursuit of a particular trail of questions about connections in the past, whatever the form in which these answers are presented. Stories are told, not because they are deemed to be simple reproductions of something that has been 'found', nor because that is the way in which human lives are actually lived (one attempted defence of narrative history 'as a way of life'), but rather because they provide plausible accounts of how something in particular came to be the way it was. Descriptions are provided of interconnections among elements because this is a means of making sense of connections from some angle in the present. Not even the attempt to escape wider syntheses – as in recent attempts at microhistory – can avoid implicit embeddedness in wider bodies of knowledge, of assumptions about period and place. And here, 'plausibility' and 'making sense' are heavily rooted in paradigms, with associated 'background pictures' and notions of what will satisfy curiosity.

Depending on these wider assumptions, the themes and characters of historical accounts will be constructed and presented very differently. Take, for example, two biographies, published within a couple of years of each other, of the same key historical individual: Oliver Cromwell. Christopher Hill's account, coming from a *Marxisant* perspective, very definitely locates Cromwell within the context of his times. We have, in the whole of the first chapter, barely a mention of Cromwell himself beyond the dates of his life. But the second paragraph of the first chapter very firmly establishes the 'real' plot:

> The seventeenth is the decisive century in English history, the epoch in which the Middle Ages ended. England's problems were not peculiar to her. The whole of Europe faced a crisis in the mid-seventeenth century, which expressed itself in a series of breakdowns, revolts and civil wars. The sixteenth century had seen the opening up of America and of new routes to the far east; a sudden growth of population all over Europe, and a monetary inflation which was also all-European. These phenomena are related (both as effect and as cause) to the rise of capitalist relations within feudal society and a consequent regrouping of social classes.[14]

It is quite clear that the story is about a major turning point, not only in English history but in the history of capitalism more generally; periodisation is set within the Marxist framework of 'feudalism to capitalism', the key actors are social classes, and, once we do finally get to some biographical details with respect to Oliver Cromwell himself in the second chapter, these primarily relate to his location within early modern English class structure. Lady Antonia Fraser's conception of her subject matter is very different. As she disarmingly puts it, her aim was 'simply to rescue the personality of Oliver Cromwell from the obscurity into which it seemed to me that it had fallen, just because there has been such an invaluable concentration on the political and social trends of the age in which he lived.'[15] In stark contrast to Christopher Hill's account, Antonia Fraser devotes the whole of the first chapter to the first eighteen years of Cromwell's life, carefully distinguishing myth from plausible surmise, and seeking to establish the direct personal influences on Oliver himself, as in the person of the Puritan master of Huntingdon Grammar School, Dr Thomas Beard.

So – to belabour the obvious – historians artificially construct the 'beginnings' of their stories; and may construct these beginnings in very different ways, even when one might plausibly expect two biographies of the same individual to 'begin' (as Antonia Fraser in fact does, and Hill very notably does not) with the birth of the person in question. Middles and ends, or – to put it in slightly less banal terms – the shapes of the whole account, may also be constructed very differently. This is true whether one is discussing 'traditional narrative' history, or history couched in more explicitly analytical terms, whichever paradigmatic perspective it comes from. There has for example been much debate (particularly among German historians) over the alleged opposition between 'structure history' and 'events history' (*Strukturgeschichte* and *Ereignisgeschichte*), a debate which has played out in slightly different ways among French historians of the *Annales* tradition and beyond. To some extent, as we have seen in Chapter 7, deep-rooted assumptions about such issues as the relative importance of structural change and individual agency will determine how an account is structured. There are also conventions of representation in particular scholarly traditions. The notion of 'revisionist' has variously had both 'good' and 'bad' connotations, depending on whether being 'innovative' and 'overturning existing views' was at a premium or not. Only a little over a third of a century ago, it appears, most American doctoral candidates in history were encouraged to exemplify, rather than challenge, the theories of their teachers in their dissertations.[16] Doctoral dissertations in the United Kingdom similarly contrast with the German system of two doctorates – the first relatively slight, the second, the *Habilitation*, massively weighty, overloaded with footnotes and drenched in detail, providing the crucial credentials to be a university professor (implicitly understood as being an expert in the sense of someone who knows more and more about less and less). While Germans appeared to be encouraged to look in exhaustive detail at closely delimited periods and problems, French historical writing, massively influenced by the *Annales* tradition, presented a quite different set of challenges and assumptions, from the notion that one needed to look at long slow sea changes over extended periods of time to the more recent trend in micro-historical investigation, occasionally characterised as the equivalent of a switch from a historical telescope to a microscope. No-one would suggest that such variations are somehow related to what is 'given' in the past; but they would claim that what is said about the selected period or problem in some sense (as understood within particular conventions) addresses important questions fairly and fully.

Not only plots, but also the cast of characters, or actors, will be constructed differently within different traditions. Key actors may be constructed as collective actors, as in, for example, Barrington Moore's focus on the landed classes in the process of modernisation, or the social classes in Marxist accounts of the French Revolution; or the primary focus may be on a selection of key historical individuals. Key 'actors' may even be construed as quantifiable trends in statistics, such as the supposed economic costs and benefits of slavery in the American South. The assumptions of cliometric historians are very different from those of social and cultural historians who focus on the interpretative reconstruction of interpreted realities; or those historians of the *Annales* school who examine the *longue durée*, underlying demographic and social structural patterns and mentalities which persist over centuries; the framing of the material by a historian interested in the history of events, or narrative, will clearly have a different focus again.

What is at issue here is not what is putatively 'given' (or not) in the past, but rather 'actors' constituted by practices of active conceptualisation, question-framing, and related assumptions. Historians have to make decisions in the context of wider debates about what sort of form will be most appropriate for a particular argument, in a particular context of debate, for a particular audience. Such decisions are not always straightforward, and positions on the theoretical issues discussed in preceding chapters will play an important role in deciding how to structure an account. Even for those historians focussing on the 'same' delimited problem and period, there is not necessarily one single way of 'emplotting' and presenting the issues. So: emplotment depends on a lot more than the individual imposition of narrative onto arbitrarily selected bits of 'historical debris'. It has a great deal to do with paradigms, collective frameworks of inquiry and argument.

Related to questions of plot and cast of characters are the roles assigned to different actors in the account. The attribution of roles of heroes, victims and villains is one of the most obvious ways in which much historical writing is very clearly slanted in one or another political direction.[17] It is striking just how much historical writing suggests guilt or pronounces exoneration, makes a criticism or arouses sympathy with one or another party in a conflictual situation. This is sometimes only implicit, almost an accidental result of the amount of space allotted by a historian to a particular person or group, trying to present matters from their perspective (as in Christopher Hibbert's fascination with the royal family's perspective in his account of the French Revolution); sometimes it is more obviously and directly related to strong political perspectives, as in the writings of East and West Germans on the Nazi period.[18]

This relates closely to the question of voice. To whom does the historian choose to give voice, and in whose voice is this given, and to what extent? The act of writing both 'adds' and 'excludes'; the role of historian is not merely one of neutral intermediary, a robotic machine for transmitting 'facts' from the past into the minds of readers in the present.

Peter Burke has interpreted this question as one of the need for presenting multiple perspectives.[19] There is clearly a case for something of this sort, though I think it is a wider question which can be addressed rather differently and perhaps less mechanically (in terms of the narrative structure) from the way in which Burke appears to conceive it. In part, it has to do with the way in which a particular substantive area is put into focus, and the kinds of questions which are put to a particular range of material. This has been argued for approaches to African history by Adu Boahen, who proposes that historians should be 'asking questions and exploring themes of relevance to the African and not the European' (although it seems to me that some of Boahen's assumptions about the 'soul' of a 'race' are somewhat dubious).[20] It is also in part what lies behind at least some post-colonial approaches to history, insofar as I understand them.[21] In part, the question is the wider one of the need for what Weber called 'interpretive under-standing' of a range of collective meanings or points of view. Much 'identity history' writing appears to have ignored or forgotten or rejected this, although it was a point which dawned even on the East German Marxist historian Jürgen Kuczynski in the early 1980s when he suddenly realised that studies of the oppressed had to be complemented by studies of the ruling classes; otherwise there would, at all times in human history, appear to be 'only one class that is doing all the struggling'.[22] And it is quite obvious when a historian badly mis-judges this point, and gets the balance wrong. A controversial recent example, contributing to the explosion of the West German 'historians' debate' of 1986–7, was that of Andreas Hillgruber's self-imposed problem of 'with whom to identify': the German civilians and soldiers battling for their fatherland on the eastern front in the closing months of the Second World War, or the inmates of concentration camps whose suffering and deaths were extended by the prolonga-tion of the war.[23] While Hillgruber's first essay was a very emotive evocation of the struggles of the soldiers on the eastern front, battling against the 'Bolshevik hordes', the second was a dry, analytical, distanced account of academic contro-versies over the Holocaust with barely a whiff of empathy to be registered. It was precisely the juxtaposition, within one book, of two essays which contrasted sharply in style and tone, which provoked angry reactions by Habermas, Wehler and others, unleashing the so-called 'historians' dispute' in Germany in 1986–7.[24]

No historical writing, however would-be 'scientific' and causal, can escape the issue of empathy – of feeling one's way into the mind and world view of other people, other cultures, other times. But we have to be quite clear what the impli-cations of these points are. It is possible to (choose to) be more or less emotive, to give 'voice' to one or more than one set of protagonists in the past. This choice may be more or less conscious. It can be blatant, as in self-confessedly politicised historical writing, whether from a right-wing or radical perspective. It can indeed be engaged in as a major purpose from the standpoint of certain his-torical paradigms (for example, the centrality of 'allowing the subaltern to speak' or given voice, in post-colonialist theory). It can be unintentional and indeed offensive. One could develop a formula or injunction about this topic: that, for example, empathy should not be confused with sympathy; and that historians should seek to restore voice to all participants. But many historians have their own agendas in the present (such as restoring voice to those whose voices have, historically, been drowned out more than others). Moreover, there is a deeper underlying problem here, namely the way in which a historian's personal sympa-thies render it easier to empathise with one viewpoint or movement than another, to highlight and re-present the aspirations, struggles, victories and defeats of one or another group with greater understanding than others, to bracket out or fail to understand viewpoints which are relatively antipathetic. Yet, if nothing else, Daniel Jonah Goldhagen's controversial work on *Hitler's Willing Executioners* demonstrated that it is possible, from the perspective of a survivor's son whose personal sympathies all lie with the victims, to seek very strongly to understand the mentality of the perpetrators.[25]

If voice presents choices for the historian, so too do questions about the evocation of time and place. Some historians are more determined to create 'atmosphere' than others; and different historians make quite different choices about how to relate structures and events, contexts and developments, to provide what Geertz termed 'thick description' or to remain at the level of dry argumentation. The most tedious histories are perhaps those which make no effort to evoke a sense of context. Yet it is not always easy to know how best to weave in what may be required – depending on how one sees it – in order to 'set the scene' or remind the reader that a scholarly discussion is about something that was, at the time, very real, very meaningful, laden with significance.[26] Nor would every historian feel as comfortable writing in quasi-novelistic tone, with privileged insight into individual mood, as Orlando Figes clearly does in the following passage from his award-winning book on the Russian Revolution:

> Trotsky's boat sailed into New York harbour on a cold and rainy Sunday evening in January 1917. It had been a terrible crossing, seventeen stormy days in a small steamboat from Spain, and the revolutionary leader now looked haggard and tired as he disembarked on the quayside before a waiting crowd of comrades and pressmen. His mood was depressed.[27]

It is clear from what follows (a direct quotation from Trotsky's own writings) that there is some justification for this imputation of mood; nevertheless the style is clearly intended to set the reader directly in the time and place. Similarly, not every historian would comfortably resort to metaphors along the lines of Ian Kershaw's: 'Self-combustion would see to it that, once lit, the genocidal fires would rage into a mighty conflagration amid the barbarism of the war to destroy "Jewish-Bolshevism"'.[28] But in the context of Kershaw's magisterial coverage of sources and consideration of controversies and evidence, such stylistic devices clearly function as accessible shorthand for a sophisticated argument.

In the context of postmodernist challenges, however, the point must be clearly reiterated: questions of style, and techniques of representation and persuasion must be clearly distinguished from questions of testability and truth.[29] One need go no further than the subtitles ('Hubris' and 'Nemesis') of Kershaw's two-volume biography of Hitler to note that Kershaw quite self-consciously provides the framework of Greek tragedy.[30] He even explicates this in the preface:

> In Greek mythology, Nemesis is the goddess of retribution who exacts the punishment of the gods for the human folly of overweening arrogance, or hubris. The English saying 'pride comes before a fall' reflects the common-place occurrence . . . The meteoric rise of rulers, politicians, or domineering court favourites has so often been followed by an

arrogance of power leading to an equally swift fall from grace. Usually, it afflicts an individual who, like a shooting star, flashes into prominence then fades rapidly into insignificance leaving the firmament essentially unchanged.[31]

One could hardly get a more concentrated example of the combination of emplotment as tragedy, and the use of metaphor and simile. But does this mean that the account which follows is 'nothing more' than a literary construction, or that, as what is already a historical 'classic', it is characterised by White's 'non-disconfirmability'? As we have seen in previous chapters, Kershaw himself clearly intends something a little more substantial by way of explanation beyond purely literary 'emplotment'.

Testability and use of metaphor are not mutually incompatible. Referring to a wider body of material, Philippe Carrard has analysed the characteristic mix or 'hybridity' of scientific and literary discourses in selected works of the New History (the latest generation of French historians working in the *Annales* tradition), pointing out their 'concurrent reliance on such diverging machineries as narrative, quantification and figurative language'.[32] Rhetorical devices are important; but they do not preclude reasoned argument.

When we actually look at the range of different historical styles and approaches, it becomes very clear that the historian is far from being the human equivalent of a photocopier or camera. The historian is the creative intermediary between selected elements of the past and selected audiences in the present; and we would hardly be likely to have any interest in history if this were not so. There are a multitude of ways in which historians choose to try to 'bring the past to life': use of visual imagery, quotations from contemporary sources, recounting particular anecdotes or incidents, making larger statistics 'personal' by the use of vivid examples, are among the more obvious ones. Quite clearly, the historian plays a major creative role in the production of a given historical account. In this respect, as well as in the others we have been looking at, it is again clear that no two historical accounts of the 'same' phenomenon will ever be the same. Yet to reduce historical writing to an act of individual creativity within a particular context of institutionally rooted historical and cultural conventions is to miss the point that any transmission of historical insight is for a purpose; whether to argue a particular case in a wider context of controversy, to solve a puzzle within an existing framework of knowledge, to present a particular interpretation against other views, to reconstruct the 'unknown', to evoke a certain atmosphere or arouse a set of sympathies. Concentration on conventions of style, rhetoric, metaphor, is important: but to reduce history to this is to overlook the possibility of historical writing achieving many ends simultaneously, in which literary form remains more the means (however much this may add) than the content.

Bridging the gaps: the historical imagination

There may be all manner of motives for reading and writing history: curiosity, escapism, 'learning the lessons of the past' (if only that there are no lessons), understanding how the present came about, preserving the memory of traditions and individuals who are, for one reason or another, important, are but a few of the more obvious and frequently repeated ones. There is a very great deal more that could be said about all the topics adumbrated, all too briefly, in this chapter. One aspect is, however, fundamental to all of these purposes: making *connections* between past and present. And here lies the power of the imagination (however limited): the imagination of both author and reader, of producer and consumer. Without this, history really is 'dead knowledge'. However much a historian may feel that he or she has solved a given puzzle, there is little point in presenting the solution in a form which will not resonate with an intended audience.

There are thus a host of wider questions which historians must face, beyond trying 'not to get the story wrong'. Should, for example, the representation be as 'factual' as possible – or would this in itself represent a distortion, excluding as it may do the pain and suffering, the experiences, the elation and joys and struggles and defeats of a particular past? Is writing on the Holocaust which focusses ever more narrowly on certain academic debates actually a *falsification* rather than a clarification; or is it essential to achieve certain perhaps merely preliminary purposes relating to clarity, precision, explanation?[33] Even the choice of attempted 'neutrality' or distance is as much a decision as the choice of emotional tone. In that sense, all historical writing is necessarily implicated, if not explicitly laden with issues concerning values, emotions, symbolisation, evocation; historians choose whether or not to write in terms of (sometimes more explicit, sometimes only implicit) heroes and villains; they choose whether or not their characterisations should evoke sympathies for one side or another, empathise better with certain points of view than others. Historians – however 'objective', archivally drenched and 'empirically adequate' their accounts – cannot help but 'colour' the past in their representation of the past to the present, whether by wilful or unwitting partisanship or by the complex attempt at the stance of omniscient narrator.

Representations are not all there is to historical analysis; the form does not determine the content. I have argued throughout this book that there is more to historical investigation than is conceded by those who over-emphasise the rhetorical aspects, the 'content of the form'. Nevertheless, the form of representation is also important. The role of the active imagination of both 'producer' and 'consumer' of historical representations is often overlooked in discussions about the nature of history. Historical consciousness is, in myriad ways, an inevitable part of any society in the present. The question of the extent to which this does and/or should affect the ways in which professional historians choose to investigate and represent the past, and the relations between history and partisanship (or value-neutrality and objectivity), are the issues to which we must now turn.

9

HISTORY AND PARTISANSHIP

In what respects are historical accounts different from myth, ideology, propaganda? What are – or should be – the relations between historical interpretations and contemporary politics? Is my account 'true', while yours is 'biased', theirs is 'ideology'? What are the relations between the types of society in which historical accounts are produced, and the nature of those accounts? Is 'objectivity' or 'value-neutrality' in principle desirable or even possible?

These questions are absolutely fundamental; we often know exactly what answers we want to be able to give; and yet, on closer inspection, such questions are not so easily answered.

On the one hand, most practising historians at least implicitly operate on the assumption that what they are pursuing, as best they can, is the 'truth' about some selected aspect of the past. Most would concede that such 'truth' is never more than partial; that they can never discover the 'whole truth and nothing but the truth'; and that the answers of one generation will be to questions in which the next generation may have little or no interest, or may be couched in terms which they no longer use or accept. But at the same time there is a widespread view among both practising historians and their lay audiences that the accounts of professional historians have a status different from fantasy and myth, subjective memory or political ideology. On the other hand, as we have seen, such claims are extraordinarily hard to justify theoretically. Different theoretical paradigms seem to correlate in practice with different political sympathies (narrative historians tend towards the right, left-wingers towards structural or class accounts, for example – before we even mention Marxism, where the connections are direct, explicit, intentional). Different conceptual frameworks may rest on widely diverging fundamental presuppositions about the nature of the world. Building on long traditions of scepticism about the relations between 'reality' and representation, postmodernists have done a remarkably good job of further rattling the unexamined foundations of the historical profession.

Not all historians would in any event even agree that history can or should be in some way 'value neutral', 'objective', uncommitted. This applies, oddly, not only to those Marxist historians who reject 'bourgeois' historiography as an ideological cover-up for what was held to be 'really' going on, but also to some historians at the opposite end of the ideological spectrum. As recent controversies over, for example, the use of the concept of totalitarianism among right-wing historians have shown, there is still no consensus over the issue of value freedom in history. One often has the impression that the observer's standpoint (whether on the right or the left) is the only one for which 'objectivity' can ever be claimed; all opposing views are readily dismissed as 'politically biased'. A variant on this is the accusation that, if an account does not take up an explicit value stance, it is deemed to have been unduly influenced by the values of the subject matter under study – a frequent right-wing critique of left-liberal historians' relatively anodyne, non-denunciatory accounts of communist regimes before 1989/90. Furthermore, contrary to what some more ivory-towered academics might (wish to) believe, not all of life is played out in battles over and through the written word. Historians are also human beings, with other aspects to their lives. Detachment, a decision not to be engaged in some way in contemporary debates about the past, is in itself a value position; refusal to take a stance is in itself a political act, in refusing to act and hence leaving the arena and allowing others to fight it out. But there are different arenas in which fights might take place; for example, battles over the nature of history teaching in schools, the criteria for appointments, the nature of historical exhibitions, may be very different from the warfare characteristic of the pages of historical journals.

In the light of these continuing controversies it is all the more urgent to ask: how far, if at all, or to what extent and with what qualifications, is it possible (or desirable) to provide a defence of any notion of history as some form of honest reconstruction of selected aspects of the past, where political sympathies are not a valid criterion for adjudication between accounts?

Explicit theoretical discussion of these questions is far from new. Over a century ago, in the famous *Methodenstreit* (controversy over methods) of the late nineteenth century, and in early twentieth-century debates over the 'abuse of the lectern' for the political manipulation of young minds, Max Weber sought to provide theoretically sophisticated answers which, for all the qualifications regarding choice of topic and conceptual framework, nevertheless sought to retain a clear demarcation between processes of inquiry, empirical findings, and moral or political evaluations.[1] Through the twentieth century, attempts at 'objectivity' have had a chequered history. Raised as the ultimate banner or academic gold standard among mid-century American historians, the notion of objectivity came under attack from a variety of quarters in subsequent decades.[2] Even the very goal was rejected by other theoretical traditions, such as the so-called 'Frankfurt School' of Critical Theory (which originated in Weimar Germany and was 'exported' to the United States, in the form of the New School of Social Research in New York, as an unintended by-product of Nazi persecution). Following along the lines laid in the 1920s and 1930s by Max Horkheimer and Theodor Adorno, later critical theorists such as Herbert Marcuse and Jürgen Habermas argued that to describe or construct generalisations about the way the world actually was at any given time constituted, in itself, an intrinsically conservative exercise: following Marx on this issue, for critical theorists the point was not so much to interpret the world as to change it.[3] Thus, in critique of the Enlightenment, critical theorists developed a notion of testing theory by active intervention to change reality, thus radically destroying any easy separation of 'science' and 'values'. And postmodernists have in any event fundamentally attacked the very possibility of objective representation.

In this chapter, I shall argue that Max Weber's proposed solutions to the question of objectivity are insufficient and inadequate in a number of respects. However, I shall also argue that it is possible to salvage a more limited version of value neutrality: that, in short, we can be somewhat more precise about the limits and the extent of objectivity within historical theory. We do not need to go down the roads of postmodernist relativism; but the solution can be found neither in some form of professional multi-culturalism, nor in a reassertion of blind faith in empiricism. It is possible to be a great deal more precise about the limits of what we are doing, and the conditions under which it is possible to make at least some circumscribed claims for the 'value-neutral' pursuit of truth under particular circumstances.

There are several respects in which the focus of the discussion needs to be shifted, with regard to features both 'internal' and 'external' to specific historical works. Much of the discussion to date has focussed on the personal prejudices and biases of individual historians. While these are no doubt important, it seems to me that there are far wider respects in which different historical approaches and their professional carriers are politically situated, and these need to be more carefully addressed. Secondly, much of the focus has been on the production of individual historical accounts, rather than on the wider presentation to, and reception of these accounts by, specified target audiences, and the related aims and purposes of certain forms of presentation of the past to the present. Thirdly, and more theoretically, I think we need to re-examine the nature of history as a discipline or collective means of actively ordering our investigation and knowledge of past worlds. The remarks I shall make on these questions build on the arguments developed in preceding chapters.

Persons and politics

Let us start with the question which is at the heart of most analyses of value freedom: the personal views and prejudices of the individual historian. The debates between Carr and Elton revolved in no small measure around the personal views of each – the one radically left-wing, the other an archetypal conservative. In a sense, their respective contributions to the debate are symptoms rather than resolutions of the issues.

Generally, historical writing is treated as a largely individual enterprise: the solution to the problem of 'bias' – as it is often phrased – is held to consist in exhortations to personal confession. In other words, the historian is generally asked to make some confession about his or her private moral and political views, in the light of which the subsequent account can be read. Injunctions to put personal prejudices aside for the duration of the historical research and writing are held to be more or less sufficient with respect to signalling (and hence on some views neutralising) any possible effects of bias. Hence Carr's injunction: before you read the history, know the historian.

This is of course important as a prerequisite. But there is more to be said about this issue; and there are further questions at stake, which are often overlooked entirely. It seems to me that we need to distinguish between, and analyse more closely, at least five respects in which the position, experience, and views of the individual historian are relevant to the nature of the historical accounts produced. These may be summarised as:

1   Empathy versus sympathy;
2   Insider knowledge: the 'worm's-eye view', or the question of 'privileged access';
3   Emotional investment, or partisanship in the production of any given account;
4   Honesty, dishonesty, 'bias' in the strong sense, and sheer blindness;
5   The choice of theoretical approach or paradigm for 'extrinsic' reasons.

Although they are all interrelated, it will be helpful to discuss them separately. The last, in particular, will be treated in a separate section of its own.

First, there is the question of 'understanding' the mindsets or mentalities of, or 'feeling with', particular protagonists in any given historical situation. The distinction between sympathy (meaning that the historian engages with a certain viewpoint or experience with a sense of personal identification and positive understanding) and 'empathy' (meaning that the historian seeks to understand, but not necessarily also evaluate positively) is often misunderstood even by prominent and experienced historians. As we saw in Chapter 8, the question of 'voice' was a key issue in the German historians' dispute of 1986–7, and in the debates in the 1990s over Goldhagen's analysis of the alleged 'eliminationist anti-Semitism' of the Germans; it is also a key issue in much identity history on gender and ethnicity. Yet emotional engagement, or 'sympathy', is arguably not what should be at stake here. Rather, the historian should use 'empathy' as a neutral tool – what Weber called 'interpretive understanding' – to try to 'get inside' the mentalities of key protagonists in the historical situation. Empathy should be viewed as a neutral tool for understanding mentalities, quite unrelated to that of the sympathy or otherwise of the historian with the motives and ideas of those whose views he or she is trying to understand. And this is so even for those historians who wish ultimately to support the cause for one or another side, although there are complications here to which we shall return.

Related to this question is the much misunderstood issue of 'who can write whose history'. On some views, this is a key question: for example, following the East German revolution of 1989–90, some East German historians argued that former communist fellow travellers should not be entitled (or at least should not hold paid positions giving them the time and means) to write the history of the GDR. Others sought to make sharp distinctions between the analyses 'imposed' by westerners with no personal experience of the GDR, and the more 'authentic' (if deeply divided) memories of those who had lived through it. Much of the thrust of post-colonialism has to do with disentangling the ways in which the colonists have talked about and interacted with the colonised, and asking (in the words of one of its prominent exponents, Spivak) 'can the subaltern speak?'[4] Similar arguments, with local variations, have raged in the area of African-American history, while some feminists have argued the need to reconceptualise women's history in terms which have not, at least hitherto, been part of the standard repertoire of male historians.

Extreme versions of this view are (rightly) dismissed at length by Richard J. Evans, who highlights the absurdity of the notion that the histories of particular groups or topics can only be written by historians belonging to, or for particular personal reasons strongly identifying with, the group or topic about which they are writing (or, conversely – a point Evans fails to make – that 'unbiased' history could never be written by someone belonging to the group in question). Taken to its most ludicrous extreme, this would in the end imply that all a historian could ever write was his or her autobiography. More seriously, such a view implies that 'interpretive understanding' is only truly possible within certain limited group parameters, whether these be defined in ethnic, class, gender or political terms. The implicit claim is hence made that there can be no shared lines of communication, of understanding, across such boundaries – a position which serves merely to sustain artificially constructed barriers between groups, and a sad conclusion about the condition of being human, however variable 'humanity' may be over time, social and geographical location. But there are some further serious aspects to this question which are worth making explicit here, and it is worth for a moment giving these positions a fair hearing and trying to consider what is at stake in such claims. It seems to me that there are some potentially important issues involved, and that these can or should be addressed in other ways.

A key underlying element in these views is the claim to 'insider knowledge', or 'privileged access' to some aspect of the experience (along the lines of 'only someone who has been through this sort of experience can know what it is really like'). This is a claim both about the authenticity of understanding, and about the extent or depth of knowledge of a certain experience or issue. In the case of the 'insider writer', there may be a peculiar wealth and depth of knowledge and understanding of particular traditions, or of a particular milieu, by saturation over a life-time. But this is essentially, in methodological terms, little more than a variant of extended 'participant observation' (however unwilling and unintentional) – and, it is worth pointing out, a form of participant observation which may have been blunted by virtue of not having the initial 'outsider' perspective through which to observe and acquire denser understanding. In any event, the principle is clear: an 'outsider' historian should be able to develop other means of acquiring such understanding and knowledge, if the 'methodology' of the accident of ethnicity, gender, class or place did not happen, retroactively, to be available to him or her. Journalists have often made use of techniques such as self-disguise to gain access to the experiences of others, as exemplified by the white American John Howard Griffin's immersion as a 'black' in the American black community, or the German journalist Günther Wallraff's account of life disguised as an immigrant Turkish worker or *Gastarbeiter* in West Germany.[5] The very fact that such techniques are not generally available to historians of past societies points up a key issue which may be uncomfortable for some of the proponents of this view to acknowledge: namely, that it is vital to be aware of precisely what claims are being made here. There may ironically be an incipient racism or sexism, however unintentional, in claims along the lines that only blacks, or women, can 'really understand' the position of their 'forebears' in the eighteenth or nineteenth centuries, irrespective of the vast historical and cultural gulfs across the centuries in contrast to the commonalities of contemporary life.

We then find ourselves back with our old friends, sympathy and empathy, discussed more generally above. It is important to note that even the 'privileged insider' would have to deploy this tool with respect to other groups in the given historical configuration: such as the mentalities of the white plantation owners, in the case of the history of African-American slaves written by a descendant; or the mentalities and actions of the capitalist classes, in the case of a Marxist sympathiser with the struggles of the oppressed proletariat; feminists, it might be pointed out, were quicker off the mark with respect to recognising the need to analyse constructions of masculinity rather than writing only 'women's history'. Equally, when we look at contemporary history, it is worth remembering that the 'worm's eye view' from a particular vantage point on the ground is not necessarily always as illuminating as the 'bird's eye view' from a detached position soaring in the skies above; it may merely provide one among many possible starting points. Comprehensive accounts will need knowledge of more than merely that which was haphazardly acquired by 'living through it all'; survivors' tales are often only a tiny part of the kind of picture that needs to be reconstructed in order to understand why they were in the position they were.

There is a further question to do with emotional involvement, or partisanship in the sense of the purpose of writing a particular account. If the 'purpose' is to construct a 'positive sense of identity and pride in our heritage', then again there is an issue which needs to be faced quite explicitly. There is little point in constructing tales of heroes if the historical account is not adequate on other grounds. The question of aims in representing the past in a certain way should be kept distinct from that of how one explores this history: emotional engagement with one party in the struggles should not preclude the possibility of comprehensive and relatively open-minded research (bearing in mind more serious qualifications we shall come to in a moment) of the whole situation. If anything, it should even sharpen determination to uncover the complexities of the context.

This brings us back, then, to the issue of honesty, dishonesty, or sheer blind spots because of the assumptions and attitudes with which one starts – the issue which has perhaps been most exhaustively discussed in most analyses of 'value-neutrality' or 'objectivity'. It is of course important, indeed crucial, to emphasise the role of what might be called the active practice of disinterested honesty in historical research. Haskell, for example, quite rightly praises the virtues of asceticism, as far as historical work is concerned:

> The very possibility of historical scholarship as an enterprise distinct from propaganda requires of its practitioners that vital minimum of ascetic self-discipline that enables a person to do such things as abandon wishful thinking, assimilate bad news, discard pleasing interpretations that cannot pass elementary tests of evidence and logic, and, most important of all, suspend or bracket one's own perceptions long enough to enter sympathetically into the alien and possibly repugnant perspectives of rival thinkers.

Haskell goes on to point out that most of us (probably even including postmodernists) have absolutely no problem with such a concept of 'objectivity' in everyday life:

> although the ideal of objectivity has been most fully and formally developed by scholars and serves importantly to legitimise their work, it was not invented by them and in fact pervades the world of everyday life. As I see it, the ideal is tacitly invoked (sometimes as a test, sometimes in a gesture of blind faith) every time anyone opens a letter, picks up a newspaper, walks into a courtroom, or decides which of two squabbling children to believe. All of us, professional or not, invoke the ideal every time we choose between conflicting interpretations with confidence that they are not simply different, but that one is *superior* to the others, superior as a representation of the way things are.[6]

This is of course important, and relates closely to Weber's discussion of 'leaving one's values at the door of the inquiry'.

Many recent controversies about 'objectivity' have indeed revolved in large part around assessing the degree to which there was dishonesty or wilful distortion of the 'facts' as a result of the historian's own political or other views. Thus the controversy about David Abraham's Marxist interpretation of the collapse of Weimar democracy – which ultimately cost him an initially promising career as an academic historian in the United States – involved discussion of whether Abraham's errors were the result merely of scholarly sloppiness, undue haste, lack of experience in taking notes in the archives, lack of a clear system for distinguishing between direct quotation and paraphrase in his own notes, and so on; or whether he was wilfully selective and distorted the evidence to fit a theory to which he was committed on grounds of left-wing political conviction.[7] Similarly, the David Irving case against Penguin Books and Deborah Lipstedt developed into an argument about whether Lipstedt's accusations of historical distortion by Holocaust deniers were grounded; the judge found that, indeed, Irving had wilfully misrepresented the Nazi past in the light of all the evidence.

If this were all that needed to be said about questions of objectivity and value-neutrality in history, life would be quite simple. We need only all be honest, ascetic, hard-working, sensitively attuned to the mentalities and experiences of others, and we could go away and write good history. Unfortunately, however, there is much more to be said about this topic.

Haskell himself is well aware that this is not the whole story: he also quite explicitly reminds the reader that 'facts only take shape under the aegis of paradigms, presuppositions, theories and the like';[8] but he does not, in this context, take us any further down the road we now need to pursue. Richard J. Evans barely even goes this far. He provides the following robust injunction: 'While historians are certainly swayed, consciously or unconsciously, by present moral or political purposes in carrying out their work, it is not the validity or desirability of these, but the extent to which their historical arguments conform to the rules of evidence and the facts on which they rest, by which they must stand or fall in the end. In other words, they have to be objective . . .'[9] This is all fair enough, and indeed very laudable as far as individual approaches to history go. Unfortunately, however, it does not quite go far enough. In the end, Evans simply reaffirms his own faith in the 'usual rules of evidence', and 'the facts on which they rest'. His attempt to examine 'the meaning and validity of [the] problematical concept' of objectivity rapidly collapses into a series of characteristically sharp comments on selected books, rather than a sustained theoretical argument focussed on the issues. Having surveyed the self-contradictory and essentially unfounded character of postmodernist assertions, and brought to our attention the hideous possibilities if we go down the road of postmodernist relativism (where fascist interpretations are in principle as valid as democratic ones), Evans concludes with a simple re-assertion of his own belief in the possibility of looking 'humbly at the past' and saying 'it really happened, and we really can, if we are very scrupulous and careful and self-critical, find out how it happened and reach some tenable though always less than final conclusions about what it all meant'.[10] Such reassertion of faith in 'the facts' – against such obvious soft targets and straw men as Holocaust deniers – does little to reconstruct the broader theoretical foundations of history. It simply redefines the issue as one of falsification of 'the evidence'. This totally misses many of the points made by, for example, Hayden White, concerning the possible construction of a wide variety of narratives on the basis of individually 'true' facts or incontrovertible single statements about the past.[11]

An emphasis on the honesty of the individual historian is of course important; similarly, injunctions not to falsify, distort, or select 'evidence' are of course well taken. But these injunctions seem to me to entirely miss some more fundamental problems, and to propose what is only a partial solution to the problem. Where there are different explanations of the same phenomenon, none of which can be seen to be obviously 'distorting the truth' (in the simple sense referred to by Richard Evans, such as denial of certain generally agreed events, omission of inconvenient facts, misinterpretation of evidence, representation out of context, and so on), we face a rather more difficult problem. There are, in short, other factors which complicate the picture of the honest, ascetic historian in earnest pursuit of the truth. Much more problematic – or at least, more difficult to resolve – than the individual biases of the historian are questions concerning competing paradigms, or cultural idioms of inquiry.

Paradigms and politics

The more difficult problem to resolve in connection with politics is not so much that of personal bias or, worse, dishonesty, but rather the filtration of individual preferences through another, more collective level: that of choice of paradigm of interpretation. The latter will, in turn, influence what are deemed to be the relevant questions to be asked, the hypotheses to be explored, the concepts through which 'facts' will be constructed, the evaluation of evidence, and so on. It is, in other words, not so much persons as paradigms that are at stake here – presupposing of course that we are talking about persons who operate as honestly as they can within a given framework of interpretation, and that we are talking about frameworks of interpretation which are deemed, at least in our current (very broadly defined) intellectual context to be at least legitimate contenders as historical paradigms.

We can see the ways in which political sympathies work in practice in a wide number of historical approaches. Many examples have been given in preceding chapters: the tendency of conservative historians to opt for 'traditional' narrative forms, and a substantive focus on individual motives and actions, particularly in the arena of 'high politics', as contrasted with left-wing historians' general preference for collective actors (classes), a focus on structure rather than agency (socio-economic conditions rather than 'great men'), and so on.

Some historians even seem quite ready to admit to a degree of subjectivity and personal preference, often based on political or 'identity' criteria, in deciding among such competing theoretical approaches. This does little for any claim to be 'telling the truth about history'. Thus Appleby, Hunt and Jacobs (whose book title I have just quoted) seek to replace the dichotomy of 'objective truth' versus 'subjective relativism' with one of 'practical realism'. They redefine 'historical objectivity as an interactive relationship between an inquiring subject and an external object'.[12] Having made these quite sensible theoretical claims, they go on to celebrate the diversity of approaches in contemporary history as a version of what might be called professional multi-culturalism, suggesting that, ultimately, only political or identity sympathies can determine which account one prefers.

This may, in my view, work quite well when what we are dealing with are what I have called, in Chapter 3, 'perspectival paradigms'. We can be perfectly happy with a notion of a multiplicity of theoretical approaches and diverse possible 'end points' of history in which different readers might be differently interested (social history approaches to the history of slavery and civil rights movements, witchcraft epidemics, Puritan settlements in New England, interactions between native peoples and colonials, and so on) and which might be perfectly compatible with other approaches and accounts of concurrent trends (economic histories of aspects of American capitalism, or narrative high politics accounts of American presidencies, diplomacy, foreign policy), which, if treated appropriately, could be held to amount additively to what is generally called a 'more comprehensive picture'. But, as we have seen, the 'multi-cultural' notion works less well when we are dealing rather with a clash of 'paradigms proper', when even the very subject matter – the constitution of individual or collective actors, the assumptions about forces and motors of history – may be construed differently. Fundamental disagreements about such issues as class versus culture (as in different interpretations of racism), or about the meaning of more abstract concepts such as 'resistance', or the construction of cases for comparison – or indeed the very legitimacy of comparative analysis at all – cumulatively pose more serious problems for this kind of 'let a thousand flowers bloom' approach. (Unless of course one has no problems about simultaneously accepting mutually contradictory approaches – the search for a potentially unifiable, if extraordinarily comprehensive, account may be a peculiarly modern western goal.) When the ultimate resting place for an explanation is held to be variously economic, or social, political, or ideological, or psychological, depending on the theoretical framework and wider informing assumptions of any particular historian, and the explanations are proferred in a spirit of competition and mutual rivalry, then we have something of a problem – or at least a controversy.

When this kind of fundamental difference in categories of inquiry and type of explanation or understanding is at stake, what do we do? Some historians explicitly allow political preferences back in as a legitimate arbiter. Ludmilla Jordanova, for example, explicitly embraces a subjective element in historical evaluation, rejecting the notion of 'truth' in favour of 'trust'. Using competing explanations of the French Revolution as an example, she argues that:

> The significant issue is, [not truth but] rather, trust, which can be established in a variety of ways. In the end, however, the decision whether to trust an individual, an institution, a source or a historical account depends on weighing up a number of factors and *making a final judgement based on previous experience, political preferences and so on*. Hence, competing accounts of the French Revolution cannot simply be evaluated according to purely rational criteria. The historian's assessment of them will necessarily depend on such issues as whether they are predisposed to be critical of the *ancien régime* or sympathetic to the difficulties of the French monarchy, to see class at the root of the

political turmoil, to consider the revolution a progressive process, the harbinger of the modern order, or an eruption of unnecessary brutality . . . In making a final judgement on a historical account, the degree of trust it elicits in us is crucial.[13]

Thus, on this view, ultimately what determines our preference for one historical account over another is personal political and emotional identification.[14] If we are prepared to follow Jordanova in saying that we can choose to opt for any particular explanation of the origins of the French Revolution in the light of our own political and moral preferences, we might as well concede that history, in the end, boils down at least in part to ideology.

If we are not prepared to accept this, then we have to think much harder, not only about individual honesty or dishonesty (the Richard Evans approach), but also about the compatibility or otherwise of competing paradigms, and the reasons why certain theoretical or methodological approaches tend to get associated with one or another position on the political spectrum.

There are intrinsic reasons, which have in part been discussed in many of the preceding chapters. For example, competing theoretical approaches may be premised on fundamentally different assumptions about the nature of being human; about the relationships between individual attitudes and motives, on the one hand, and social and political circumstances on the other; about the relationships between what are presumed to be 'real' class interests, and cultural frameworks of interpretation; and so on. These could be summarised as revolving, in some way, around issues of alternative philosophical anthropologies, on which historians do not all agree. For example, some historians will be perfectly willing to treat as a historical given what to them are alien religious views, the significance of which can be explored without making any comment on their validity or otherwise; while other historians will continue to view such beliefs as reducible (if only 'in the last instance') to something else (such as presumed material interests, or the effects of a dominant ideology).

Why do budding historians land up in one rather than another theoretical camp? Clearly personal beliefs, of the sort just mentioned, will have something to do with it. A committed Christian is unlikely to accept all of the assumptions of the Marxist framework, however much he or she may agree on the importance of social class analysis as one element among many. There are also what might be called 'extrinsic' reasons, to do with the particular institutional, political and social 'situatedness' of different historical professions at different times. Paradigms are, as we have seen, to some extent, 'language communities' of scholars sharing certain socialisation experiences and conforming to common institutional values. Once a particular theoretical approach has become firmly associated with a particular subculture or 'school', students are likely to gravitate towards that with which they feel most comfortable for a wide range of reasons, not all of which may be purely intellectual. Peer group pressure is as evident in the recurrent cycles of historical fashion – the successive stampedes into and again out of neo-Marxism, societal history, structuralism, post-structuralism, 'new cultural history', the 'linguistic turn', and so on – as it is in other areas of life. There is also an element of exploration involved: a good idea or approach may be worth pursuing, investigating, thinking through, applying, extending, critiquing – and then jettisoning as the conversations move on. And this is even before we add in the question of what substantive topics or questions 'about the real world' are uppermost or seen as the most urgent, pressing, interesting, at different times.

The tendency for competing paradigms to be associated with different political subcultures (for want of a better expression) is one which can be observed empirically, but with a relatively wide range of variation, particularly in institutional settings where a range of approaches coexist quite peacefully (and one has to ask why, occasionally, historical tempers flare up). There is, in short, not an absolute and intrinsic relationship between politics and paradigms, with the possible exception of Marxism. One does not necessarily have to be 'left-wing' to be interested in social history, 'right-wing' to be interested in narratives of high politics, however much these may have been conflated in practice. The Jordanova answer about the French Revolution is, thus, not entirely adequate. Sympathy with particular protagonists or outcomes is not what is (or should be) at issue in choosing among paradigms. Before we return more explicitly to this question, however, we need more directly to shift our attention away from the individual level of the personal identities and biases of the historian discussed above, to the wider profiles of those groups producing competing historical accounts in different sociopolitical situations.

Historians as gatekeepers and tour guides to the past

If the past is a foreign country, we should ask the question: who issues the visas, who constructs the itineraries, and who brings back what snapshots?

There are complex links here between intellectual history, on the one hand, and, on the other, the sociopolitical history of the institutional landscape promoting, supporting, marginalising or excluding those doing particular types of history. Without wishing to reduce the question of paradigms to some sort of sociology of knowledge, it is nevertheless worth explicitly reminding ourselves that the discipline of history is, too, a part of the contemporary world and is in some considerable measure shaped by the circumstances in which historical knowledge is produced and received. This will readily become clear if we look briefly at a few examples.

The 'worst', or most obvious, cases of bias are of course to be found in the case of historical professions under dictatorships. The character of such regimes has strong influences on personnel, on topics and themes for research and teaching, and on frameworks of interpretation. Quite obviously, for example, those historians in the Third Reich who were not prepared to conform to the broad conservative-nationalist aims of the regime (without necessarily going down the full road of Nazi racism), and those whose own personal 'biological credentials' were unacceptable to the Nazis (such as Jews), were more or less rapidly excluded from the profession. Those who remained had to pay at least lip-service to the aims and concepts of a racist state, and in some cases adopted and internalised the whole conceptual framework of Social Darwinism, which had, in any event, pre-Nazi intellectual roots. A quite different form of conformity was soon imposed in the German Democratic Republic, the dictatorship which succeeded the Third Reich on East German soil. Those 'bourgeois' historians who had survived across the great divides of 1933 and 1945 found, in the course of the 1950s, that their positions became ever more tenuous under the new circumstances of a Marxist-Leninist state. By the mid- to later 1960s, the new orthodoxy of writing history in terms of the great heroic struggles of the labouring classes had taken hold in the self-proclaimed 'workers' and peasants' state' (*Arbeiter- und Bauernstaat*). Accounts (even, in the later 1970 and 1980s, of 'great men' such as Bismarck or Frederick the Great, or previously denigrated cultural movements such as the Lutheran Reformation) had to be framed in terms of the progressive history of class struggles, within the broader Marxist-Leninist framework. The correspondence between the ideological bias of the preferred historical paradigms and the (contrasting) political ideologies of these two dictatorships iss too obvious to require further discussion.

What is less immediately apparent to the naked eye, however, particularly for those fortunate enough to be able to take political democracies for granted, is the extent to which institutional and political circumstances affect the development of the more variegated historical professions even in democratic states. We can see this in all manner of aspects: in, for example, the social and gender profile of those in different levels of the professional hierarchy; the topics and types of questions asked in historical research, or considered to be important enough to be put on the syllabuses of schools and universities; and the public reception of different aspects of and slants on selected historical topics.

Let us stick for a moment with the German example, and glance at some key features of post-war West German historiography, with an eye for what one might call the interrelations between contexts and texts. There was remarkably little sustained turnover in the West German historical profession after 1945; many conformist conservative-nationalist historians (sometimes with intermissions for 'denazification') succeeded in retaining or regaining their jobs by the 1950s, or in finding, for example, editorial work which allowed them to continue making a contribution to the development of history.[15] These 'grand old men', largely socialised in the Wilhelmine and Weimar eras, held the rising generation of post-war historians for some time in relationships of apprenticeship, entailing both professional and financial dependence, and in large measure controlling choice of research topics and outlets for publication. It was not until the combination of generational turnover and expansion of the higher education system in the 1960s that a wider range of voices began to find paid positions, though the curious German system of 'political' appointments to chairs sustained a remarkably close alignment between political outlook and preferred theoretical and thematic approaches, and women remained in a tiny minority among the higher ranks.

There continued to be peculiarities with respect to the thematic concerns and theoretical approaches of the West German historical profession. The Nazi past posed particular problems: the Holocaust, for a long time virtually a taboo topic among historians, was surrounded by explosive sensitivities once it mushroomed onto the public stage of discussion in the 1970s and 1980s; and peculiar pieties surrounded discussion of resistance and opposition in Nazi Germany. The divided present also posed a problem: given the proximity of the GDR, Marxism was more or less not an option for left-wing historians in the Federal Republic in the way that it could be in, say, Britain. More generally, given a legacy of an official political culture of shame, it was all too easy for historical interpretations to be evaluated in the light of external criteria, such as whether or not they seemed to 'relativise' the Nazi past, whether or not there was something uniquely awful about German history (a 'special path' to modernity), and whether or not it was acceptable to attempt to harness historical consciousness for the construction of an acceptable national identity in the present. All these factors lent a peculiarly vitriolic and controversial character to West German historical debates, and stamped a political mark on different theoretical approaches. Thus for example the so-called Bielefeld School of societal history was always characterised as 'left-liberal', while the history of everyday life (*Alltagsgeschichte*) was held to be the stamping ground of those further to the left who, in other contexts, might have been tempted by Marxism; and gender history tended to be restricted to the tiny minority of women who succeeded in entering a highly male-dominated historical profession. The often very heated debates over approach and method characteristic of the West German historical profession tended to be almost unthinkingly, automatically, associated with personal and political differences.

Lest we be tempted by a sneaking suspicion that Germany has trodden a 'special path' in historiography as well as in history, it will be as well to remember that no modern historical profession is constituted entirely by, in Karl Mannheim's term, 'free-floating intellectuals'. In somewhat different outlines, and without some of the unique characteristics of the German case – the Nazi heritage, the national division – comparable stories can be told about the development of other historical professions. In Britain, there was perhaps a longer and broader tradition of institutional coexistence of opposing views: consider the fact that those two great sparring opponents of the 1960s, whose debates for decades held centre stage in discussions of 'the nature of history', Carr and Elton, both held distinguished positions in the University of Cambridge. But, with very broad brush strokes and much sideways muttering about qualifications and individual exceptions, we can still see some striking features of the development of historical approaches in Britain.

It has been said that 'traditional' (narrative, diplomatic and political) history was 'history written by men, for men, about men' (and, it might be added, usually only about, for and by upper-class men). It was in large part in protest against aspects of this (perspectival) paradigm that 'new' forms of approach emerged in the latter half of the twentieth century – social history, labour history, women's history, and so on – often supported and trumpeted by those considering themselves on the left of the political spectrum. Of course various forms of 'underdog' history were not entirely new in the latter half of the twentieth century: one has only to think of earlier writers such as G. D. H. Cole or Sidney and Beatrice Webb to realise that the emergence of the English working class was not a discovery of E. P. Thompson (although he provided a genuinely innovative perspective on its agency, or self-making). What was new in the British historiographical landscape of the later twentieth century was, rather, that there were perhaps more, and more diverse groups of, people engaged in historical research and writing. This was in part due to a number of inter-related contextual developments. There was the massive expansion of higher education, with the creation of the 'new universities' of the 1960s (not to be confused with the then polytechnics); the subsequent abolition of the 'binary divide' between universities and polytechnics in 1992 (at which point the former 'new' universities acquired overnight the status of 'old universities', as former polytechnics colonised the label of 'new'); the massive expansion of publications (in part fuelled by the government-driven research assessment exercises, prompting periodic explosions onto the printed page), and the associated proliferation of new outlets for publication in ever more specialised journals or periodicals. Alongside these expansionary trends went the often contested expansion and institutionalisation of relatively new perspectival paradigms, with sometimes less than polite debates about whether there should or should not be programmes and positions in, for example, 'women's studies' or 'cultural studies'. There was a professional culture in which a premium was placed, not only on the 'discovery of new facts', or 'filling gaps in our knowledge', but also on 'theoretical innovation', 'revisionism', the development of 'new approaches' and the like.

All this took place in a climate of what was euphemistically called 'research selectivity' and associated funding mechanisms, with a constant need to reassert values of academic freedom in face of preferences for one or another type and topic of research (with buzz words such as 'inter-disciplinarity' and 'collaboration' coming into favour as the flavour of the month at one time, 'relevance' to the wider community or the 'needs of the nation' at another). To this list might be added further dimensions: that of the public role (intended or unintended) played by different accounts; questions concerning the syllabuses to be followed by children in state schools, with the introduction of a uniform National Curriculum; debates over the relative importance of 'skills' versus 'facts', 'national heritage' versus 'multi-culturalism', and so on.

In short: even in a democracy with a relatively long tradition of public debate, the character and location of the historical profession is not irrelevant to the nature of the history produced.[16] The degree to which history is instrumentalised, appropriated, distorted, of course varies widely according to the specific political context (and perceived uses) of the production and reception of works of history. But it is worth pointing out that the contrast frequently drawn between the political instrumentalisation and often also distortion of history in former Soviet bloc states, on the one hand, and the supposedly 'objective' historical accounts produced in western democratic states, on the other, is often greatly exaggerated. What is more interesting, in some respects, is the issue of why and when history is actually held to be relevant by governments (of left or right), public bodies and funding institutions; what is deemed to be 'essential' with respect to teaching the rising generation of school and university students; and what the implications are for those who wish to pursue particular forms of historical inquiry. It is also worth noting that virtually all of this operates or functions at a collective level, rather than directly or only relating to the private views of individual historians.

The politics of history relates not only to producers, but also to consumers. As we have seen in Chapter 8, history is not only about the pursuit of the irretrievably lost past, but also about its reconstruction or representation in varying forms and for varying purposes in the present. As any analysis of aspects of 'collective memory' reveals, historical symbols and commemorations may arouse strong and often conflicting emotions in the present. Professional historians play widely differing roles in such popular presentations of the past, ranging from the serious involvement in the making of major historical television series by historians of the stature of Ian Kershaw and Simon Schama, through acting as advisers to historical museums and exhibitions, to minor advisory roles. The point here, however, is that at some stage the reception of a historical representation (whether through film, theatre, television documentary; or museum, memorial, commemoration) and its transformation into 'historical consciousness' takes on a life of its own, divorced from the biases of the historian(s) associated with it.

The character of the audience is thus to some extent an element of the equation, in terms of the effects of historical accounts. Let us just consider briefly that very old 'history', the story of Abraham and Isaac in the Old Testament. Part of the anguish and pathos in the receipt of the story by a modern audience is precisely in the terrible disjuncture between what Abraham is about to do – to sacrifice his only son because he believes that is what God has commanded him to do – and how a modern audience reacts to this situation. The vast majority of contemporary westerners (including committed Christians) would probably have doubts in their own minds, on reading this story, as to whether Abraham was not simply deluded in believing that God had commanded him to do such a terrible thing, particularly in the face of the earlier promises made by God to Abraham about founding a great nation. They might go on to think Abraham was suffering further delusions on hearing an angel telling him not to sacrifice his son, after all, and seeing a convenient ram caught by the horns in the bushes, which could be sacrificed in place of Isaac. Nor do contemporary readers of the account live in a culture where child sacrifice to appease the Gods is common.

We could take many examples closer to hand. But I use this example, not because I think the story exemplifies the sort of works which pass as historical accounts today, but rather because the enormous gulf between the assumptions of the storyteller and the readership in this case points up in particularly acute form the ways in which the meaning and impact of a story can vary according to the context of reception.

The extent and limits of objectivity

Wherein, then, lies 'objectivity'? It is often argued that objectivity resides, not in the work itself, nor in the mind of the historian, but solely in the context of the discussion: in the conditions of pluralism, the multiplicity of perspectives which can engage in mutual and tolerant debate. It is argued that, on this basis, there is at least a collective (if not necessarily individual) openness to change in the light of new arguments and evidence.

However, this view seems to me inadequate for a number of reasons. For one thing, even in the supposedly 'free market' of ideas, there is no reason in principle why an idea that happens to win the democratic vote, as it were, is necessarily more 'true' than an idea which is less popular or receives less powerful backing in any given context. On the contrary, in fact: ideas popular at one time (such as 'racial superiority') may be deeply unpopular at another; powerful backers of certain views may be no more privy to 'the truth' about the past than are minorities or subordinate groups; the blasts and counter-blasts of journal warfare may simply end in mutual exhaustion and a moving on to other topics rather than any definitive resolution of the issues at stake. The appeal to a notional 'free market place of ideas' is something of a classic American (or capitalist?) way out of the real underlying issues; in principle little different from, if in practice infinitely preferable to, the communist notion of the Party as the vanguard Guardian of Truth against an all-pervading False Consciousness.

In short: we have a problem which has frequently (at least among non-Marxist historians) been stated in the following terms. The individual historian inevitably suffers from (or at least is influenced by) his or her own private political and moral views. These should be stated explicitly and thus to some extent neutralised. The answer to the problem is not that we should ask of historians the impossible, namely to shed their views; but that we should duly take this influence into account, and then let battle reign in the public arena of debate and controversy. Somehow, in this cut-and-thrust of controversy, it is held that The Truth will out; and that, irrespective of differences in personal viewpoint, there are shared rules, procedures, criteria of evidence, by which any account is to be judged, regardless of the author's own prejudices.

However, in this context it is worth reminding ourselves that there are some very serious 'internal' issues concerning how we choose between competing paradigms which are more or less closely associated with different political colourings. In particular there are serious questions concerning: the ways in which paradigms affect questions and concepts, which in turn highlight and filter what is significant about the past; the use of empathy and interpretive understanding for exploring facets of past lives and translating these to the present; and the character of writing, or other forms of representation, to different audiences in the present. Thus, Weber was wrong in assuming that values end with the selection of the problem. They are intrinsically implicated in the initial appropriation of a metatheoretical framework, or paradigm; in the employment of associated concepts and categories of analysis, including both 'theory-drenched concepts' and 'essentially contested concepts', or concepts over which there can in principle be no agreement; and in the way in which the story is told, its re-presentation, with related questions of emplotment, characterisation, the identification of heroes and villains, the evocation of sympathies, the relation to identity claims in the present, and the construction of traditions – as discussed above.

Secondly, we have to remember that, even within any putative 'free market place of ideas' – were one really to exist or persist – such debates would be capable of some rational resolution only within the parameters of a common language community or paradigm, and in the context of shared wider presuppositions about the relations between the individual and society, structure/agency, and so on. There has to be a shared commitment to the possibility of revising concepts and hypotheses in the light of what is mutually agreed to be an appropriate empirical test or appropriate evidence. The 'facts' unfortunately do not always 'speak for themselves'. If there are alternative paradigms coexisting, there is no particular intrinsic reason why a 'free market place' should do anything other than ensure (or at least permit or remove barriers to) the availability in principle of a plurality of perspectives. It could foster the conditions for debate and development of a variety of ideas and approaches. But in no way is pluralism necessarily a route to or guarantee of 'objectivity', let alone 'truth'.

The real issues, thus, relate to the arguments developed in earlier chapters with respect to the relative openness of certain paradigms and concepts for revision, extension, jettisoning, as part of a tolerant collective conversation about the past, and the mutual translation, however imperfect, across different mental worlds.

In relation to the views of some postmodernists, I have sought in preceding chapters to argue for the importance of the 'real world out there' which can empirically 'answer back', limit and refine what explanations and concepts are or are not viable, in the light of the essentially neo-Kantian viewpoint developed above. But this can only be done within the framework of given paradigms of inquiry. There is, in short, no way of escaping the 'hermeneutic circle' – of achieving a standpoint entirely outside all paradigms, from which they can, in some Olympian way, be judged. Note, incidentally, that even the framework of paradigms in which I am discussing these questions is in some senses itself a paradigm, with its own set of questions and concepts and assumptions.

It is, however, possible, in a limited sense, to provide a set of more differentiated answers to the question about the extent and limits of value neutrality in history (though these answers will not necessarily resolve the question of its desirability). I would now refine the Weberian model of value freedom as follows.

Insofar as choice of paradigms and associated purposes of inquiry and forms of representation are affected by politics, then political considerations directly or indirectly affect the following aspects of historical inquiry:

1   the questions posed;
2   the character(s) of the group(s) empowered to search for the answers;
3   the frameworks of inquiry chosen;
4   the associated concepts in terms of which the 'empirical evidence' is sought (there is no such thing as 'the facts' which are in some way innocent, 'naked', prior to, or outside, a prior framework of interpretation – hence there are real problems of the theoretical filtration of what is to count as a 'fact');
5   even the methodology or 'rules' through which explanations and interpretations are sought;
6   the choice of style, presentation, intended audience – and, to some degree, the reception of historical accounts by the latter.

The only level which seems to be relatively unaffected by political considerations is a level of internal reasoning somewhere between the choice of questions and concepts, on the one hand, and the production of answers, valid within a particular paradigm, on the other. So we might conclude the following:

If we can agree on a (situated, historically specific) conceptual framework, *then* we can at least in principle agree on the results of the analysis; or at least on what would be relevant criteria ('in the light of further research') for deciding between different views on any given controversy, for which all the (relevant, pre-defined) material might not be readily available at the time of debate. But, equally, we might still disagree on the purposes and manner of the presentation of the results of the inquiry; we may, for example, disagree over whether all Holocaust representations should or should not be couched in particularly emotive terms, to warn, remind, and so on; whether it is doing a disservice to those who were victims and those touched by their fates, even distorting the historical events, to attempt to retain a dry-as-dust academic manner of scholarly discussion, or whether this is not a crucial prerequisite for moving beyond a restraining plane of emotionalism. (I use this example again because there are more likely to be large numbers of people willing to concede a degree of force to the arguments on both sides, unlike more straightforward politically divisive issues.)

But I started the last paragraph with a rather large 'if'. When we look again at particular differences in approach – such as those between historians emphasising structure, in whatever version, and those emphasising individual motives and action – the area of metaparadigmatic agreement may be less; similarly, what serves to satisfy curiosity may differ quite widely. For an intentionalist, 'the (explanatory) buck stops' with Hitler's anti-Semitism, his fanaticism, personality traits, and personal power; for a functionalist, it comes to rest only with examination of the enabling context in the peculiar, ever more radical conditions of war-time and the ever more chaotic power struggles, with underlings competing to carry out the Führer's will, 'working towards the Führer'. The story will, in short, be told differently; the ultimate burden of explanation will come to rest in different places.

Thus, it is not sufficient for the author/observer simply to declare his or her private political standpoints before embarking on analysis. Historical research is a collective endeavour, situated (like its subject matter) in specific social and political circumstances. The issue of objectivity is not only a personal one, of individual bias or the temptation to 'distort the evidence'; we are not dealing only with questions of dishonesty, falsification, fabrication, misrepresentation, as in the case of the Irving trial. We are also dealing with the character of history as a set of language communities, historically situated collective endeavours. The more difficult problems have to do with these collective frameworks of inquiry, which are in part – but not entirely – coloured by political considerations and sympathies. It is these theoretical approaches which provide the mediating level between 'the historian', on the one hand, and 'the evidence' or 'the facts', on the other.

Let me start another paragraph with a big 'if'. *If* we are looking for the broadest extent of 'objectivity', *then* the honesty and personal views of the individual historian are not all that is at stake. The theoretical and conceptual apparatus must be as transparent and as open to dialogue and reasoned amendment as the research methodology and empirical subject matter more narrowly defined. This may be possible to a greater or lesser extent depending on what sort of paradigm and conceptual apparatus is deployed; as indicated in preceding chapters, some are more readily translatable, or open to development and change, than others; some levels are more compatible with competing frameworks than others. And the bottom line is that, while many paradigms (such as those I have called perspectival paradigms) are in principle far more compatible with one another than their practitioners might occasionally like to concede, others (particularly certain 'paradigms proper') are divided by vast and empirically unbridgeable gulfs. Some of these chasms have been indicated in preceding chapters: views on the social construction of individual or collective identities, on the nature of belief systems, on the relative importance of 'deep structures' versus 'surface appearances', are but some of the issues resting ultimately on different kinds of anthropological assumption which are scarcely amenable to any straightforward form of empirical refutation or rational persuasion.

The question then arises of how much, if at all, these considerations matter. If we can accept that there will never be a fixed, universally accepted, historical Table of the Elements *à la* natural science, we could simply accept historical interpretations as just another form of creative interpretation – part of the human condition and human endeavours to make sense of an ever-changing position in the world. And for those who reject the 'if' with which the last paragraph began, the pursuit of history may be an integral, indeed essential, part of political projects in the present. But a word of caution is in order here for those who want to adopt these positions. It is perhaps even more important for those who want to use history for contemporary ends to arrive at interpretations which are in some respects 'accurate', which represent the past in ways which can be engaged with and potentially amended by those of other perspectives; otherwise, to adopt a quite utilitarian attitude, actions based on inadequate interpretations will be less likely to succeed.

This does not preclude the possibility of saying that, however things have been seen in the past, they can be seen differently in the future: that, for example, the roles of women, blacks, other previously marginalised groups, can be radically reconceived; and that historical reconstruction is an integral part of such reconceptualisation. Nor does it preclude a recognition that the ways in which we think, and the things we choose to think about, affect our collective actions and range of possible futures. In these senses, historical inquiries and representations inevitably are and remain intrinsically political.

I do not pretend to have resolved these knotty issues. But I think it is worth at least proposing that we think about them in this somewhat more differentiated manner, which goes beyond the level of individual bias and dishonesty and examines more fully the various levels and possibilities of historical research as a collective endeavour. Nevertheless this chapter will conclude with a set of questions.

What if the choice of paradigm is uncoupled from political connotations? What if historians finally have the courage to query the almost automatic linking of certain approaches to certain positions on the political spectrum? What if a frontal assault is launched on unexamined notions that it is 'left-wing' to look for social and economic forces, 'right-wing' or 'traditional' to write accounts in terms of individual motives and intentions, 'postmodern' to prioritise a metanarrative of chaos over the search for ordered explanations? What if the practice of history abandons tidal waves of fashion, and refocusses on questions and the pursuit of answers? Is it indeed possible to overcome deep divisions on fundamental questions of philosophical anthropology? And what implications do answers – or failures to find answers – to these questions have for the nature of historical inquiry?

10

CONCLUSION

Partial histories

Historical accounts are both potentially infinite in number, and yet at the same time subject to the possibility of disconfirmation. History is both an art and a science (in the loose sense of the latter word). History involves creative leaps of the imagination; but it is at the same time a discipline characterised by collective discourses with a variety of concepts, questions, methods, procedures, and standards of evaluation. And, for all the differences of approach across paradigms, even if we cannot agree on 'supra-paradigmatic' or 'theory-neutral' criteria for evaluating competing accounts, we can at least attain some clarity about the issues involved in deciding for one approach over another. We are not, in short, left with history as fiction. Nor do we have to buy into a notion of one single historical truth to be able to develop ways of rationally deciding between competing accounts of selected aspects of the past; rejecting a notion of progress in history does not simultaneously entail rejecting a notion of progress in historical understanding.

History; seeing through a glass, darkly?

We have seen, in Part I, some competing views on the nature of history. While some claim history to be a form of transparent window on the past, others see it rather as a picture, constructed in the present, replacing a past which we can never really know. If one must resort to metaphors, I would prefer that of 'seeing through a glass, darkly', to adopt the biblical phrase (where the contrast is with seeing 'face to face').[1] Alternatively, one might resort to the metaphor of looking down into murky, rippled water and watching fish swimming in and out of view, of which one only catches glimpses and with which one cannot very sensibly communicate, but about which one can nevertheless say quite a lot (and actually historians can probably talk with more understanding about the actions of fellow humans in the past than they can about the imputed meanings of the actions of fish). The question, however, is not so much what metaphor one chooses to summarise the nature of history, but rather how one explicates this in detail.

I have sought in this book to present some of the parameters that are, I think, inescapable and perennial issues for all historians. There is no possibility of evasion of historical theory. But at the same time, there is no reason why an awareness of theoretical issues should lead one into an obsessive fascination with them to the extent that – having realised there can be no perfect mimetic representation of the past – one gives up any attempt to explore that past and bring versions, interpretations, fragments to the present. There is no reason why one cannot pose questions, pursue puzzles, seek to develop solutions, and represent them in appealing and accessible ways for the benefit of those who do not have the means or luxury of being able to go exploring for themselves. And, if one accepts this, then one can also present a few criteria which are, admittedly, professional criteria developed in a particular time and a particular place, but which are at least relatively widely shared across international academic culture.

The key issue, it seems to me, is not the question of whether we can make individual statements about the past which can be shown to be true or false in terms of a very basic notion of factual accuracy. In that sense, the 'appeal to Auschwitz' argument, and related appeals to assumed 'rules of historical method', are more or less irrelevant in seeking to resolve current theoretical debates. The factual accuracy of individual statements is an important, indeed vital, prerequisite to the production of any adequate historical knowledge; but an assertion that such limited, accurate, factual knowledge (which we might wish to call, perhaps, 'information') is possible is by no means a complete answer to the more fundamental questions about the nature of history as providing interpretation and/or explanation as well as a true compilation of factual knowledge.

The fundamental, underlying issue posed by the challenges we considered in Part I, may perhaps be summarised as follows: what are the implications of the fact that a multiplicity of interpretations (or stories) can be constructed out of the 'same' past?

Postmodernists tend to take the conclusion to be that, because a plurality of stories can be written on the basis of the 'same' (but, in some versions, essentially unknowable) past, then all are 'just constructs', and none can be shown to be more adequate 'windows on' or 'pictures of' the past than others. Hence (for those such as Ankersmit or Jenkins), we are heading down the path of relativism, and the only criteria for judging are either those based on aesthetic grounds, or those rooted in political and personal sympathies. By a slightly different route, which does not go as far as saying we cannot 'really' know what the past was like, but which nevertheless suggests that there are different stories which can be written from different perspectives in the present, others (such as Appleby, Jacobs and Hunt, and Jordanova) suggest that ultimately the arbiter will again be, at least in many cases, that of personal and political sympathies.

Unfortunately, appeals to (unexplicated) 'rules of historical method' (Richard J. Evans and others) do not adequately answer these points. Different 'individual facts' may be selected, each selection being as 'true' (or, in the worst case, as distorted, inaccurate, and so on) as any other selection; the selections may be construed in terms of any set of substantive concepts or analytical constructs, on a whole variety of bases, and combined to form an almost infinite variety of analyses, interpretations, and narratives.

There do, however, seem to be some sensible roads forward in (if not actually routes right out of) this theoretical jungle of competing approaches, each of which is at one remove from the individual factual statements about limited aspects of the past. We do not need to agree with the relativist and sceptical conclusions of postmodernists; nor do we need to accept simple empiricist assertions of faith. History is a far more complicated endeavour than either of these positions recognise. It seems to me that, on closer analysis, we can begin to distinguish grounds for accepting, rejecting, or amending different perspectives in more detail; and for determining whether in some areas at least a relatively broad scholarly community can collectively engage in closer approximations to adequacy in accounts of the past in the present, while certain issues will prove to be insurmountable stumbling blocks. Thus, the notion of 'perspectival paradigms' still implies that, at least in principle if never in practice, some grand synthesis might be possible; but the mutual incompatibility of certain approaches under the headings of both implicit paradigms and paradigms proper suggests that this is not the case. So where, and in terms of what supra-paradigmatic ground rules, might we look for a broad terrain of agreement?

We may not be able to resolve all the issues adumbrated in the chapters above. But if we are to move forward to some more theoretically sophisticated notion of history which, while recognising the degree of contemporary construction and imagination involved in the practice, still retains a belief in the possibility of searching for more adequate representations of the past, we do need to agree to some supra-paradigmatic guidelines or ground rules. These would entail certain fundamental commitments, as follows:

1   In general: to the comprehensiveness and exhaustiveness of the historical endeavour in principle, and to the honesty of the inquiry (irrespective of outcome);

2   In terms of method: to the use of concepts which are as value-neutral as possible, as culturally broad and as supra-paradigmatic as possible; and hence which have the maximum chance of mutual intelligibility, translatability and revision in the light of new (conceptually netted) 'findings';

3   and to deployment of empathy with respect to a variety of voices and positions, seeing interpretive understanding as a historical tool, in contrast to eliciting sympathy as a misplaced personal engagement of the historian and partisan appeal to the audience;

4   In terms of discussions and representation: to participation in controversies about the past in as clear and 'disengaged' a manner as possible, irrespective of personal political and moral views;

5   but also to recognition of: the creativity of the human imagination; the importance of empathic understanding of other cultures, other viewpoints; the contemporary situatedness of historical representations; and the

inescapability of engagement (whether by action or inaction) as citizens of the present.

There may be further guidelines which one could explicate, in the interests of having as wide a collective conversation in the present about the past as possible. There may also be areas where no resolution will be possible, particularly where there are conflicting, competing views on the nature of being human and on the relations between the individual and society. A philosophical anthropology is, it seems, to me, unavoidable.

If, then, we return for a moment to the metaphor of 'seeing through a glass darkly'; there may be a variety of colours and degrees of distortion in the lenses (or glass) used by different scholars to look at the past. But we will be able to say something sensible, and with a heightened degree of self-awareness, about these different lenses, and the sources and effects of the colouring and distortions they produce. We will also be able to say, with some degree of confidence, when we can agree to share lenses, and what it is we are able to discern – however dimly, inadequately, partially – through them. We can still retain a notion of history as a disciplined investigation of that which has gone before – a discipline which is self-reflective, aware of the implications of the choices practitioners must make in terms of the concepts, approaches and methods they use.

Thus, the character of historical knowledge is intrinsically both coloured and structured by contemporary concerns and concepts, but at the same time accessible to alteration in the light of (culturally bound and theoretically saturated) empirical evidence and inter-subjective professional dialogue. Of course historical writing involves imagination and literary flair. But it is not sufficient to point to the gap between the past and the reconstruction, or to recite as a mantra that narrative imposes a content which is not given in the kaleidoscopic maelstrom of the past as it really was. One has rather to analyse carefully the character and implications of this gap. Historical writing is neither purely literary and imaginative, nor inevitably mythologising and politically biased; it is about real issues and real questions (which are of course politically and morally informed); the ways in which the questions are phrased and the answers which historians give are nevertheless context- and theory-bound. These contexts and theories are, however, communal, social constructions which are open to debate, revision and advancement.

Historical representations

It may be helpful to participate briefly in a game which seems popular among writers on the 'nature of history': that of reflecting more broadly on the ways in which history compares to other subjects.[2]

There are clearly respects – many of which have been mentioned above – in which history shares elements of scientific method with some areas of natural science (particularly those such as geology or astronomy which deal with the historically emergent, possibly unique, and do not rely on the repeatability of the experimental method). These include detailed techniques and methods relating to, for example, the logic of case selection or comparative analysis, clarity of design and argument. There are also, clearly, distinctions relating to the differences in subject matter between inert natural worlds and the subjectivities and cultural meanings of the human world, and the associated lack of a common conceptual framework for capturing and analysing the latter. Not least among the differences is the fact that the character of the social world may self-reflexively change as a result of our analysis of it; this is only the case in a rather different way with respect to the natural world. Perhaps one of the oddest things to think about as a historian is the fact that our very knowledge of, engagement with, and relationship to what we know of the past actually changes the way we ourselves are, and the ways in which we act in the present and strive to affect the future. This is evidenced in countless ways: for example, the effects on politics of knowledge of past wars (think of the willingness to engage in what it was thought was going to be a short war in 1914) or genocides (the Holocaust has sensitised us to all subsequent attempts at 'ethnic cleansing') or political systems (learning from the constitutional errors of the past) – all perhaps summarised as 'the benefit of hindsight'. The old saying that 'the only lesson of history is that we cannot learn from history' is off the point: even if we cannot learn any simple lessons, in that history simply does not 'repeat itself' (not even the first time as tragedy, the second time as farce, as Marx had it), we nevertheless act, as human beings, in the knowledge or perception of what we think has gone before and in the light of what we think of it. We inhabit human worlds which are intrinsically suffused with a sense of history and a placement within webs of historical significance. To turn the postmodernist point on its head: historical consciousness is not a choice; it is an inevitable part of the human condition.

We are, too, constituted differently as a result of historical change. The people of today live longer, and with better health, than did their forebears; they travel more, over longer distances, and communicate with an increased number of different cultures and different parts of the world; they operate with different (and highly varied) conceptions of what is good and bad, moral and immoral, to be sought after and shunned. Not only the economic and technological systems, the political and social structures, but also cultures, mentalities, patterns of attitude and behaviour, shift and change constantly over time. And our knowledge and interpretation of what has passed informs and is informed by those shifts.

What, then, of the comparison of history with fiction? This has been played out at perhaps by now inordinate length by those theorists drawing their insights from post-structuralist literary theory. Some valuable insights have been gained from postmodernist challenges to unthinkingly positivist and empiricist assumptions, although some of the subtleties on both sides may occasionally have been drowned out in the storms of over-polarised theoretical battles. In particular, the challenge to historians mounted by literary critics, who view history writing as itself a form of creative literature, has been discussed extensively above, and needs no further discussion here.

However, it is worth briefly engaging with the less well-rehearsed comparison between historians and literary critics as practitioners of two arguably different disciplines. Historical evidence may be of various kinds; but, as we have seen, much of it consists in 'texts' which can be read in very similar ways to the works of creative literature. There may also of course be other totally non-textual (in the strict sense) historical clues; and not all of what historians may be looking for in historical texts need be as ambiguous and open to 'multiple readings' as literary critics may like to think. And, of course, literary texts may themselves provide one form of historical evidence. 'Realism' in, for example, prose narratives, need not necessarily take the form of detailed and factually accurate accounts of the physical world; even when all the characters are figments of the imagination, and the plots never took place in reality; even when there are no telling details of social life, of extremes of wealth and poverty (on the lines of Dickens), there can nevertheless – as Martin Swales has shown – be a 'realism' of the inner world.[3] Fiction can often – at least appear to – represent mentalities and emotions in a way that no other sources from the past appear able to do – at least not as vividly, compellingly. Literary texts can thus be read alongside, say, diaries, letters, court records, as a historical source for reconstructing the general character of interpersonal relations, assumptions, emotions, the definition of social situations, in past societies. They may give us (admittedly pre-interpreted) insights into bygone mental worlds which cannot necessarily be attained from – although they may be confirmed or queried by – other sources. Accounts in diaries, letters, or creative literature may open up worlds of feeling, and explore ambiguities and ambivalences in an open-ended way. Yet literary works, too, can be tendentious, wilfully misleading, distorted for a purpose – and indeed take a delight in parody and satire to make a contested point.

Not all historians are interested in such inner worlds of mentalities or culturally varying conceptualisations. And even where there is overlap between the focus of historians and of literary critics, there remain large differences in the character and purposes of their inquiries. The literary critic would have quite different purposes and focus: particular literary texts, far from being background and suggestive material in service of a wider investigation, would themselves be forefronted. They would not be scavenged for evidence of 'something else', but analysed in their own right. Features such as the role of narrator, the structuring of the account, the use of language, the development of atmosphere, plot, characters, the interweaving of subtexts, would be the primary focus of attention. It is clearly not my place here to describe what literary critics do; the point, merely, is that what they do, and their purposes, are somewhat different from what historians do – even with the very same material in front of them.

The debate couched in terms of 'history between science and fiction' has had its uses, but it seems to me that there are other poles of comparison, or types of representation, which may at this point yield more insights into the unique character of history – which is in the end *sui generis*. Let us take a mental wander around some of the possible variations in the game of comparing history to other human endeavours, in order to highlight the distinctive features of the historical enterprise.

There are many respects in which the comparison between geography and history can yield useful insights; here, let us concentrate solely on one element to do with the representation of 'other places'. The past, as we have just seen, may usefully be interpreted as a foreign country (albeit one, to appropriate Shakespeare, 'from whose bourne no traveller returns'). One of the most fruitful conceptions of history is perhaps that of 'mapping the past'. We know that maps of the Paris Metro, the Boston T, the New York subway or the London Underground are hardly realistic representations of the meanderings of the dark tunnels under the earth. These tunnels do not follow the neat loops of the maps; their real colours bear little resemblance to the coded reds, greens and browns of the sketch plans. But we do know that such forms of representation have their uses: to get to Heathrow from Holborn, it is better to embark on the Piccadilly Line than the Central Line; to go to Harvard from downtown Boston, take the Red Line. The same terrain may be represented very differently for different purposes: a walker will want a different scale of map from a motorist, and will find the marking of bridle paths and hill contours more useful than motorway service stations. Mental maps too can vary according to purpose: one person's directions (left past the Shamrock, right at McDonalds) may use very different landmarks from another's (left at the traffic lights, right at the Church of Latter Day Saints).

But what all maps have in common – at least in principle – is the notion that they refer to real landmarks which can in principle be located; that they assist travellers unfamiliar with the area in finding their way; and that there is an explicit and reliable consistency about scale, proportions, principles of inclusion and exclusion. If some motorways are marked, then all motorways should be marked; 'blank spots' are as much unprofessional distortions as are inventions and displacements. Maps which are simply wrong are infuriating, and it is quite clear that some are better than others for finding one's way.

No one would suggest that all maps should be mimetic representations of reality (although advances in computer technology, with virtual reality and CD-Roms, are tending in the direction of bringing disembodied aspects of the 'whole experience' of other parts of the world – minus mosquitoes, malaria and malaise – into one's home or office). Nor would anyone criticise maps on the grounds that they impose grids (latitude, longitude) on the world which do not really exist out there. Maps are evaluated according to other criteria – fitness for purpose, consistency, clarity – than simple realism. It is somewhat strange that, among many theorists of history, there is an almost arbitrary imposition of the artificially limited choice between realism or fiction.

Our discussions of ways of writing, of empathy and the evocation of atmosphere, may perhaps lead into some brief analogies with other art forms. There are different styles, different media, different techniques for the representation of artistic subjects, ranging from the realism of certain sculptures of human bodies or paintings of bowls of fruit on the one hand, to impressionism or surrealism on the other. Perspectives on the human world can be conveyed in a wide variety of ways: few would deny that photography and film, for example, both purport to bring us 'real' subjects, and yet at the same time select, frame and present these subjects in ways which are open to a high degree of imagination, creativity, and alternative forms of expression. For some reason, this is an occasion for rejoicing in most areas classified as 'art', while it appears to be a reason for censure in historical representations which depart from some notional ideal – or straw man – of an unattainable realism.

History can in many respects be compared to detective work. The historian poses puzzles to which he or she seeks the answers. A good historian, like a good detective, knows what are the most pertinent questions to ask (including those about that which did not take place, as in Sherlock Holmes' question about why the dog did not bark in the night), what to find surprising, what leads to pursue. The historian knows what clues to look for, which suspects to interrogate, which of the diversity of contemporaneous elements can be safely ignored. But the historian is not only the detective; he or she is also the author of the mystery book, who had to write it up, with appropriate structuring to lead the readers through, to engage their minds with the puzzle that the author/detective has already solved, to present the clues and the evidence in such a way that the conclusion is both eagerly sought for and also satisfyingly accepted. The story can of course be written in different ways, but the 'facts' of the case – who was murdered, when and where – are givens that cannot be evaded. The clues could in principle be different ones, there could be fewer or more clues, but they have to lead to the 'correct' conclusion: the right person must ultimately be identified as the murderer.

There is, however, a variant of this last version. Not all cases that come to court are open and shut. The job of the historian is in some cases as akin to that of barrister as to that of detective or mystery writer. The barrister takes the case in which he or she is instructed, and presents it in the light which has the best possible chances of success for the client. Clearly the 'facts of the case' are of vital importance, as is the mustering of appropriate witnesses, the collation of evidence, the clarity of argument. But, when it comes to the final appeal to judge or jury, rhetorical powers of persuasion may very often tip the balance.

The historian also, in some respects, acts as a translator of one society to another. The historian 'learns the language' of a past society and represents it in terms which a culturally compatible audience in the present will understand. The arena of what is 'culturally compatible' may of course be more tightly or more broadly drawn: highly paradigm-specific concepts and terms will be accessible only to members of that particular theoretical language community (ranging from the technical complexities of some branches of econometric or demographic history, to the theoretical abstruseness of certain versions of neo-Marxism or post-structuralism); while other historians may seek to present their interpretations in language which is accessible to a much broader literate public. On this view, history cannot be a cumulative endeavour in the sense that each generation could build on the achievements of a previous generation. There may perhaps be an accumulation of 'knowledge' or 'facts'; but the translations will always have to be accomplished anew, as questions shift and terminology changes. The unexamined, unquestioned existence of 'races' and 'nations' in the textbooks of a previous age give way to the constructed (or deconstructed) collective identities of today; narratives of great men give way to thematic analyses of the struggles of classes; classes subside in importance as women and subalterns are discovered. It is impossible to predict what future modes of categorising the world will arise in other groups and subsequent generations.

History as a political endeavour has already been discussed at some length in the previous chapter. Here, it is worth briefly reiterating that, whatever we may think the nature of history is, we do it and will go on doing it. Our sense of both individual and collective identity is intrinsically rooted in a sense of where we have come from; and we constantly, as part of our very existence, seek to understand our paths through the world, the opportunities seized and lost, the openings and closures that constitute our own lives. For all the discussions of this and preceding chapters, the search for historical understanding, whether collective or merely individual and autobiographical, is – and this I would hazard without the usual cluster of qualifications when one embarks on any remark of this sort – an intrinsic element of the condition of being human, in the same way as the physical functions of eating, sleeping and reproduction.

Let me then finally elaborate a little on the bare assertions made at the start of this chapter.

1. Plurality does not preclude falsifiability

There is a potentially infinite number of possible historical accounts, for several reasons. For one thing, there are innumerable possible standpoints in the present, and potential questions which can be posed to the past. For another, each historian engages in a creative act of the imagination in the ways he or she selects to re-present the answers brought back about that question to the present. To write history entails a leap of the imagination in both directions – immersion into the atmosphere of a particular moment, time or place in the past, attempting to interpret and understand an alien world; and an imaginative re-creation of that past to make the connections with particular groups in a particular time and place in the present. The historian is a creative intermediary. Yet it is not the case that 'anything goes'; not all accounts are equally 'empirically adequate'. It is possible to design ways of testing hypotheses, of checking the validity of particular interpretations or explanations, the accuracy or otherwise of particular statements of fact, and the plausibility of statements about relations between facts. Historians can get things wrong – and stand to be corrected.

2. The art and science of historical practice

Historians engage in some very creative, idiosyncratic activities; individual historians are in some respects themselves a 'tool' for the acquisition of historical knowledge and understanding, and the representation of their findings in the present. But they do this, not as isolated 'artists' (actually when has an artist ever really worked as an isolated genius, rather than as part of a society that saw fit, for example, to maintain sculptors who produced marble statues of the ideal human body, or painters who produced portraits of the great and good, or architects who produced temples to the gods or representations of worldly status, or even ironists to produce some form of anti-art?), but rather as contributors to collective bodies of what is deemed to be knowledge. Such knowledge may not necessarily be cumulative, since the concepts of history are not 'given' in the world out there. But it is organised knowledge about which there may be rational debate; and where there may be limited progress with respect to particular questions within the constraints of particular frameworks of inquiry.

3. Imaginative leaps and disciplinary frameworks

Historical writing is not simply the product of an individual brain, or an individual historian's creative imagination. 'Emplotment' is not just an arbitrary imposition by a creative individual on selected historical bones. Historians work within a collective framework of assumptions about 'what is already known', what 'gaps need filling', what puzzles remain to be solved. While for extended periods of time background 'historical pictures' may remain relatively unexamined, taken for granted, scholarly communities focus on particular questions and issues to be explored. And they interrogate the surviving traces of the past through concepts, tools and methods which are, to a greater or lesser extent, shared by the wider theoretical community or communities. Within such communities, there are generally shared standards of evaluation, including, for example, criteria such as more exhaustive exploration and compilation of relevant evidence, interpretations accounting for more aspects of the evidence, or reconceptualisation in new ways that enhance understanding and illuminate certain features in more productive ways.

4. Mutual compatibility and criteria for evaluation of competing approaches

With the exception of (the actually rather amorphous and many-headed example of) Marxism, there seems to be almost no necessary or intrinsic linkage between different theoretical approaches, or paradigms, and particular positions on the political spectrum. The key issues determining differences between 'paradigms proper' appear to have to do with far more deep-rooted questions of philosophical anthropology. These revolve around fundamentally irresolvable questions concerning, for example, the relations between the social or historical construction of cultural patterns, characteristic attitudes and behaviour, on the one hand, and assumptions about the irreducible uniqueness of individual personality and creativity on the other; or about long-term trends and 'structures' versus human capacity for innovation and willed change. While many historians would probably wish to acknowledge a variety of aspects, in practice historians tend towards different ends of the spectrum concerning what they prioritise in their writing. So too do the consumers of historical writing: for some, an explanation couched in terms of general forces and trends will be more compelling than one in terms of individual motives; for others, the reverse will be the case. Perspectival paradigms which share common underlying assumptions may in principle be more readily compatible with one another – irrespective of the fact that many are situated quite differently in the contemporary institutional and political landscape.

5. The possibility of enhanced historical understanding

If we analyse in more detail the nature of the 'gap' between lost past and historical representations in the present, we find that the postmodernist case for the death of history has been overstated. There are ways of seeking to bridge that gap. Some of these ways are mutually compatible; others less so. But there are also ways of adjudicating between competing accounts. More importantly, the fact that there is no single 'final account' is not necessarily a reason either for not doing history at all (as some postmodernists occasionally seem to believe), or for suggesting that all accounts are in principle equally valid, or equally invented (as other postmodernists appear to suggest).

Within the kinds of qualifications discussed above, there remains the possibility of achieving enhanced historical understanding and explanation of selected questions about the past.

Making sense of the past

The processes of historical investigation and representation are about making sense of the past. Making sense is of course an activity in the present; and it is an active practice, not a matter of passive reception and reflection of what has gone before. Making sense means imposing categories, looking for patterns, searching for connections, seeking answers to questions, imbuing the past with meaning. And this is what we, as humans, do all the time. Professional historians (should?) have more time, resources, and training, more sophisticated methodology, familiarity with key traditions, knowledge, and sets of debates, more willingness and capacity to explore totally unknown territory, than other people; but humans are inevitably historically conscious creatures. Historical practices – the activity of seeking to make sense of those aspects of the past that are important in the present – will continue, however contested their character may be. It is all the more important that we are highly aware of what we are doing as historians.

I have argued in this book that, as far as history as a discipline is concerned, there clearly are key areas of debate which will never be resolved. Metanarratives which see wider meanings in historical patterns will never be universally shared, and must remain ultimately matters of faith. There will also be different views on fundamental questions concerning how our lives, aspirations, emotions, behaviour patterns, are in part shaped and formed by the distinctive historical environments or even 'structures' into which we are born, our socialisation and formative experiences, the symbolic worlds of belief and value systems into which we enter, and the extent to which we can alter our world. But this does not prevent historians from interpreting symbolic, cultural and intellectual webs of significance; analysing the consequences of meaningful human action within given circumstances; and engaging in rational debates over the relative importance of different factors in their own analyses and representations. I have sought to show that, within given parameters and when adhering to certain rather general tenets – to do with honesty, openness and willingness to revise conceptual, interpretive and explanatory frameworks in the light of new evidence, however theoretically 'contaminated' all such evidence inevitably will be – it is possible to say that historical knowledge is of a different order from that of fiction, myth, and ideology.

I do not claim to have covered, let alone fully discussed, all the relevant issues in this book. But I hope that if nothing else, it will have served to raise a heightened awareness of key issues which all historians face, and a realisation that processes of historical investigation and representation are inevitably, intrinsically theoretical enterprises. It is thus all the more important that we are aware of the parameters of what we are doing, and the assumptions on which our practices rest, rather than blindly conforming to whatever the varied contemporary pressures may be: whether towards repeated exemplification of particular traditions or innovative proclamation of 'new approaches'; towards explicit partisanship or often equally partisan pretences of neutrality; or towards the rejection of all rational attempts to make sense of the past because of the sheer difficulty of grounding those attempts philosophically. Historical debates are about issues which matter; and therefore the nature of historical understanding matters.

NOTES

1 INTRODUCTION

1 See, for example, Beverley Southgate, *History: What and Why? Ancient, Modern and Postmodern Perspectives* (London: Routledge, 1996).
2 See, for example, P. Burke (ed.), *New Perspectives on Historical Writing* (Cambridge: Polity Press, 1991); and any number of historiographical works and edited collections on specific historical topics.
3 See, for example, John Tosh, *The Pursuit of History* (Harlow: Pearson, 3rd edition, 2000).
4 G. R. Elton, *The Practice of History* (Glasgow: Collins, Fontana edition, 1969; first published 1967), Preface, p. vii.
5 Lawrence Stone, 'Notes: History and Postmodernism', *Past and Present*, no. 131, May 1991, p. 217, p. 218; Patrick Joyce, 'History and Postmodernism I', *Past and Present*, no. 133, November 1991, p. 205.
6 I am grateful to John Breuilly for pointing out the issues relating to the construction of the Holocaust as an integrated set of events. For an interesting set of essays on the issues raised by postmodernism and the Holocaust, see Saul Friedländer (ed.), *Probing the Limits of Representation* (Cambridge, MA: Harvard University Press, 1992).
7 For an excellent overview of controversies on Nazi Germany, see Ian Kershaw, *The Nazi Dictatorship* (London: Arnold, 3rd edition, 1993).
8 Daniel J. Goldhagen, *Hitler's Willing Executioners* (London: Little, Brown and Co., 1996).
9 Richard J. Evans, *In Defence of History* (London: Granta, 1997).
10 Ludmilla Jordanova, *History in Practice* (London: Arnold, 2000) esp. p. 96; Joyce Appleby, Lynn Hunt and Margaret Jacobs, *Telling the Truth about History* (New York and London: W. W. Norton and Co., 1994).
11 For an overview of these developments, see Mary Fulbrook, *German National Identity after the Holocaust* (Cambridge: Polity Press, 1999).

2 THE CONTESTED NATURE OF HISTORICAL KNOWLEDGE

1 'Man hat der Historie das Amt, die Vergangenheit zu richten, die Mitwelt zum Nutzen zukünftiger Jahre zu belehren, beigemessen: so hoher Ämter unterwindet sich gegenwärtiger Versuch nicht: er will blos zeigen, wie es eigentlich gewesen.' Leopold von Ranke, 'Vorrede zur ersten Ausgabe, Okt. 1824', *Geschichten der romanischen und germanischen Völker von 1494 bis 1514 zur*

Kritik neuerer Geschichtsschreiber (Leipzig: Verlag von Duncker und Humblot, 3rd edition, 1885), p. vii.

2 For surveys of the development of some relevant traditions in European and American history, see, for example, Georg Iggers, *Historiography in the Twentieth Century: From Scientific Objectivity to the Postmodern Challenge* (Hanover, NH: Wesleyan University Press, 1997); Peter Novick, *That Noble Dream: the 'Objectivity Question' and the American Historical Profession* (Cambridge: Cambridge University Press, 1988).

3 On East German versus West German historical approaches, cf. my discussions in Mary Fulbrook, *German National Identity after the Holocaust* (Cambridge: Polity Press, 1999).

4 For a more extensive discussion and references, see Mary Fulbrook, *Interpretations of the Two Germanies, 1945–1990* (Basingstoke: Macmillan, 2000).

5 David Harvey, *The Condition of Postmodernity. An Enquiry into the Origins of Cultural Change* (Oxford: Blackwell, 1990), p. 9. For a useful overview of developments from the 1970s, and intellectual history of the philosophical precursors of postmodernism, see David Roberts, *Nothing but History. Reconstruction and Extremity after Metaphysics* (Berkeley, CA: University of California Press, 1995).

6 Useful overviews and selections of contributions to these debates may be found in a number of recent edited collections, such as: Brian Fay, Philip Pomper, and Richard T. Vann (eds), *History and Theory: Contemporary Readings* (Oxford: Blackwell, 1998); Keith Jenkins (ed.), *The Postmodern History Reader* (London: Routledge, 1997); Geoffrey Roberts (ed.), *The History and Narrative Reader* (London: Routledge, 2001); see also Frank Ankersmit and Hans Kellner (eds), *A New Philosophy of History* (London: Reaktion Books, 1995).

7 Keith Jenkins, *On "What is History?" From Carr and Elton to Rorty and White* (London: Routledge, 1995), p. 6. See also F. R. Ankersmit, 'Historiography and Postmodernism', *History and Theory*, vol. 28, no. 2, 1989, pp. 137–53; and Perez Zagorin's nice reply, 'Historiography and Postmodernism: Reconsiderations', *History and Theory*, vol. 29, no. 3, 1990, pp. 263–74. A flavour of Lyotard can be gained from Jean-François Lyotard, 'The postmodern condition', in Jenkins (ed.), *The Postmodern History Reader*.

8 Ankersmit, 'Historiography and Postmodernism', *History and Theory*, vol. 28, no. 2, 1989, pp. 137–53, p. 137.

9 F. R. Ankersmit, 'Reply to Professor Zagorin', *History and Theory*, vol. 29, no. 3, 1990, pp. 275–96, at p. 281.

10 Keith Jenkins, *On "What is History?" From Carr and Elton to Rorty and White*, pp. 37–8; emphasis added.

11 See, for example, *ibid.*, p. 30.

12 Patrick Joyce, 'History and Postmodernism I', *Past and Present*, no. 133, November 1991, pp. 204–9, at pp. 208–9.

13 Cf., for example, Simon Schama, *Dead Certainties (Unwarranted Speculations)* (London: Granta Books, 1991), p. 322.

14 Cf. the interesting review by John Toews, 'A New Philosophy of History? Reflections on Postmodern Historicising', *History and Theory*, vol. 36, no. 2, 1997, pp. 235–48.

15 Cf. the rather muddled discussion of historical 'facts' in E. H. Carr, *What is History?* (New York: Random House, 1961), and Elton's typically acerbic comments on Carr in *The Practice of History*.

16 Hayden White, 'The question of narrative in contemporary historical theory', *The Content of the Form: Narrative Discourse and Historical Representation* (Baltimore, MD, and London: The Johns Hopkins University Press, 1987), p. 27.

17 Hayden White, 'The value of narrative in the representation of reality' in White, *Content of the Form*, p. 24.
18 Hayden White, 'Historical Emplotment and the Problem of Truth' in Saul Friedländer (ed.), *Probing the Limits of Representation* (Cambridge, MA: Harvard University Press, 1992).
19 Ankersmit, 'Reply to Zagorin', *loc. cit.*
20 See particularly Hans Kellner, *Language and Historical Representation: Getting the Story Crooked* (Madison, WI: University of Wisconsin Press, 1989).
21 Robert Berkhofer, *Beyond the Great Story: History as Text and Discourse* (Cambridge, MA: Harvard University Press, 1995), pp. 282–3.
22 Appleby, Hunt and Jacobs, *Telling the Truth*, p. 227.
23 *Ibid.*, pp. 201–2.
24 In addition to the works cited in previous footnotes, see also, for example: Victoria Bonnell and Lynn Hunt (eds), *Beyond the Cultural Turn: New Directions in the Study of Society and Culture* (Berkeley, CA: University of California Press, 1999); Alex Callinicos, *Theories and Narratives: Reflections on the Philosophy of History* (Durham, NC: Duke University Press, 1995); Roger Chartier, *On the Edge of the Cliff: History, Language and Practices* (Baltimore, MD, and London: The Johns Hopkins University Press, 1997; transl. Lydia G. Cochrane); Elizabeth Deeds Ermarth, *Sequel to History: Postmodernism and the Crisis of Representational Time* (Princeton, NJ: Princeton University Press, 1992); Richard J. Evans, *In Defence of History* (London: Granta, 1997); David Harlan, *The Degradation of American History* (Chicago: University of Chicago Press, 1997); Eric Hobsbawm, 'Postmodernism in the Forest', in *On History* (London: Weidenfeld and Nicolson, 1997); Chris Lorenz, *Konstruktion der Vergangenheit* (Cologne: Böhlau Verlag, 1994); C. Behan McCullogh, *The Truth of History* (London: Routledge, 1998); Terence J. McDonald (ed.), *The Historic Turn in the Human Sciences* (Ann Arbor, MI: University of Michigan Press, 1996); Alun Munslow, *Deconstructing History* (London: Routledge, 1997); Beverley Southgate, *Why Bother with History?* (Harlow: Pearson, 2000).
25 Gertrude Himmelfarb, 'Introduction' to *On Looking into the Abyss. Untimely Thoughts on Culture and Society* (New York: Alfred Knopf, 1994), p. xii. A heated Australian response to a range of theoretical developments, including social theory as well as postmodernist and literary perspectives, will be found in Keith Windschuttle, *The Killing of History. How Literary Critics and Social Theorists are Murdering Our Past* (New York, NY: Free Press, revised edition, 1997; orig. 1994). For a rather different set of polemics over the alleged death of 'national history' in Canada, see John Granatstein, *Who Killed Canadian History?* (Toronto: University of Toronto Press, 1998), responded to by A. B. McKillop, 'Who Killed Canadian History? A View from the Trenches', *Canadian Historical Review*, 90 (1999), pp. 269–99.
26 Very often these debates are to be found in the pages of specialist journals such as *History and Theory* or *Rethinking History*; there have also recently been flourishing debates on the *History and Theory* list on the internet.
27 See, for example, Ludmilla Jordanova, *History in Practice* (London: Arnold, 2000); Arthur Marwick, *The New Nature of History: Knowledge, Evidence, Language* (Basingstoke: Macmillan, 2001); John Tosh, *The Pursuit of History* (Harlow: Pearson, 3rd edition, 2000).
28 See, for example, Geoffrey Roberts, 'Narrative History as a Way of Life', *Journal of Contemporary History*, vol. 31 (1996), pp. 221–8 – a piece stimulated by the desire to rescue Arthur Marwick in his more pre-philosophical incarnation by providing some philosophical underpinnings.

29 Cf., for example, Arthur Marwick, *The Nature of History* (Basingstoke: Macmillan, 3rd edition, 1989) and Arthur Marwick, '"A fetishism of documents?" The salience of source-based history' in H. Kozicki (ed.), *Developments in Modern Historiography* (Basingstoke: Macmillan, 1993); also the debate between Marwick and Hayden White sparked by Arthur Marwick's typically pugnacious Open University lecture, published in altered form as 'Two Approaches to Historical Study: the Metaphysical (including "Postmodernism") and the Historical', *Journal of Contemporary History*, vol. 30 (1995), pp. 5–35; Hayden White, 'Response to Arthur Marwick', *Journal of Contemporary History*, vol. 30 (1995), pp. 233–46; Geoffrey Elton, *The Practice of History* (London: Fontana, 1969); Geoffrey Elton, *Return to Essentials* (Cambridge: Cambridge University Press, 1991). Marwick has significantly modified his position in (the substantially rewritten fourth edition of) his *The New Nature of History*.
30 Cf. Evans, *In Defence of History*.
31 Cf. Elton, *Practice of History*, Chapter 4.
32 Hayden White, 'The Question of Narrative in Contemporary Historical Theory', *The Content of the Form* (Baltimore, MD, and London: The Johns Hopkins University Press, 1987), p. 31.
33 *Ibid.*, p. 31.
34 See, for example, Lawrence Stone, 'History and Postmodernism III', *Past and Present*, no. 135 (May 1992), pp. 189–94; or Evans, *In Defence of History*, as well as their various substantive historical works.
35 See, for example, the juxtaposition of the views of Gertrude Himmelfarb and Joan Wallach Scott in *American Historical Review*, vol. 94, no. 3, June 1989, pp. 661–70 and pp. 680–92. These issues are discussed further in Chapter 9, below.
36 Marwick, 'Two Approaches', *loc. cit.*, p. 8; Jenkins, *Rethinking History*, Chapter 1. In any event, Marwick holds a pretty dim view of Jenkins' book, which he thinks 'will come to be regarded as the classic of postmodernist ineptitude and contempt for accepted scholarly practice' (*ibid.*, p. 26).
37 Indeed, one of the referees for this book suggested to me on reading an early draft of the manuscript that I 'should avoid giving this fashionable nonsense more space than it merits'. Since then, I fear I have probably written slightly more, rather than less, about it.
38 Interestingly for a nation more usually noted for its assiduous attention to matters philosophical and theoretical, Germans have been caught up mostly by the politicisation issue alone. The postmodernist wave has – with distinguished exceptions, such as Iggers and Jarausch, both of whom are highly influenced by a North American intellectual climate – barely touched Germany, where 'theory' still remains, for the most part, a matter of *Quellenkritik* or source criticism. The collapse of the GDR and the consequent need either to take the views of East German historical colleagues seriously, or to provide rational grounds for their rejection, has in fact – as an unintended side effect – prompted a wave of more explicit thinking in Germany about the nature of history; but it has at the same time reinforced a 'fetishism of the sources', with the rush for the newly opened archives.
39 I have to confess that, in my own scholarly endeavours, I am still rather committed to the motto of my second *alma mater*, Harvard: the pursuit of truth, or *veritas*.

3 HISTORICAL PARADIGMS AND THEORETICAL TRADITIONS

1 Thomas Kuhn, *The Structure of Scientific Revolutions* (Chicago, IL: University of Chicago Press, 1962; 2nd edition, 1970).

2 See, for example, Imre Lakatos and Alan Musgrave (eds), *Criticism and the Growth of Knowledge* (Cambridge: Cambridge University Press, 1970).

3 See, for example, Joyce Appleby, Lynn Hunt, and Margaret Jacobs, *Telling the Truth about History* (New York, NY: W. W. Norton and Co., 1994); G. Iggers, *Historiography in the Twentieth Century: From Scientific Objectivity to the Post-modern Challenge* (Hanover, NH: Wesleyan University Press, 1997); Peter Novick, *That Noble Dream: the 'Objectivity Question' and the American Historical Profession* (Cambridge: Cambridge University Press, 1988); Peter Burke (ed.), *New Perspectives on Historical Writing* (Cambridge: Polity Press, 1991).

4 See, for example, Perry Anderson, *Arguments within English Marxism* (London: New Left Books, 1980); and *Considerations on Western Marxism* (London: New Left Books, 1976); E. P. Thompson, *The Poverty of Theory* (London: Merlin Press, new edition, 1995).

5 Carr, p. 54.

6 See, for example, John Morrill, Brian Manning and David Underdown in P. Gaunt (ed.), *The English Civil War: Essential Readings* (Oxford: Blackwell, 2001).

7 G. M. Trevelyan, *English Social History* (London: Longmans Green and Co., 1944; reprinted 1948), p. vii.

8 For histories of different historiographical traditions, see, for example, S. Berger, *The Search for Normality* (Oxford: Berghahn Books, 1997); P. Burke (ed.), *New Perspectives on Historical Writing* (Cambridge: Polity Press, 1991); G. Iggers, *Historiography in the Twentieth Century* (Hanover, NH, and London: Wesleyan University Press, 1997). On differences among different national traditions, see, for example, Carl Berger, *The Writing of Canadian History* (Toronto: University of Toronto Press, 1986); Stefan Berger, Mark Donovan and Kevin Passmore (eds), *Writing National Histories: Western Europe since 1800* (London: Routledge, 1999); and (including Eastern European perspectives) Geoffrey Hosking and George Schöpflin (eds), *Myths and Nationhood* (London: Hurst and Company, 1997).

9 See, for example, Lynn Hunt (ed.), *The New Cultural History* (Berkeley: University of California Press, 1989).

10 Cf., for example, Keith Thomas, *Religion and the Decline of Magic* (Harmondsworth: Penguin, 1973).

11 See, for example, Joan Wallach Scott (ed.), *Feminism and History* (Oxford: Oxford University Press, 1996).

12 See, for example, Bill Ashcroft, Gareth Griffiths and Helen Tiffin (eds), *The Postcolonial Studies Reader* (London: Routledge, 1995); Partha Chatterjee, *The Nation and its Fragments: Colonial and Postcolonial Histories* (Princeton, NJ: Princeton University Press, 1993); Robert Young, *White Mythologies: Writing History and the West* (London: Routledge, 1990).

13 The field of twentieth-century Marxism is far too wide to be encompassed in a single footnote. For introductory surveys and interesting discussions, see, for example, Dick Howard and Karl E. Klare (eds), *The Unknown Dimension. European Marxism since Lenin* (New York: Basic Books, 1972); Paul Connerton, *The Tragedy of Enlightenment. An Essay on the Frankfurt School* (Cambridge: Cambridge University Press, 1980).

14 See, for example, E. P. Thompson's classic, *The Making of the English Working*

Class (Harmondsworth: Penguin, 1968; orig. 1963); or the works of Christopher Hill, such as *Society and Puritanism* (New York: Schocken Books, 1964) or *The World Turned Upside Down* (Harmondsworth: Penguin, 1975; orig. 1972). The complexity of these historians' approaches cannot be discussed fully here. For further analysis, see, for example, Harvey Kaye *The British Marxist Historians* (Cambridge: Polity Press, 1984); Theda Skocpol (ed.), *Vision and Method in Historical Sociology* (Cambridge: Cambridge University Press, 1984); for my own more detailed analysis of the theoretical underpinnings of Christopher Hill's work, Mary Fulbrook, 'Christopher Hill and Historical Sociology' in Geoff Eley and William Hunt (eds), *Reviving the English Revolution: Reflections and Elaborations on the Work of Christopher Hill* (London: Verso, 1988).

15 See, for example, Louis Althusser, *For Marx* (Harmondsworth: Penguin, transl. Ben Brewster, 1969; orig. 1966); Louis Althusser and Étienne Balibar, *Reading Capital* (New York: Random House, transl. Ben Brewster, 1970; orig. 1968); Nicos Poulantzas, *Political Power and Social Classes* (London: New Left Books, transl. Timothy O'Hagan, 1973; orig. 1968).

16 See, for example, E. P. Thompson, *The Poverty of Theory*.

17 For recent examples of attempts to apply psychoanalytic insights to social phenomena (rather than purely individual biographies) see: H.-J. Maaz, *Der Gefühlsstau. Ein Psychogramm der DDR* (Berlin: Argon, 1990); Lyndal Roper, 'Witchcraft and fantasy in early modern Germany', in J. Barry, M. Hester and G. Roberts (eds), *Witchcraft in Early Modern Europe* (Cambridge: Cambridge University Press, 1996). See also the general discussion of 'History and Psychology' by Arthur Marwick, *The Nature of History* (Basingstoke: Macmillan, 3rd edition, 1989), pp. 165–70.

18 See, for example, Michael Lane (ed.), *Structuralism* (New York: Basic Books, 1970); on the contrast between structuralism proper and structural-functionalism in anthropology, David Goddard, 'Anthropology: the Limits of Functionalism' in Robin Blackburn (ed.), *Ideology in Social Science* (New York: Random House, 1972); see also Maurice Godelier, 'Functionalism, Structuralism and Marxism', Foreword to *Rationality and Irrationality in Economics* (New York: Monthly Review Press, transl. Brian Pearce, 1972; orig. 1966). For more detailed discussion of a number of variants of a 'structural approach' in the field of history, see Christopher Lloyd, *The Structures of History* (Oxford: Blackwell, 1993). See also Chapter 7 below.

19 On structuralism in literary criticism, see the account in Terry Eagleton, *Literary Theory* (Oxford: Blackwell, 2nd edition, 1996).

20 Edmund Leach, *Lévi-Strauss* (London: Fontana, 1970).

21 See, for example, R. J. Evans, *Rituals of Retribution: Capital Punishment in Germany 1600–1987* (Oxford: Oxford University Press, 1996) for the application of concepts derived from the works of Michel Foucault, Norbert Elias, and Philippe Ariès to the areas of discourse, culture and experience.

22 This relates to a much wider theoretical issue about the question of historical generalisations versus ('idiographic') explanations of unique sets of developments which cannot be discussed further here.

23 Most explicitly developed first in his book on Hitler in the Longman 'Profiles in Power' series: Ian Kershaw, *Hitler* (London: Longman, 1991); see also his two-volume Hitler biography, *Hitler. Vol. 1: Hubris* (Harmondsworth: Penguin, 1998); *Hitler. Vol. II: Nemesis* (Harmondsworth: Penguin, 2000).

24 Why did Max Weber not become the founder of a school? Is it merely because his name did not lend itself readily to the addition of '-ism' ('Marxism' trips more lightly off the tongue than 'Weberianism'); or is it because he withdrew

from ultimate commitment to any underlying premises, allowing us to revolve in a world of uncertainties and acts of faith as far as metatheoretical commitments were concerned?

4 BEYOND METANARRATIVE: PLOTS, PUZZLES AND PLAUSIBILITY

1 Thus I am not directly concerned in this chapter with the narrower question of 'narrative' versus 'social scientific', 'analytical' (and so on) approaches to history. For contributions to those debates, some of which directly critique Hayden White's approach, see Geoffrey Roberts (ed.), *The History and Narrative Reader* (London: Routledge, 2001); see also Chapter 8, below.
2 See above, Chapter 2.
3 Hayden White, 'The Historical Text as Literary Artefact', in *Tropics of Discourse* (Baltimore, MD, and London: The Johns Hopkins University Press, 1985; orig. 1978), p. 88.
4 *Ibid.*, p. 89.
5 *Ibid.*, p. 94 (emphasis on 'only' added).
6 White, 'The Historical Text as Literary Artefact', p. 99.
7 For a very clear account of the diverse intellectual traditions which coalesced in the 1970s and 1980s, see David Roberts, *Nothing but History: Reconstruction and Extremity after Metaphysics* (Berkeley: University of California Press, 1995), Chapter 1, including discussions of Northrop Frye, Roland Barthes, Joan Scott, Peter Novick, Simon Schama and others. Roberts suggests that Himmelfarb's spirited attacks entailed no real rethinking of the 'traditional' position which she herself occupied; while Haskell and Struever provided 'elements for an alternative' which is as yet not fully developed (p. 15).
8 For variations on these themes, see, for example, the reprinted selections in Keith Jenkins (ed.), *The Postmodern History Reader* (London: Routledge, 1997). The Barthes quotation in translation is at p. 121; the original essay may be found in Roland Barthes, 'Le Discours de l'Histoire', *Oeuvres Complètes*, vol. II (Paris: Éditions du Seuil, 1994), pp. 417–27.
9 Hans Kellner, *Language and Historical Representation* (Madison, WI: University of Wisconsin Press, 1989), p. 10.
10 *Ibid.*, Preface, p. vii.
11 Keith Jenkins, *Why History? Ethics and Postmodernity* (London: Routledge, 1999), p. 8.
12 *Ibid.*, pp. 11–12.
13 See, for example, the selections from Plumb, Carr and Butterfield in John Tosh (ed.), *Historians on History* (Harlow: Pearson, 2000).
14 Given the sheer scale, complexity, ambiguity and often self-contradictory nature of Marx's oeuvre, this may be to simplify somewhat; but I think my brief summary here does not do a serious injustice to the gist of Marxist theory.
15 H. A. L. Fisher, *A History of Europe* (London: Edward Arnold, 1936), p. v.
16 Elton, pp. 56 ff.
17 Cf. Jürgen Kocka, *Vereinigungskrise. Zur Geschichte der Gegenwart* (Göttingen: Vandenhoeck and Ruprecht, 1995).
18 See Catherine Clinton, 'Gerda Lerner', in Robert Allen Rutland (ed.), *Clio's Favorites: Leading Historians of the United States 1945–2000* (Columbia, MO: University of Missouri Press, 2000), pp. 98–110.
19 E. P. Thompson, *The Making of the English Working Class* (Harmondsworth: Penguin, 1980 edition; orig. 1963), p. 12.

20 Joan Wallach Scott, 'Women in *The Making of the English Working Class*' in *Gender and the Politics of History* (New York, NY: Columbia University Press, 1988).
21 See also Alan Megill's discussion of cognate issues (although his conceptual schema does not neatly map onto the points I want to make here): Alan Megill, '"Grand Narrative" and the Discipline of History' in F. Ankersmit and H. Kellner (eds), *A New Philosophy of History* (London: Reaktion Books, 1995).
22 Obviously I have my own view on this question, which I think is more differentiated than the widely prevalent positions outlined here. My own position will only be fully developed by the end of the book.
23 I am grateful to John Breuilly for pointing out these differences to me in relation to an earlier draft of this chapter which focussed exclusively on 'endpoint-driven' histories.
24 For summaries of and contributions to these debates, see, for example, Peter Burke, *The Renaissance* (Basingstoke: Macmillan, 2nd edition, 1997); Thomas Munck, *The Enlightenment. A Comparative Social History 1721–1794* (London: Arnold, 2000); Roy Porter, *The Enlightenment* (Basingstoke: Macmillan, 1990); James Sharpe, *Witchcraft in Early Modern England* (Harlow: Pearson, 2001); Darren Oldridge (ed.), *The Witchcraft Reader* (London: Routledge, 2002).
25 For examples taken almost at random from my shelves, see Louis Masur (ed.), *The Challenge of American History* (Baltimore, MD: The Johns Hopkins University Press, 1999); William Lamont (ed.), *Historical Controversies and Historians* (London: UCL Press, 1998).
26 Alfred Cobban, *The Social Interpretation of the French Revolution* (Cambridge: Cambridge University Press, 1964).
27 W. Doyle, *Origins of the French Revolution* (Oxford: Oxford University Press, 3rd edition, 1999); W. Doyle, *The Oxford History of the French Revolution* (Oxford: Oxford University Press, 1989); T. C. W. Blanning, *The French Revolution: Class War or Culture Clash?* (Basingstoke: Macmillan, 2nd edition, 1998); D. Townson, *France in Revolution* (London: Hodder and Stoughton, 1990).
28 Lynn Hunt, *Politics, Culture, and Class in the French Revolution* (London: Methuen, 1986; orig. 1984).
29 *Ibid.*, p. 12.
30 *Ibid.*, p. 15.
31 Simon Schama, *Citizens* (London: Penguin, 1989), p. xiv.
32 *Ibid.*, p. xiv.
33 Theda Skocpol, *States and Social Revolutions* (Cambridge: Cambridge University Press, 1979).
34 A. Soboul, *The French Revolution 1787–1799* (New York: Vintage Books, 1975; orig. French, 1962), p. 24.
35 Schama, *Citizens*, p. xvi.

5 LABELLING THE PARTS: CATEGORIES AND CONCEPTS

1 See further Chapters 8 and 9, below.
2 In principle, the theoretical problems relating to the application of concepts to describe society are the same whether we call what we are doing history, sociology, or anthropology: the problem is that of devising categories through which to capture the complexities of another (a past, a foreign, a different) 'reality'.
3 See Hans-Georg Gadamer, 'Der hermeneutische Zirkel und das Problem der Vorurteile', *Wahrheit und Methode* (Tübingen: Mohr Verlag, 1960); on the

Habermas–Gadamer debate, see also Anthony Giddens, *New Rules of Sociological Method* (London: Hutchinson, 1976), pp. 54–70.

4 See, for example, Keith Wrightson, 'Estates, degrees and sorts; changing perceptions of society in Tudor and Stuart England' and Geoffrey Crossick, 'From gentlemen to the residuum: languages of social description in Victorian Britain' in Penelope J. Corfield (ed.), *Language, History and Class* (Oxford: Basil Blackwell, 1991).

5 Roy Porter in Juliet Gardiner (ed.), *The History Debate* (London: Collins and Brown, 1990), p. 15.

6 See Robert Berkhofer, *Beyond the Great Story. History as Text and Discourse* (Cambridge, MA: Harvard University Press, 1995).

7 John W. Derry, *Politics in the Age of Fox, Pitt and Liverpool* (Basingstoke: Macmillan, 1990), p. 1.

8 Louis Fischer, *The Life of Mahatma Gandhi* (New York: Harper and Row, 1983), p. 12.

9 Penelope J. Corfield, 'Introduction: Historians and language' in P. J. Corfield (ed.), *Language, History and Class*, p. 11.

10 Joan Wallach Scott, *Gender and the Politics of History* (New York, NY: Columbia University Press, 1988), 'Introduction', p. 2.

11 Benedict Anderson, *Imagined Communities* (London: Verso, revised edition, 1991); John Breuilly, *Nationalism and the State* (Manchester: Manchester University Press, 2nd edition, 1993); Ernest Gellner, *Nations and Nationalism* (Ithaca, NY: Cornell University Press, 1983); E. J. Hobsbawm, *Nations and Nationalism since 1780* (Cambridge: Cambridge University Press, 1990); Anthony Smith, *National Identity* (Harmondsworth: Penguin, 1991); for a more extended discussion, see also Mary Fulbrook, *German National Identity after the Holocaust* (Cambridge: Polity Press, 1999), Chapter 1.

12 Cf. the debate between Saul Friedländer and Martin Broszat in Peter Baldwin (ed.), *Reworking the Past: Hitler, the Holocaust and the Historians' Dispute* (Boston, MA: Beacon Press, 1990).

13 We shall discuss these questions more directly in Chapter 9, below.

14 W. Gallie, 'Essentially contested concepts', in Gallie, *Philosophy and the Historical Understanding* (New York: Schocken Books, 1964).

15 There is an immense literature in this area. For select examples to show some of the ends of the spectrum, see the early crude Marxist version presented by Christopher Hill in *The English Revolution 1640* (London: Lawrence and Wishart, 1940), and his more sophisticated analysis in Christopher Hill, *Century of Revolution 1603–1714* (New York: W. W. Norton, 1966); and, by contrast, the revisionist views in, for example, John Morrill, *The Revolt of the Provinces* (London: Longman, 1980); Conrad Russell, *The Crisis of Parliaments 1509–1660* (London: Oxford University Press, 1971) and some of the contributions to Russell (ed.), *The Origins of the English Civil War* (London: Macmillan, 1973). See also a recent collection of significant contributions to the debates over the past two or three decades in P. Gaunt (ed.), *The English Civil War: Essential Readings* (Oxford: Blackwell, 2001).

16 Christopher Hill modified his views considerably over time; and there are differences in degree of sophistication and complexity of analysis in the revisionist camp. See Mary Fulbrook, 'Christopher Hill and Historical Sociology' in G. Eley and W. Hunt (eds), *Reviving the English Revolution: Reflections and Elaborations on the Work of Christopher Hill* (London: Verso, 1988); and M. Fulbrook, 'The English Revolution and the Revisionist Revolt', *Social History*, vol. 7, no. 3, 1982, pp. 249–64.

17 Wrightson, 'Estates, degrees and sorts', in Corfield (ed.), *Language, History and Class*, p. 44.
18 See the very useful overview in Brian Levack, *The Witch-hunt in Early Modern Europe* (London: Longman, 1987).
19 The last phrase quoted, in which the word 'psychic' should probably read 'psychoanalytic' or 'in terms to do with the psyche', comes from Lyndal Roper, 'Witchcraft and fantasy in early modern Germany', in Jonathan Barry, Marianne Hester and Gareth Roberts (eds), *Witchcraft in Early Modern Europe* (Cambridge: Cambridge University Press, 1996), p. 232. For classic social functionalism, see Keith Thomas, *Religion and the Decline of Magic* (London: Weidenfeld and Nicolson, 1971); see also Alan MacFarlane, *Witchcraft in Tudor and Stuart England* (London: Routledge and Kegan Paul, 1971). On witchcraft as misogyny, see Anne Llewellyn Barstow, *Witchcraze. A New History of the European Witch Hunts* (London: HarperCollins, 1994), who wants to emphasise 'the sexual terror and brutality at the heart of the witch-hunts, a topic too little discussed' (p. 15).
20 H. R. Trevor-Roper, *The European Witch-craze of the Sixteenth and Seventeenth Centuries* (Harmondsworth: Penguin, 1969); Levack, *Witch-hunt*; see also the very perceptive review essay by Alison Rowlands, 'Telling witchcraft stories: new perspectives on witchcraft and witches in the early modern period', *Gender and History*, vol. 10, no. 2, August 1998, pp. 294–30.
21 Joan Wallach Scott, 'Women in *The Making of the English Working Class*' in Scott, *Gender and the Politics of History*.
22 For an excellent overview of these debates in English, see particularly Ian Kershaw, *The Nazi Dictatorship* (London: Arnold, 3rd edition, 2000).
23 Cf. Alf Lütdke, *Eigen-Sinn: Fabrikalltag, Arbeitererfahrungen und Politik vom Kaiserreich bis in den Faschismus* (Hamburg: Ergbenisse Verlag, 1993); for applications to the GDR, Thomas Lindenberger (ed.), *Herrschaft und Eigen-Sinn in der Diktatur* (Cologne, 1999).
24 There is a vast literature on Weber, of which it would be impossible to give more than a hint in any footnote seriously determined to resist epic proportions (notwithstanding the precedent set by Weber's own often totally overgrown footnotes). For those not familiar with Weber's works, a good starting point is the overview provided in W. G. Runciman (ed.), *Weber: Selections in Translation* (Cambridge: Cambridge University Press, 1978).
25 *Ibid.*, p. 237.
26 Max Weber, 'Die "Objektivität" sozialwissenschaftlicher Erkenntnis' in J. Winckelmann (ed.), *Max Weber: Soziologie, Weltgeschichtliche Analysen, Politik* (Stuttgart: Alfred Kröner Verlag, 1956), p. 235.
27 *Ibid.*, p. 227.
28 Contrast the views presented in the essay on objectivity, from which extensive quotations have just been made, with the elaboration of seemingly exhaustive conceptual frameworks in M. Weber, *Wirtschaft und Gesellschaft* (Tübingen: J. C. B. Mohr (Paul Siebeck), 1980) and the systematic deployment of relatively abstract conceptual categories in his comparative-historical studies of the world religions.
29 On the questions of objectivity and value neutrality raised by this argument, see further Chapter 9, below.
30 Weber, 'Die "Objektivität"', p. 227.
31 *Ibid.*, p. 194.
32 See, for example, E. Jesse (ed.), *Totalitarismus im 20: Jahrhundert* (Bonn: Bundeszentrale für politische Bildung, 1996).

33 In my view, for example, it is very much less than helpful for understanding the GDR. See, for example, Klaus Schroeder, *Der SED-Staat* (Munich: Carl Hanser Verlag, 1998); and my critique of Klaus Schroeder's approach, in 'Jenseits der Totalitarismustheorie? Vorläufige Bemerkungen aus sozialgeschichtlicher Perspektive' in Peter Barker (ed.), *The GDR and Its History* (Amsterdam: Rodopi, 2000).

34 The meaning of church membership in the Federal Republic of Germany, for example, was quite different from the meaning of church membership in the German Democratic Republic.

6 LOOKING FOR CLUES: THE QUESTION OF EVIDENCE

1 Increase Mather, *A Further Account of the Tryals of the New-England Witches with the Observations of a Person who was upon the Place Several Days when the Suspected Witches Were First Taken into Examination to Which Is Added, Cases of Conscience Concerning Witchcrafts and Evil Spirits Personating Men* (London: John Dunton, 1693).

2 Laurie Winn Carlson, *A Fever in Salem: A New Interpretation of the New England Witch Trials* (Chicago, IL: Ivan R. Dee, 1999).

3 Charles W. Upham, *Salem Witchcraft; with an Account of Salem Village and a History of Opinions on Witchcraft and Kindred Subjects* (Boston, MA: Wiggin and Lunt, 1867), vol. 1, p. 405.

4 Let me in my turn lend an air of scholarly verisimilitude to this statement: see, for example, Roland Barthes, 'Le Discours de l'Historie', in Barthes, *Oeuvres Complètes*, vol. II (Paris: Éditions du Seuil, 1994), pp. 417–27.

5 Dominick LaCapra, *History and Criticism* (Ithaca, NY, and London: Cornell University Press, 1985), p. 18.

6 G. R. Elton, *The Practice of History* (London: Fontana, 1969; orig. 1967), p. 88.

7 John Tosh, *The Pursuit of History* (London: Longman, 2nd edition, 1991), p. 30.

8 Ludmilla Jordanova, *History in Practice* (London: Arnold, 2000), pp. 28–34, pp. 100–2.

9 Neville Morley, *Writing Ancient History* (London: Duckworth, 1999), Chapter 2.

10 Richard J. Evans, *In Defence of History* (London: Granta, 1997), p. 126.

11 See what were in their time the pioneering works of Keith Thomas, *Religion and the Decline of Magic* (New York: Charles Scribner's Sons, 1971) and Peter Burke, *Popular Culture in Early Modern Europe* (London: Temple Smith, 1978).

12 See, for example, Henrietta Leyser, *Medieval Women: A Social History of Women in England 450–1500* (London: Weidenfeld and Nicolson, 1995).

13 See, for example, Roy Foster, *Modern Ireland 1600–1972* (London: Penguin, 1989), where Chapter 1 evokes a real sense of place and people in Ireland *c.* 1600. Many historians, however, continued to find it difficult to integrate traditional political history with social and cultural history, and adopted a strategy of effectively 'ghettoising' the latter in stand-alone chapters as, for example, in Gordon Craig's *Germany 1860–1945* (Oxford: Oxford University Press, 1981).

14 See, for example, Pieter Spierenburg, *The Broken Spell: A Cultural and Anthropological History of Pre-industrial Europe* (Basingstoke: Macmillan, 1991), building on the pioneering works of Norbert Elias first published in 1939; and Theodore Zeldin, *An Intimate History of Humanity* (London: Sinclair-Stevenson, 1994).

15 On oral history, see, for example, Paul Thompson, *The Voice of the Past: Oral History* (Oxford: Oxford University Press, 1988).

16 See, for example, W. G. Hoskins *The Making of the English Landscape* (London: Hodder and Stoughton, 1955).
17 David Hackett Fischer, *Historians' Fallacies* (New York: Harper and Row, 1970).
18 Robert Darnton, 'Workers Revolt: The Great Cat Massacre of the Rue Saint-Séverin', reprinted in Tamsin Spargo (ed.), *Reading the Past* (Basingstoke: Palgrave, 2000).
19 Evans, *In Defence of History*, pp. 116 ff; David Abraham, *The Collapse of the Weimar Republic* (Princeton, NJ: Princeton University Press, 1981).
20 Evans, *In Defence of History*, p. 127.
21 On post-structuralism in literary theory, see, for example, Terry Eagleton, *Literary Theory* (Oxford: Blackwell, 2nd edition, 1996). For alternative 'readings' of the same object – in this case a picture – see, for example, the juxtaposition of the New Historicist and post-structuralist 'readings' of Holbein's painting of *The Ambassadors*, with its curious 'anamorphotic' skull that can be seen only when viewing the painting from the 'wrong', or unusual, perspective, one from which the main characters and ostensible worldly subjects of the painting cannot be properly seen: Stephen Greenblatt, 'At the Table of the Great: More's Self-Fashioning and Self-Cancellation' and Jürgen Pieters, 'Facing History, or the Anxiety of Reading: Holbein's *The Ambassadors* according to Greenblatt and Lyotard' in Spargo (ed.), *Reading the Past*.
22 I have discussed this case at greater length in my *Anatomy of a Dictatorship: Inside the GDR, 1949–89* (Oxford: Oxford University Press, 1995).
23 Hans Kellner, *Language and Historical Representation: Getting the Story Crooked* (Madison, WI: University of Wisconsin Press, 1989), p. 9.
24 *Ibid.*, p. 10.
25 Ankersmit, 'Reply to Professor Zagorin', *History and Theory*, vol. 29, no. 3, 1990, pp. 275–96, p. 281; also quoted above, Chapter 2, p. 20.
26 Kellner, *Language and Historical Representation*, pp. 10–11.
27 *Ibid.*, p. 11.
28 For an excellent overview of recent debates, see William Doyle, *Origins of the French Revolution* (Oxford: Oxford University Press, 3rd edition, 1999).
29 Alfred Cobban, *The Social Interpretation of the French Revolution* (Cambridge: Cambridge University Press, 1964).
30 Lynn Hunt, *Politics, Culture and Class in the French Revolution* (London: Methuen, 1986; orig. 1984).
31 Theda Skocpol, *States and Social Revolutions* (Cambridge: Cambridge University Press, 1979); T. C. W. Blanning, *The French Revolution: Class War or Culture Clash?* (Basingstoke: Macmillan, 2nd edition, 1998).
32 See John Hardman, *Louis XVI* (New Haven, CN: Yale University Press, 1993); John Hardman, *Robespierre* (London: Longman, 1999).
33 See, for example, Hugh Gough, *The Terror in the French Revolution* (Basingstoke: Macmillan, 1998).
34 Ian Kershaw, *Hitler. Vol. II: Nemesis* (Harmondsworth: Penguin, 2000), p. 468.
35 Alan Bullock, *Hitler: A Study in Tyranny* (London: Penguin, 1990; orig. 1952), pp. 702–3.
36 The debate has indeed moved so fast that within four years Nick Stargardt felt he had radically to rewrite his chapter on this topic: compare Nick Stargardt's chapters on 'The Holocaust' in Fulbrook (ed.), *German History since 1800* (London: Arnold, 1997), and in the revised separate volume, *Twentieth-century Germany* (London: Arnold, 2001).
37 Weber was somewhat ill-served by Talcott Parsons, the first major social theorist and translator who introduced Weber to the English-speaking world. Parsons

tended to represent a more 'idealist' Weber than was really there in the original German; see, for example, the rather slanted translation of the introduction to Weber's comparative studies of the world religions.

38 Barrington Moore, *The Social Origins of Dictatorship and Democracy* (London: Penguin, 1977), p. xviii.

39 Skocpol, *States and Social Revolutions*.

40 See, for example, the analyses of a number of key historical scholars in Theda Skocpol (ed.), *Vision and Method in Historical Sociology* (Cambridge: Cambridge University Press, 1984).

41 Marcel Faucheux, *L'Insurrection Vendéenne de 1793* (Paris: Imprimerie Nationale, 1964); Marc Bloch, 'La lutte pour l'individualisme agraire dans la France du XVIIIe. siècle', *Annales d'Histoire Économique et Sociale*, vol. 11, no. 7, July 1930, pp. 329–81 and no. 8, October 1930, pp. 511–56.

42 See, for example, Hamish Scott (ed.), *Enlightened Absolutism* (Basingstoke: Macmillan, 1990).

43 C. Behan McCullogh, *The Truth of History* (London: Routledge, 1998), p. 275.

44 Leszek Kolakowski. 'Emperor Kennedy Legend: A New Anthropological Debate' in Tamsin Spargo (ed.), *Reading the Past* (Basingstoke: Macmillan, 2000).

7 SATISFYING CURIOSITY: STRUCTURE, AGENCY AND UNDERLYING ASSUMPTIONS

1 Thomas Carlyle, *On Heroes, Hero-worship and the Heroic in History*, Lecture 1, delivered 5 May 1840 (Oxford: Oxford University Press, 1946 edition; orig. 1841), p. 1, p. 17.

2 Peter Burke (ed.), *New Perspectives on Historical Writing* (Cambridge: Polity Press, 1991), p. 4. See also above, Chapter 3.

3 For a nice eighteenth-century answer to the individualist approach, see, for example, Montesquieu, *The Spirit of the Laws*, English edition translated by Thomas Nugent with Introduction by Franz Neumann (New York: Hafner Publishing Company, 1949).

4 See, for example, H. Veeser (ed.), *The New Historicism* (London: Routledge, 1989); T. G. Ashplant and Gerry Smith, *Explorations in Cultural History* (London: Pluto, 2001).

5 This was recognised even by East German Marxist historians in the 1960s, who realised that West German coffee-table biographies of great men seemed to have far greater impact on popular historical consciousness than did the East German histories in which only social classes appeared as collective actors on the historical stage. This recognition prompted the subsequent and at first sight rather surprising production in the GDR of Marxist biographies of 'great men': Ernst Engelberg, *Bismarck*, 2 vols (Berlin: Akademie Verlag, 1985, 1990); Ingrid Mittenzwei, *Friedrich II. von Preußen. Eine Biographie* (Berlin: VEB Deutscher Verlag der Wissenschaften, 1979; revised edition, 1982).

6 Cf. Steven Lukes, 'Methodological Individualism Reconsidered', *Essays in Social Theory* (London: Macmillan, 1977), Chapter 9.

7 R. G. Collingwood, *The Idea of History* (Oxford: Clarendon Press, 1946); E. Durkheim, *The Rules of Sociological Method* (New York, NY: Free Press, 1938); and particularly Durkheim's attempted exemplification of his injunction, in analysing the presumed social causes of that most apparently individual and private of actions, suicide, in *Suicide* (London: Routledge and Kegan Paul, 1952).

8 For analyses of theoretical lineages, surveying past debates in order to come to a new, and still relatively abstract, formulation of a notion of 'structuration' over

time, see, for example, Anthony Giddens, *Central Problems in Social Theory: Action, Structure and Contradiction in Social Analysis* (Basingstoke: Macmillan, 1979); Christopher Lloyd, *The Structures of History* (Oxford: Blackwell, 1993).

9 For an excellent discussion of many of these issues, see C. Behan McCullogh, *The Truth of History* (London: Routledge, 1998).

10 Cf. E. H. Carr, *What is History?* (New York, NY: Vintage Books, 1961), Chapter II; Richard J. Evans, *In Defence of History* (London: Granta, 1997), Chapter 6.

11 G. R. Elton, *The Practice of History* (Glasgow: Collins, Fontana edition, 1969), p. 20.

12 See, for example, the numerous biographies of important historical figures by the popular historian Christopher Hibbert.

13 R. G. Collingwood, *The Idea of History* (Oxford: Clarendon Press, 1946).

14 Arthur Marwick, 'Two Approaches to Historical Study: The Metaphysical (Including "Postmodernism") and the Historical', *Journal of Contemporary History*, vol. 30, 1995, pp. 5–35; Geoffrey Roberts, 'Narrative History as a Way of Life', *Journal of Contemporary History*, vol. 31, 1996, pp. 221–8.

15 Roberts, *loc. cit.*, p. 223. Roberts includes in this list (rather than reaching the conclusion from it) the assertion that 'the stories told by historians (if they are good enough) correspond to those that have been played out and lived in the past'. This assertion – essentially an article of faith – is of course diametrically opposite in principle to the views of postmodernists who follow Hayden White's argument that there are no stories 'simply given in the past'.

16 R. G. Collingwood, *The Idea of History* (Oxford: Oxford University Press, 1946; repr. 1956), p. 282, p. 305.

17 See, for example, Claude Lévi-Strauss, *Anthropologie Structurale* (Paris: Librairie Plon, 1958); Louis Althusser, *For Marx* (Harmondsworth: Penguin, transl. Ben Brewster, 1969; orig. 1966); see also above, Chapters 2 and 3.

18 A. Gramsci, *Selections from the Prison Notebooks* (New York, NY: International Publishers, 1971); G. Lukacs, *History and Class Consciousness* (London: Merlin Press, 1971).

19 See, for example, Christopher Hill's studies of Oliver Cromwell and Milton, in addition to his disinterment of the views of Levellers, Diggers, and other members of a forgotten underworld.

20 E. P. Thompson, *The Poverty of Theory* (London: Merlin Press, new edition, 1995).

21 Theda Skocpol, *States and Social Revolutions* (Cambridge: Cambridge University Press, 1979). Skocpol was a student of Barrington Moore, and her work was greatly stimulated by, and formulated in partial reaction to, his *Social Origins of Dictatorship and Democracy* (London: Penguin, 1977).

22 However, Skocpol subsequently somewhat modified her explanatory framework to concede a larger role to the power of particular political ideologies in different circumstances. See in particular her debate with William Sewell in T. Blanning (ed.), *The Rise and Fall of the French Revolution* (Chicago, IL: University of Chicago Press, 1996).

23 See also my own attempt to explain the very different contributions, in terms of both levels and directions of political activity, of three similar movements for religious reform; Mary Fulbrook, *Religion and the Rise of Absolutism in England, Württemberg and Prussia* (Cambridge: Cambridge University Press, 1983).

24 Cf. Mary Fulbrook, 'Max Weber's "Interpretive Sociology": a Comparison of Conception and Practice', *British Journal of Sociology*, vol. 29, 1978, pp. 71–82.

25 Burke, *New Perspectives*, p. 5.

26 I am of course begging a huge number of questions regarding the rise of

absolutism in European states, not to mention highly contentious debates over the revolutionary crises in England (1640) and France (1789). The point here, however, is merely to indicate some of the general theoretical issues at stake; not to enter into the substance of detailed historical controversies on these particular topics.

27 See, for example, Kershaw, *Hitler: A Profile in Power* (London: Longman, 1991).

28 Simon Schama, *Citizens: A Chronicle of the French Revolution* (London: Penguin, 1980).

29 For the debates over the alleged Nazi roots of post-1945 societal history, see Winfried Schulze, *Deutsche Geschichtswissenschaft nach 1945* (Munich: Oldenbourg, 1989); Ernst Schulin (ed.), *Deutsche Geschichtswissenschaft nach dem zweiten Weltkrieg (1945–1965)* (Munich: Oldenbourg, 1989).

30 Thomas Holt, 'Explaining Racism in American History' in Anthony Molho and Gordon Wood (eds), *Imagined Histories: American Historians Interpret the Past* (Princeton, NJ; Princeton University Press, 1998), p. 108.

31 Judith Butler, *Gender Trouble. Feminism and the Subversion of Identity* (New York, NY, and London: Routledge, 1990), p. 6.

32 *Ibid.*, p. 2.

33 See E. J. Hobsbawm, *The Age of Revolution* (London: Weidenfeld and Nicolson, 1962), Chapter 3; Christopher Hill, *The Century of Revolution 1603–1714* (New York, NY: W. W. Norton and Co., 1961).

34 A. Soboul, *The French Revolution, 1787–1799* (New York, NY: Vintage Books, 1975; orig. 1962), pp. 7–8.

35 As I have sought to argue for the case of the awkward construction of divergent national identities in the two post-war German states, east and west: Mary Fulbrook, *German National Identity after the Holocaust* (Cambridge: Polity Press, 1999).

36 I have to agree with Weber here. One would have to be a very convinced atheist to insist on 'reducing' religion, in one way or another, to class interests or social experience or – following Durkheim's functionalist view – to some alleged collective 'need' for social cohesion. The variations in religious experience across different periods and cultures are indeed immense, posing serious problems for any particular faith claiming a monopoly on truth, whether revealed or otherwise; Weber's determination to bracket out these questions would seem the wisest course for any agnostic or religiously committed historian.

8 REPRESENTING THE PAST

1 There is a large literature on all these fields; see particularly the pathbreaking and wide-ranging David Lowenthal, *The Past is a Foreign Country* (Cambridge: Cambridge University Press, 1985). For analyses of specific examples, see, for example, Ian Buruma, *The Wages of Guilt: Memories of War in Germany and Japan* (Harmondsworth: Penguin, 1995); Tina Rosenberg, *The Haunted Land: Facing Europe's Ghosts after Communism* (London: Vintage, 1995); James Young, *The Texture of Memory: Holocaust Memorials and Meaning* (New Haven, CN, and London: Yale University Press, 1993).

2 Catherine Belsey, 'Reading Cultural History', in Tamsin Spargo (ed.), *Reading the Past* (Basingstoke: Palgrave, 2000), pp. 104–5.

3 Cf., for example, Douglas Greenberg, '"History is a Luxury": Mrs Thatcher, Mr Disney and (Public) History', in Louis Masur (ed.), *The Challenge of American History* (Baltimore, MD: The Johns Hopkins University Press, 1999).

4 Lowenthal, *The Past is a Foreign Country*, p. xxv.

5 Hans Kellner, *Language and Historical Representation: Getting the Story Crooked* (Madison, Wisconsin: University of Wisconsin Press, 1989).
6 *Ibid.*, p. 2.
7 Roland Barthes, 'Le discours de l'histoire', *Oeuvres Completes*, vol. 2 (Éditions du Seuil, 1994), pp. 417–27.
8 It is not always the case that an awareness of the importance of these issues actually serves to improve style. Max Weber did think about these questions, but only to dismiss them; he told his wife, Marianne, that he saw no reason to make concessions to the reader, since it had been so difficult for him to think things through in the first place. Such disregard for accessibility would now be seen as unacceptable in most quarters, although in some circles a degree of (supposedly deep) impenetrability simply disguises a lack of clear thinking.
9 See the by now classic essay by Lawrence Stone, 'The Revival of Narrative: reflections on a new old history', originally published in *Past and Present*, no. 85, 1979, pp. 3–24; for a clear overview and selection of contributions to some of these debates, including a reprint of the Stone article, see Geoffrey Roberts (ed.), *The History and Narrative Reader* (London: Routledge, 2001).
10 This was, for example, a crucial feature in the controversy surrounding the attempted demolition of David Abraham's work on the Weimar Republic; see David Abraham, *The Collapse of the Weimar Republic* (Princeton, NJ: Princeton University Press, 1981), and the discussions in *Central European History*, vol. 17, 1984, and Peter Novick, *That Noble Dream: the 'Objectivity Question' and the American Historical Profession* (Cambridge: Cambridge University Press, 1988).
11 John Hardman, *Robespierre* (London: Longman, 1999), p. 202.
12 Michael Crawford, *The Roman Republic* (London: Fontana, 2nd edition, 1992), p. 158.
13 Natalie Zemon Davies, *The Return of Martin Guerre* (Cambridge, MA: Harvard University Press, 1983), pp. vii–viii.
14 Christopher Hill, *God's Englishman. Oliver Cromwell and the English Revolution* (Harmondsworth: Penguin, 1972; orig. 1970), p. 13.
15 Antonia Fraser, *Cromwell. Our Chief of Men* (London: Granada edition, 1975; orig. 1973), p. xiii.
16 See, for example, the evocation of the changing historical culture of the United States in the 1950s and 1960s which appears, perhaps unintentionally, through the discussion of failures of logic in historical thought in David H. Fischer, *Historians' Fallacies* (New York, NY: Harper and Row, 1970).
17 I have discussed historical works on the GDR under this aspect, in 'Reckoning with the Past: Heroes, Victims and Villains in the History of the German Democratic Republic' in Reinhard Alter and Peter Monteath (eds), *Rewriting the German Past* (New York, NY: Humanities Press, 1997).
18 Christopher Hibbert, *The French Revolution* (London: Penguin, 1982; orig. 1980); on East and West German historical writing in political context, see my *German National Identity after the Holocaust* (Cambridge: Polity Press, 1999).
19 Peter Burke, 'History of Events and the Revival of Narrative' in Roberts (ed.), *The History and Narrative Reader*.
20 A. Adu Boahen, 'Clio and Nation-Building in Africa', reprinted in John Tosh (ed.), *Historians on History* (Harlow: Pearson, 2000), p. 80.
21 It has to be said that, for those committed to finding new 'discourses' against the previous 'hegemonic discourse', some of the writing in this area appears to the uninitiated as unnecessarily opaque and pretentious. For a good overview, see Bill Ashcroft, Gareth Griffiths and Helen Tiffin (eds), *The Postcolonial Studies Reader* (London: Routledge, 1991). See also: Homi Bhabha (ed.), *Nation and*

Narration (London: Routledge, 1990); Gayatri Chakravorty Spivak, *In Other Worlds. Essays in Cultural Politics* (London: Methuen, 1987); and Robert Young, *White Mythologies* (London: Routledge, 1990).

22 Jürgen Kuczynski, 'The History of the Everyday Life of the German People' (the preface to the first volume of his *Geschichte des Alltags des Deutschen Volkes*), reprinted in English translation in Georg Iggers (ed.), *Marxist Historiography in Transformation: New Orientations in Recent East German History* (Oxford: Berg, 1991), p. 38.

23 Andreas Hillgruber, *Zweierlei Untergang. Die Zerschlagung des deutschen Reiches und das Ende des europäischen Judentums* (Stuttgart: Siedler, 1986).

24 The key texts of the historians' dispute are reprinted in English translation in *Forever in the Shadow of Hitler?* (Atlantic Highlands, NJ: Humanities Press, 1993, transl. J. Knowlton and T. Cates).

25 Daniel Jonah Goldhagen, *Hitler's Willing Executioners: Ordinary Germans and the Holocaust* (New York, NY: Knopf, 1996).

26 On a personal note, I can vividly remember feeling overwhelmed by this problem when writing about the Holocaust in my *History of Germany 1918–1990: The Divided Nation* (London: Fontana, 1991; 2nd edition, Oxford: Blackwells, 2002). One of the readers of the original manuscript, the late William Carr, suggested I should replace my own paragraph attempting to imagine the arrival of a train at Auschwitz with an account from a contemporary source; I could find nothing that evoked the atmosphere in the way I imagined it, and yet – despite the lack of a key quotation – felt that my paragraph was in some way authentic, if only as a recognition of the need of later generations to attempt to imagine as well as to understand, intellectually, the parameters of the academic debates over explanation.

27 Orlando Figes, *A People's Tragedy. The Russian Revolution 1891–1924* (London: Random House, 1996; Pimlico edition, 1997), p. 291.

28 Ian Kershaw, *Hitler, Vol. II: Nemesis* (London: Penguin, 2000), p. 461.

29 See particularly C. Behan McCullogh, *The Truth of History* (London: Routledge, 1998), pp. 80–1: 'There is no good reason for thinking that metaphorical descriptions of the past cannot be true, in a metaphorical, not a literal, sense . . . An examination of historical practice has revealed that historians are very conscious of the need to find evidence for their general descriptions, not only to prove them true, but to ensure that they are fair, not misleading, as well.'

30 Ian Kershaw, *Hitler 1889–1936: Hubris* and *Hitler 1936–45: Nemesis* (London: Penguin, 1998 and 2000).

31 Kershaw, *Hitler, Vol. II: Nemesis*, p. xvi.

32 Philippe Carrard, *Poetics of the New History: French Historical Discourse from Braudel to Chartier* (Baltimore, MD: The Johns Hopkins University Press, 1992), p. 222. See also more generally Sande Cohen, *Historical Culture. On the Recoding of an Academic Discipline* (Berkeley, CA: University of California Press, 1986).

33 Cf. the debate between Martin Broszat and Saul Friedländer in Peter Baldwin (ed.), *Reworking the Past: Hitler, the Holocaust and the Historians' Dispute* (Boston: Beacon Press, 1990).

9 HISTORY AND PARTISANSHIP

1 In English translation, see: Max Weber, 'The Meaning of "Ethical Neutrality" in Sociology and Economics", and '"Objectivity" in Social Science and Social Policy' in Edward Shils and Henry Finch (eds), *The Methodology of the Social*

Sciences (New York, NY: Free Press, 1949); and 'Politics as a Vocation' and 'Science as a Vocation' in H. H. Gerth and C. Wright Mills, *From Max Weber* (London: Routledge and Kegan Paul, 1948); formulations which proved profoundly influential for an Anglo-American audience in the post-war era.

2 On belief in history as the pursuit of truth about the past in America, see particularly Peter Novick, *That Noble Dream. The 'Objectivity Question' and the American Historical Profession* (Cambridge: Cambridge University Press, 1988). On truth in history more generally, see the clear analysis by C. Behan McCullogh, *The Truth of History* (London: Routledge, 1998).

3 See, for example, Max Horkheimer and Theodor Adorno, *Dialectic of Enlightenment* (New York, NY: Herder and Herder, transl. John Cumming, 1972); Max Horkheimer, *Critical Theory* (New York, NY: Herder and Herder, transl. Matthew J. O'Connell, 1972); Max Horkheimer, *Eclipse of Reason* (New York, NY: Oxford University Press, 1947); Martin Jay, *The Dialectical Imagination. A History of the Frankfurt School and the Institute of Social Research, 1923–1950* (Boston, MA: Little, Brown and Co., 1973); Paul Connerton, *The Tragedy of Enlightenment: An Essay on the Frankfurt School* (Cambridge: Cambridge University Press, 1980).

4 Gayatri Chakravorty Spivak, 'Can the Subaltern Speak?' in Bill Ashcroft *et al.* (eds), *The Postcolonial Studies Reader* (London: Routledge, 1995).

5 John Howard Griffin, *Black Like Me* (London: Granada, 1964; orig. 1962); Günther Wallraff, *Ganz Unten* (Cologne: Kiepenheuer and Witsch, 1985).

6 Thomas Haskell, *Objectivity is Not Neutrality: Explanatory Schemes in History* (Baltimore, MD, and London: The Johns Hopkins University Press, 1998), pp. 148–9, pp. 158–9.

7 See the discussion and references in Chapter 8 (footnote 10).

8 Haskell, *Objectivity*, p. 157.

9 Richard J. Evans, *In Defence of History* (London: Granta, 1997), p. 223.

10 *Ibid.*, p. 253.

11 I have sought to deal with the Hayden White points in preceding chapters, so will not rehearse the arguments again here.

12 Joyce Appleby, Lynn Hunt and Margaret Jacobs, *Telling the Truth about History* (New York, NY, and London: W. W. Norton and Co., 1994), p. 261.

13 Ludmilla Jordanova, *History in Practice* (London: Arnold, 2000), p. 96. Emphasis added.

14 Jordanova actually slides from a notion of trust in individual sources to a notion of trust in historical accounts. I shall argue that the latter are, in various ways, open to critique and evaluation on the grounds of more than 'trust' based on personal sympathies.

15 For further discussion and references, see my *German National Identity after the Holocaust* (Cambridge: Polity Press, 1999); on recent debates, see, for example, Rüdiger Hohls and Konrad Jarausch (eds), *Versäumte Fragen: Deutsche Historiker im Schatten des Nationalsozialismus* (Stuttgart: Deutsche Verlags-Anstalt, 2000) and subsequent reviews and debates on the H-Soz.u.Kult. internet site.

16 On debates on history in the United States, see, for example, Elizabeth Fox-Genovese and Elizabeth Lasch-Quinn (eds), *Reconstructing History. The Emergence of a New Historical Society* (London: Routledge, 1999), Part IV: 'An educational mission: standards for the teaching of history'.

10 CONCLUSION: PARTIAL HISTORIES

1 In the Bible, of course, (I Corinthians, 13) the contrast refers to our knowledge

of the transcendental or divine now and in the post-redemption future, rather than to our mundane knowledge of our own secular past.

2 I presented some of these comparisons (and the wider ideas of this book) in preliminary form in the 1999 Annual Lecture to the German Historical Institute Washington, and am grateful to Konrad Jarausch and others present for their comments.

3 M. Swales, *Studies of German Prose Fiction in the Age of European Realism* (Lewiston: Edwin Mellen Press, 1995).

SELECT BIBLIOGRAPHY

This very selective bibliography lists primarily recent English-language works on theoretical issues of particular significance in the context of the arguments developed in the book. In the interests of space in an area which is virtually limitless, I have had to be brutal about principles of exclusion. I have therefore decided not to include a wide range of relevant works on methodological issues, theoretical approaches, the philosophy of history, the ruminations of eminent historians, and substantive areas of historical controversy; I have also on the whole chosen not to include what might be called the 'classics' (although a couple of key essays by Max Weber have been allowed to creep in). The works listed below will, however, serve to guide interested readers further into the respective areas of debate.

Specific references to other works cited in the text, including substantive historical works used as examples in relation to particular issues, will be found in the endnotes to each chapter. However, even in notes I have chosen on the whole to 'under-reference' rather than provide general guides to wider reading, given the extent of relevant debates in certain areas of controversy. Interested readers should, however, again be able to 'pick their way outwards' from the particular references given in endnotes to the relevant wider reading in those areas.

P. Abrams, *Historical Sociology* (Shepton Mallet: Open Books, 1982)

Perry Anderson, *Considerations on Western Marxism* (London: New Left Books, 1976)

Perry Anderson, *Arguments within English Marxism* (London: New Left Books, 1980)

F. R. Ankersmit, 'Historiography and Postmodernism', *History and Theory*, vol. 28, no. 2 (1989): 137–53

F. R. Ankersmit, 'Reply to Professor Zagorin', *History and Theory*, vol. 29, no. 3 (1990): 275–96

F. Ankersmit and H. Kellner (eds), *A New Philosophy of History* (London: Reaktion Books, 1995)

Joyce Appleby, Lynn Hunt and Margaret Jacobs, *Telling the Truth about History* (New York, NY, and London: W. W. Norton and Co., 1994)

Bill Ashcroft, G. Griffiths and Helen Tiffin (eds), *The Postcolonial Studies Reader* (London: Routledge, 1995)

T. G. Ashplant and Gerry Smith, *Explorations in Cultural History* (London: Pluto Press, 2001)

Michael Bentley (ed.), *Companion to Historiography* (London: Routledge, 1997)

S. Berger, *The Search for Normality* (Oxford: Berghahn Books, 1997)

Robert Berkhofer, *Beyond the Great Story: History as Text and Discourse* (Cambridge, MA: Harvard University Press, 1995)

Victoria Bonnell and Lynn Hunt (eds), *Beyond the Cultural Turn: New Directions in the Study of Society and Culture* (Berkeley, CA: University of California Press, 1999)

P. Burke (ed.), *New Perspectives on Historical Writing* (Cambridge: Polity Press, 1991)

Judith Butler, *Gender Trouble: Feminism and the Subversion of Identity* (New York, NY, and London: Routledge, 1990)

E. H. Carr, *What is History?* (New York, NY: Vintage Books, 1961)

Philippe Carrard, *Poetics of the New History* (Baltimore, MD: The Johns Hopkins University Press, 1992)

Roger Chartier, *On the Edge of the Cliff: History, Language and Practices* (Baltimore, MD, and London: The Johns Hopkins University Press, Lydia C. Cochrane (transl.), 1997)

Sande Cohen, *Historical Culture: On the Recoding of an Academic Discipline* (Berkeley, CA: University of California Press, 1986)

R. G. Collingwood, *The Idea of History* (Oxford: Clarendon Press, 1946)

Penelope J. Corfield (ed.), *Language, History and Class* (Oxford: Basil Blackwell, 1991)

Terry Eagleton, *Literary Theory* (Oxford: Blackwell, second edition, 1996)

Geoffrey Elton, *The Practice of History* (London: Fontana, 1969; orig. 1967)

Geoffrey Elton, *Return to Essentials* (Cambridge: Cambridge University Press, 1991)

Richard J. Evans, *In Defence of History* (London: Granta, 1997)

Brian Fay, Philip Pomper and Richard T. Vann (eds), *History and Theory: Contemporary Readings* (Oxford: Blackwell, 1998)

David Hackett Fischer, *Historians' Fallacies* (New York, NY: Harper and Row, 1970)

R. W. Fogel and G. R. Elton, *Which Road to the Past?* (New Haven, CN: Yale University Press, 1983)

Saul Friedländer (ed.), *Probing the Limits of Representation* (Cambridge, MA: Harvard University Press, 1992)

Hans-Georg Gadamer, *Truth and Method* (London: Sheed and Ward; J. Weinsheimer and D. G. Marshall (transl.), 1989; orig. 1960)

Juliet Gardiner (ed.), *The History Debate* (London: Collins and Brown, 1990)

Anthony Giddens, *New Rules of Sociological Method* (London: Hutchinson, 1976)

Anthony Giddens, *Central Problems in Social Theory: Action, Structure and Contradiction in Social Analysis* (Basingstoke: Macmillan, 1979)

Thomas Haskell, *Objectivity is Not Neutrality: Explanatory Schemes in History* (Baltimore, MD, and London: The Johns Hopkins University Press, 1998)

Geoffrey Hawthorn, *Plausible Worlds* (Cambridge: Cambridge University Press, 1991)

Gertrude Himmelfarb, 'Some Reflections on the New History', *American Historical Review*, vol. 94, no. 3 (June 1989): 661–70

Eric Hobsbawm, *On History* (London: Weidenfeld and Nicolson, 1997)

Lynn Hunt (ed.), *The New Cultural History* (Berkeley, CA: University of California Press, 1989)

Georg Iggers, *Historiography in the Twentieth Century: From Scientific Objectivity to the Postmodern Challenge* (Hanover, NH: Wesleyan University Press, 1997)

Martin Jay, *The Dialectical Imagination: A History of the Frankfurt School and the Institute of Social Research, 1923–1950* (London: Heinemann, 1973)

Keith Jenkins, *On "What is History?" From Carr and Elton to Rorty and White* (London: Routledge, 1995)

Keith Jenkins (ed.), *The Postmodern History Reader* (London: Routledge, 1997)

Keith Jenkins, *Why History? Ethics and Postmodernity* (London: Routledge, 1999)

Ludmilla Jordanova, *History in Practice* (London: Arnold, 2000)

Patrick Joyce, 'History and Postmodernism I', *Past and Present*, no. 133 (November 1991): 204–9

Hans Kellner, *Language and Historical Representation: Getting the Story Crooked* (Madison, WI: University of Wisconsin Press, 1989)

Ian Kershaw, *The Nazi Dictatorship* (London: Arnold, 3rd edition, 1993)

H. Kozicki (ed.), *Developments in Modern Historiography* (Basingstoke: Macmillan, 1993)

Thomas Kuhn, *The Structure of Scientific Revolutions* (Chicago, IL: University of Chicago Press, 1962; 2nd edition, 1970)

Dominick LaCapra, *History and Criticism* (Ithaca, NY, and London: Cornell University Press, 1985)

Imre Lakatos and Alan Musgrave (eds), *Criticism and the Growth of Knowledge* (Cambridge: Cambridge University Press, 1970)

Christopher Lloyd, *The Structures of History* (Oxford: Blackwell, 1993)

David Lowenthal, *The Past is a Foreign Country* (Cambridge: Cambridge University Press, 1985)

Steven Lukes, *Essays in Social Theory* (London: Macmillan, 1977)

Jean-François Lyotard, *The Postmodern Condition: A Report on Knowledge* (Manchester: Manchester University Press, Geoff Bennington and Brian Massumi (transl.), 1984)

Arthur Marwick, *The Nature of History* (Basingstoke: Macmillan, 3rd edition, 1989)

Arthur Marwick, 'Two Approaches to Historical Study: the Metaphysical (including "Postmodernism") and the Historical', *Journal of Contemporary History*, vol. 30 (1995): 5–35

Arthur Marwick, *The New Nature of History: Knowledge, Evidence, Language* (Basingstoke: Palgrave, 2001)

Louis Masur (ed.), *The Challenge of American History* (Baltimore, MD: The Johns Hopkins University Press, 1999)

C. Behan McCullogh, *The Truth of History* (London: Routledge, 1998)

Terence J. McDonald (ed.), *The Historic Turn in the Human Sciences* (Ann Arbor, MI: University of Michigan Press, 1996)

Allan Megill (ed.), *Rethinking Objectivity* (Durham, NC: Duke University Press, 1994)

Anthony Molho and Gordon Wood (eds), *Imagined Histories. American Historians Interpret the Past* (Princeton, NJ: Princeton University Press, 1998)

Neville Morley, *Writing Ancient History* (London: Duckworth, 1999)

Peter Novick, *That Noble Dream: the 'Objectivity Question' and the American Historical Profession* (Cambridge: Cambridge University Press, 1988)

David Roberts, *Nothing but History: Reconstruction and Extremity after Metaphysics* (Berkeley, CA: University of California Press, 1995)

Geoffrey Roberts, 'Narrative History as a Way of Life', *Journal of Contemporary History*, vol. 31 (1996): 221–8

Geoffrey Roberts (ed.), *The History and Narrative Reader* (London: Routledge, 2001)

W. G. Runciman (ed.), *Weber: Selections in Translation* (Cambridge: Cambridge University Press, 1978)

Joan Wallach Scott, Gender and the Politics of History (New York, NY: Columbia University Press, 1988)

Joan Wallach Scott, 'History in Crisis? The Others' Side of the Story', *American Historical Review*, vol. 94, no. 3 (June 1989): 680–92

Joan Wallach Scott (ed.), *Feminism and History* (Oxford: Oxford University Press, 1996)

Theda Skocpol (ed.), *Vision and Method in Historical Sociology* (Cambridge: Cambridge University Press, 1984)

Beverley Southgate, *History: What and Why? Ancient, Modern and Postmodern Perspectives* (London: Routledge, 1996)

Beverley Southgate, *Why Bother with History?* (Harlow: Pearson, 2000)

Tamsin Spargo (ed.), *Reading the Past* (Basingstoke: Palgrave, 2000)

Gabrielle M. Spiegel, *The Past as Text: The Theory and Practice of Medieval Historiography* (Baltimore, MD: The Johns Hopkins University Press, 1997)

M. Stanford, *A Companion to the Study of History* (Oxford: Blackwell, 1994)

M. Stanford, *The Nature of Historical Knowledge* (Oxford: Blackwell, 1986)

M. Stanford, *An Introduction to the Philosophy of History* (Malden, MA: Blackwell, 1998)

Lawrence Stone, 'History and Postmodernism III', *Past and Present*, no. 135 (May 1992): 189–94

E. P. Thompson, *The Poverty of Theory* (London: Merlin Press, new edition, 1995)

Willie Thompson, *What Happened to History?* (London: Pluto Press, 2000)

John Toews, 'A New Philosophy of History? Reflections on Postmodern Historicising', *History and Theory*, vol. 36, no. 2 (1997): 235–48

John Tosh (ed.), *Historians on History* (Harlow: Pearson, 2000)

John Tosh, *The Pursuit of History* (Harlow: Pearson, 3rd edition, 2000)

H. A. Veeser (ed.), *The New Historicism* (London: Routledge, 1989)

Max Weber, 'Politics as a Vocation' and 'Science as a Vocation' in H. H. Gerth and C. Wright Mills, *From Max Weber* (London: Routledge and Kegan Paul, 1948)

Max Weber, 'The meaning of "Ethical Neutrality" in Sociology and Economics', and '"Objectivity" in Social Science and Social Policy' in Edward Shils and Henry Finch (eds), *The Methodology of the Social Sciences* (New York, NY: Free Press, 1949)

Max Weber, *Economy and Society*, 2 vols. (Berkeley, CA: University of California Press, C. Gerth and C. Wittich (eds), E. Fischoff *et al.* (transl.), 1978)

Hayden White, *Tropics of Discourse* (Baltimore, MD, and London: The Johns Hopkins University Press, 1985; orig. 1978)

Hayden White, *The Content of the Form* (Baltimore, MD, and London: The Johns Hopkins University Press, 1987)

Hayden White, 'Historical Emplotment and the Problem of Truth' in Saul Friedländer (ed.), *Probing the Limits of Representation* (Cambridge, MA: Harvard University Press, 1992)

Hayden White, 'Response to Arthur Marwick', *Journal of Contemporary History*, vol. 30 (1995): 233–46

Robert Young, *White Mythologies: Writing History and the West* (London: Routledge, 1990)

Perez Zagorin, 'Historiography and Postmodernism: Reconsiderations', *History and Theory*, vol. 29, no. 3 (1990): 263–74

INDEX